The Historical Defense Of 1 John 5:7-8 -- The Unjustly Exscinded Text Of The Three Divine Witnesses

By Michael Maynard

the BIBLE FOR TODAY
900 Park Avenue
Collingswood, N. J. 08108
Phone: 609-854-4452

B.F.T. #2008

"God so loved the world, that He gave His only begotten Son, that whosoever believeth in Him should not perish, but have everlasting life." (John 3:16)

DIRECTED BY: REV. D. A. WAITE, Th.D., Ph.D.

900 PARK AVENUE, COLLINGSWOOD, NEW JERSEY 08108 • 609 854-4452

JUNE 5, 1991

"THE HISTORICAL DEFENSE OF 1 JOHN 5:7-8--

THE UNJUSTLY EXSCINDED TEXT OF THE THREE DIVINE WITNESSES"

****

B.F.T. #2008

By:

Michael Maynard

(March, 1991)

Published and Copyrighted by: THE BIBLE FOR TODAY, INCORPORATED
1991, ALL RIGHTS RESERVED

900 Park Avenue, Collingswood, New Jersey 08108
Phone: 609-854-4452

#2008

[No portion of this research may be reproduced in any form without written permission from the author and the publisher, THE BIBLE FOR TODAY, 900 Park Avenue, Collingswood, NJ 08108, except by a reviewer, who may quote brief passages in connection with a review.]

****

PUBLISHER'S NOTE:

This document, (BFT #2008), is an uncorrected draft copy sent upon individual request only. The book in its final form is still being revised. We hope the information will be helpful in its present form, and we look forward to the final copy when ready.

D. A. Waite

Rev. D. A. Waite, Th.D., Ph.D.
Director, THE BIBLE FOR TODAY, INC.
900 Park Avenue
Collingswood, NJ 08108
Phone: 609-854-4452

April 9, 1992

THE UNJUSTLY EXSCINDED TEXT

OF THE

THREE DIVINE WITNESSES;

An Account of 1 John 5:7-8, Exhorting Baptists to Preach

"all the counsel of God"

from the Entire Greek Received Text

by
Michael Maynard

An Enlargment upon a Paper
Originally Prepared for
Classical Philology 510
submitted to
Dr. Holt Parker
of the
Classics Department
University of Arizona

B.F.T. #2008

March 1991

Forward:

"And after him was Shammah the son of Agee the Hararite. And the Philistines were gathered together into a troop, where was a piece of ground full of lentiles: and the people fled from the Philistines. But he stood in the midst of the ground, and defended it. . ." (II Samuel 23:11, 12)

It is my privilege and joy to commend the work of a man whom God has raised up to defend one of the most vital "pieces of ground" in all of Scripture- I John 5:7,8. Here is a passage full of lentiles; but the Philistines have gathered, and the people fled! Those who feel a kindred spirit in their stand for the Received Text and Authorized Version will be thankful that God has endowed the author with the spritural insight, scholarship, and linquistic ability for such a defence. It is tragic that so many in fundamentalism are prepared to surrender what is in fact the Bible's central Trinitarian passage, but it is here that the stand must be made, and it is with gratitude that such a landmark contribution has now been made.

Ostensibly the work is a bibliography, but in reality it gives a succinct history of the debate that has raged over the *Johannine Comma* through the centuries. It is also a promise of further research from the author, and it is my prayer that he be encouraged and given every assistance in the crucial areas in which he is working.

Jack A. Moorman
Shropshire UK

> Now what is the influence upon the community of rejecting a part of it [the Bible],-of calling a verse, here and there, spurious? Other verses are soon suspected, expecially if they reveal an unpleasant doctrine, or inculcate an unpleasant duty. The public confidence is shaken, and infidelity is encouraged.

Rev. William W. Hunt (as quoted from Orme's *Memoirs*, p. 192)

B.F.T. #2008

THE EXSCINDED TEXT OF THE THREE DIVINE WITNESSES;

step one: split verse 6 in two,
1-6a This is he that came by water and blood, *even* Jesus Christ; not by water only but by water and blood. >>6b. And it is the Spirit that beareth witness, because the Spirit is truth. 7. For there are three that bear record in heaven, the Father, the Word, and the Holy Ghost: and these three are one. 8. And there are three that bear witness in earth, the spirit, and the water, and the blood: and these three agree in one.

Step two: Renumber verse 6b to 7 and verse 7 to 8. Separate the lower clause as shown:

2-6 This is he that came by water and blood, *even* Jesus Christ; not by water only but by water and blood. >>> 7. And it is the Spirit that beareth witness, because the Spirit is truth. 8. For there are three that bear record --->in heaven, the Father, the Word, and the Holy Ghost: and these three are one. X. And there are three that bear witness in earth, <--the spirit, and the water, and the blood: and these three agree in one.

Step three: Take away the marked clause
3-6 This is he that came by water and blood, *even* Jesus Christ; not by water only but by water and blood. >>> 7. And it is the Spirit that beareth witness, because the Spirit is truth. 8. For there are three that bear record -->.. ......, ..., ..., ...; ... . X. ... ., <---the spirit, and the water, and the blood: and these three agree in one.

Step four. Pull the verses together, so no one notices any tampering.
5-7 This is he that came by water and blood, *even* Jesus Christ; not by water only but by water and blood. >> 7. And it is the Spirit that beareth witness, because the Spirit is truth. 8. For there are three that bear record --><-- the spirit, and the water, and the blood: and these three agree in one.

1) Manuscripts and editions which include the Received Text clause:
61 88^{mg} 221^{mg} 429^{mg} 629 635^{mg} 636^{mg} 918 2318 vg^c vg^{dem} vg^{div} it^l it^m it^p it^q=it^r lat^{Bede} SYR^{Tr-mg} SYR^{Hu} SYR^{Gu} SYR^{Sch} ARM^{Usc} arm^{Zohr} GEO^{Mosc} vg$^{mss:}$ VG^{Six} VG^{Cl} VG^{WW} vg^{Leon} vg^{9000+} TR^{600+} ger^{Tepl} slav^x slav^y Ch.F^8

2) Current versions which have expunged the clause
ASV RSV LB New American Standard, New Internation Version, NRSV +others

Abbreviations

ADB	*Allgemeine Deutsche Biographie* 56 vols.
ANTF	*Arbeiten Zur Neutestamentlichen Textforschung*
DNB	*Dictionary of National Biography* 53 vols + supp.
ISBE	*International Standard Bible Encyclopdia* 4 vols. ['79-'88]
ME	*Mennonite Encyclopedia* 4 vols.
NBrit	*New Encyclopædia Britannica* (15th ed.)
NCE	*New Catholic Encyclopedia* 15 vols.
NDB	*Neue Deuutsche Biographie* 15 vols. (to date)
NSHE	*New Schaff-Herzog Encyclopedia* 12 vols.
RPTK	*Realencyklopädie für protestantische Theologie und Kirche* 24 vols.
TRE	*Theologische Realenzyklopädie* 18 vols.

INTF	Institut für Neutestamentliche Textforschung (Münster, Germany)
VLI	Vetus Latina Institut (Beuron, Germany)

Library sources:

in Tübingen:
a) Eberhard-Karls-Universität:
1. Fakultätsbibliothek Neuphilologie [Brecht Bau] 270,000 vol.
2. Katholisch-Theologisches Seminar [Theologicum]
3. Universitätsbibliothek [Wilhelmstraße 32], 2,443,000 vol.
b) Stadt:
4. Kulturamt/Stadtbücherei [Nonnengasse 19]

in Leipzig:
a) Universitätsbibliothek der Karl-Marx-University
5. Hauptbibliothek [Beethovenstraße 6] ~3,000,000 vol.
6. Section Theologie[1] [Emil-Euchs Straße]
b) Stadtbücherei
7. Deutsche Bücherei [18. Oktober Straße]

in Augsburg
8. Staats- und Stadtbibliothek [Schaezlerstraße 25]

---

1. This sign on the exterior of this library actually reads "Karl-Marx-Universität Section Theologie"

INTRODUCTION

-----The famous Bible commentator, Adam Clarke, claimed "the *seventh verse* of the *fifth chapter* has given rise to more theological disputes than any other portion of the sacred writings."[2] The following words in italics from verse 7 and 8 of 1 John 5 are referred to as the "comma" (κόμμα from κοπτειν, "to cut off"). "For there are three that bear record *in heaven; the Father, the Word, and the Holy Ghost; and these three are one. And there are three that bear witness in earth;* the spirit, and the water, and the blood; and these three agree in one."

There has been immense interest[3] in the disputed verse for several reasons. It is one example of those few verses included in the *Received Text* which have a "weak attestation" from Greek MSS, and which have caused many a student to pace "his study for hours struggling with the question"[4] whether the verse was an actual error.

Before proceeding, the terms will be defined. There are over 5300 Greek manuscripts (hereafter MSS) of the New Testament. A debate exists concerning which MSS are best. Though there are scholars of several viewpoints, all of them admit that 85% (+/- 5%) per cent of the MSS generally agree with each other.

MAJORITY TEXT = The name assigned to this bulk of MSS (85% of NT Greek MSS). It has several alternative names, but for simplicity, the term Majority Text (whose symbol is 𝔐)[5] will be employed. Those advocating that these MSS are the more trustworthy, will be referred to as Majority Text Advocates (hereafter "MTA")

MINORITY TEXT = The Greek manuscripts which comprise about 15% (+/- 5%) of the MSS, are also referred to with a variety of terms. Its advocates prefer the term "critical text", but for simplicity, the term Minority Text will be employed. Those advocating that

---

2. *The New Testament of Our Lord and Savior Jesus Christ Carefully Printed from the . . .Authorized Translation*.
3. Consider, e.g., the quantity of pages in entire books devoted to this *one verse* from five authors: Orme, Knittel, Porson, Armfield, and Forster: respectively 213pp + 251pp +406pp + 219pp + 271pp. Five authors combined wrote 1360 pages on this one verse!
4. "Baptists and Changing Views of the Bible" *Baptists; The Bible, Church Order and the Churches* (New York: Arno Press, 1980) 73. This phrase is being borrowed from an original context of doubts resulting from a question of higher criticism. However, the phrase is appropriate as well for our present question of lower criticism.
5. Old Testament scholars for years have already been applying the *MT* abbreviation for Massoretic Text).

these MSS are more trustworthy, will be referred to as the Minority Text Advocatates (hereafter "mta").

TEXTUS RECEPTUS (hereafter "TR"). This Latin expression is often applied to the *printed* Greek editions of the New Testament which dominated all other editions during the 16th, 17th, 18th, and 19th century. These editions are based upon a certain strand of MSS within the 𝔐. Hence the TR and 𝔐 agree in thousands of readings. But differences, "non-majority readings,"[6] exist. Because this Latin term is often referred to these *printed* editions, it is often said that the TR began in the 16th century. Martin Luther and William Tyndale used the TR as the Greek basis for their translations.[7]

RECEIVED TEXT: Rather than redefine the Latin term *textus receptus*, or *TR*, it seems best if we allow it to be further applied to be these *printed* Greek editions. But it becomes necessary to refer to Greek and non-Greek (French, German, Latin, Syriac) readings from pre-16th century manuscripts and incunabula which bear testimony to and pre-date the *printed* TR readings. Hence, these readings will be referred to with the English term *Received Text* (hearafter *RT*) readings. Advocates of this view, will be referred to as Received Text advocates (hereafter "RTa").

In addition to the aformentioned three groups, a fourth group believes that most of the RT readings are accurate, but not all. Depending on their criteria, they believe the RT should be corrected. The advocates of this position, will be referred to as partial Received Text advocates (hereafter "pRT").

In summary, these four veiwpoint are represented by:

mta = minority text advocate(s)
MTA = majority text advocate(s)
pRT = partial received text advocate(s)
RTa = received text advocate(s)

Those who claim the *Comma* does not belong in Scripture, delight to "count noses", i.e., they emphasize that the quantity of Greek support for a reading is small. With respect to the *Comma*, they count Greek MSS. Yet, when the vast bulk of Greek manuscripts do not support readings [8] favored by the mta, they accuse the MTA of "counting noses". If the

---

6. These few difference are often called "Latin Vulgate readings". The problem which this expression will be explained later.
7. Both Tyndale and Luther defied the Papacy, and both repudiated the papist doctrine of free will.
8. An example of a poorly attested reading favorable to the *mta* is the omission of the verb ὑποτάσσεσθε in Ephesians 5:22. The corrected edition of UBS3 (1983) says the verb occurs in K 181 326 614 629 630 1984 and in the vast majority of Byzantine MSS as well as in the lectionaries. The verb also appears as in D G 1985 1[55] in a different location within the verse. The verb appears as ὑποτασσέσθωσαν in Ψ cop[sa,bo], aleph. Further,

Comma were set aside, the New Testament textual debate would be simplified to a majority text view against a minority text view. But if this verse is taken into account, then the debate (concerning which Greek MSS of the New Testament are most reliable) expands to the four views mentioned above. Advocates of the first three views all agree that the *Johannine Comma* does not belong in Scripture. They say it is spurious. The fourth view has received most scorn from textual scholars. Yet the RT view is unique in that it recognizes that most of its text is supported by the majority of Greek MSS, but in the few verses where the RT differs from the 𝔐, it relies upon readings from Latin MSS which pre-date Jerome's version.

CATHOLIC EPISTLES: Baptists and others prefer the term General Epistles, but we must understand the term, which others use. The term refer to 5 books of the New Testament: James, 1 Peter, 2 Peter, 1 John, 2nd John, 3rd John, and Jude. If a student is interested whether one or more of these 5 books are contained in a certain MS, he will often encounter the abbreviations "c", "cath", or "*epist. cath.*" which do not suffice if he wants to know which MSS contain the 5th chapter of 1 John.

VULGATE: In modern days, this term is applied to the Latin MSS of Jerome. But the term was "previously given to the LXX and then to the Old Latin version."[9] Thus, the statement "Peter Waldo used the Vulgate." has several interpretations. Even further, the term was later used for the Greek Received Text. The Latin translation of "common Greek text" is *vulgatam Graecum editionem*. Sepulveda is an example of a scholar who used this Latin expression to refer to the Greek RT.

CATHOLIC: (In reference to one's denominational beliefs). One may say that Girolamo

---

ὑποτασσέσθωσαν appears in different locations within of the verse in aleph A I P 33 81 88 104 330 436 451 1241 1739 1877 1881 1962 2127 2492 2495. Apart from the vagueness of "Greek mss$^{acc\ to\ Jerome}$", of all the Greek manuscripts containing Ephesians ch. 5, the UBS3 editors indicate ONLY TWO distinct Greek manuscripts omit the verb. Only p^{46} and B omit it! In the Greek text, the UBS omits it. The NASB puts the verb in italics: *submit*. But one asks "How does this affect doctrine?" John F. MacArthur, Jr. demonstrates how in cassette #1 of his series *Family Feud* (1979). To his congregation (which numbers up to 6000), he preached

"Do you know that the verb *submit* does not appear in the original manuscript in verse 22. That might surprise you. You say "WHAT !!! There goes my whole theory" Your wife is saying "Hallelujah." Yeah, the verb doesn't appear there. It's only applied."

He repeated the error in 1986. In *The MacArthur New Testament Commentary; Ephesians*. On p. 280, he says: "As indicated by italics in most translations *be subject* is not in the original text. . ."

9. A. Vööbus, "Versions" *ISBE* 4:973.

Savonarola[10], John Hus, and Erasmus never left the Roman Catholic Church. Nor did the "Morning Star of the Reformation" leave it! (John Wycliffe died of a stroke "while hearing Mass.") But they were not loyal to it. They constantly rebuked the clergy and tried to reform it.

POPE: A definition employed by the signatories of the 2nd London Baptist Confession: "neither can the Pope of Rome in any sense be head thereof [of the church], but [he] is that antichrist, that man of sin, and son of perdition, that exalteth himself in the church against Christ and all that is called God; whom the Lord shall destroy with the brightness of his coming."[11]

PAPIST: This a term our Baptist forefathers used for those who are truly loyal to the Pope, to his teachings, and to his editions of the Latin Vulgate. Many Ecumenists find this term too harsh. Sepulveda and Lopez de Zuñiga are examples of Papists. They were zealous in their defense of "the Latin Vulgate."

---

10. As for Roman Catholicism, "He did not call in question a single one of its dogmas (cf Pastor, *Popes*, vi. 51). His only departure from the ecclesiastical belief of the time was his denial of the pope's infallibility." *NSHE* 10: 215. Yet "Protestants are inclined to regard him as in a sense a precursor of the Reformation, a seer of a new era in the Church. So Luther regarded him, and wrote a preface to an edition of his meditation on Pss 51 and 31 (1523)."
11. *The London Baptist Confession of Faith of 1689*, chap 26, #4, (Choteau, MT: Gospel Missions, 1980).

CODEX VATICANUS: This manuscript is "the glory of the great Vatican Library at Rome." Also known as "Codex B", this Greek MS differs from the TR throughout the entire NT. According to Philip Schaff, Burgon asserted on p. 164 of the *Quarterly Review* in October 1881, that in the Gospels alone, "B omits at least 2877 words, adds 536, substitutes 935, transposes 2098, modifies 1132 (total changes 7578)"[12] In a.1553, Sepulveda, a Papist, selected 365 reading from Codex B, to demonstrate how closely it agrees with their own Roman Catholic Latin Vulgate edition .

CODEX SIANITICUS This is also known as "Codex Aleph". Once again, according to Philip Schaff, Burgon asserted on p. 164 of the *Quarterly Review* in October 1881, that in the Gospels alone, "the corresonding figures in Aleph being severally 3455, 839, 1114, 2299, 1265, (in all 8972). This is one of the reasons for which the Dean. . . condemns Aleph and B as the most corrupt of MSS., and of course all the critical editions based on them. His list of departures is indeed formidable. . ."[13]

ECUMENISM: Its essence, is a disregard for Scriptual truth, for the sake of visible unity and harmony. The popular Greek Testaments of today are dependant upon two ecumenical institutes in Germany, founded in the 20th century; the VLI (1927), for Latin MSS, and the INTF (1959), for Greek MSS. In these institutes Papists and Protestants work side by side with the MSS, undoubtedly deciding which to suppress from the public, and which to include in the critical notes. The fact that Kurt Aland announced in 1977 that the cirulation of Nestle[26] "will be done in co-operation with the appropriate agencies of the Roman Catholic Church"[14] proves that the ecumenical institues have had the production of an ecumenical Greek N.T. as their underlying motive.

POPERY: John Gill said "Popery may be considered as a system of antichristian doctrines and practices, some of the prinicipal of which the apostle Paul has prophetically given notice of 1 Tim. iv. 1-3 . . .All of which are notorious doctrines and practices of the Papists."[15]

TEXTUAL CRITICISM: This term, as defined by mta, and MTA, is only properly used by non-RTa. Presumably, it originated in Germany. In the early 1860's Tischendorf called it his "new weapon",[16] against unbelieving criticism. In the final analysis, the underlying difference among the MTA, mta, RTa, pRT groups, is that only the RTa believe that the true Greek text has been forever settled. All other positions are century after century

---

12. P. Schaff *Companion to the Greek Testament* (London: MacMillan, 1883) 119.
13. Ibid.
14. K. Aland *United Bible Societies Bulletin 108/109 (1977)*
15. John Gill, "A Dissertation Concerning the Rise and Progress of Popery" *Sermons and Tracts by the Late Reverend and Learned John Gill* (Streamwood, IL: Primitive Baptist Library, Reprint 1981) 10.
16. K. Tischendorf. *When Were Our Gospels Written?* (London: Religious Tract Society, 1866) 113.

"faced with the problem of recovering the original wording"[17] of their lost text. Before the term *textual criticism* is even defined, the non-RTa presuppose that the true Greek text is lost and must be "recovered" or "restored". Only after this assumption is made by faith, without any proof, do they proceed with their definitions. For example: "The purpose and goal of texual criticism is the recovery, within the limits of possibility, of the original text."[18]

THE SYRIAC: The modern definition is the combined testimony of recent *editions* [not MSS] of the Syriac New Testament. Thus, the statement "The *comma Johanneum* does not appear in the Syriac!" means, that according to NA[26] (which does NOT cite Syriac MSS), the verse does not appear in a certain five printed editions, each of which is based on 1 or 2 MSS, or a slender portion of all exant Syriac MSS: sy^s(1910), sy^c(1904), sy^p(1920), sy^{ph}(1909), and sy^h(1778)(1803)(1889).[19] But if we deal with only editions of the Syriac, it is fair to say that the *Comma* does appears in at least four Syriac editions. See (1983: UBS3c) in this paper.

LATIN VULGATE: The term is associated with Jerome's Latin translation of the 5th century. But the term without clarification is vague. The following usages of the term, reveal the vagueness:

1. The Latin version completed by Jerome himself (after A.D. 384).
2. The Latin MSS of Jerome's version, said to be in use for 1000 years.
3. The predominace of these MSS which occurred "but not until the 9th century"[20]
4. *Codex Amiantinus*, said to be the best MS of the Vulgate tradition.
5. The latest edition of the printed Vulgate, e.g., Stuttgart 1975.

A discussion as to whether the *Comma* was in "the Latin Vulgate" is meaningless without a definition of the term. Some of the attempts to restore Jerome's version include: Alcuin's Vulgate (c.800), Theodulf's Vulgate (c.811), Lanfranc's Vulgate (1089), Stephan Harding's Vulgate (1109), etc. Erasmus said the *Comma* was in his Vulgate. The *Comma* was also found in the Mazarin Vulgate (1456), Froben's Vulgate (1509), Estienne's Vulgate (1528) the Sixtine Vulgate (1590), the Clementine Vulgate (1592), and Matthei's Vulgate (1782). In the 19th century, some editions of the Vulgate were based on one manuscript, *Codex Amantianus*, which does not contain the *Comma*. Besides the ironic exception of its appearance in the Latin editions by Nestle, the *Comma* is not found in 20th century Vulgates: the Wordsworth-White- Sparks-Adams Vulgate (1954), Stuttgart Vulgate, 1st ed.(1969), Stuttgart Vulgate, 2nd ed. (1975).

---

17. W. Pickering. *The Identity of the New Testament* (Nashville & New York: Thomas Nelson, 1977) 15. Notice that this presupposition is on the first page of his introduction.
18. G. Zuntz. *The Text of the Epistles; Disquisitions upon the Corpus Paulinus* (London: Oxford Univ. Press, 1953) 1.
19. For the idenification of these Syriac editions, see pages 56-57 of NA[26].
20. Vööbus. *ISBE* (Grand Rapids: Eerdmans, 1988) 4:973

BIBLE OF THE PAPACY: is the ever-changing "Latin Vulgate," which underwent a series of rescensions. One might use the term "Early Vulgate" to speak of the Vulgate MSS from A.D. 450- 800. Thus, the "Late Vulgate MSS" begin with Alcuin's rescension (c. 800). Theodulf's rescension was next. "During subsequent centuries the Alcuinian recension suffered the same fate that befell other earlier attempts at purifying the Vulgate text."[21] But corruptions of the text continued. "Within a few generations, therefore, complaints of corruption of the text were heard once again, and other efforts were made to arrest the decline in purity of the text."[22] Thus, Lanfranc worked at correction. In the 12th century Stephen Harding "purged the text of a large number of interpolations. . ."[23] Even further, in the 13th century, various societies of scholars (*correctorium*) were established to remove still further scribal corruptions. Thus, the character of the Vulgate MSS is that of corruption and correction, unlike the homogeneous character of the majority of Greek MSS. But despite all these corruptions and corrections of the Latin Vulgate MSS, many scholars agree that they still forms a type of text distinctly different from the Latin MSS prior to Jerome: the "Old Latin MSS". Further, whether they are 7th century Vulgate MSS or 16th century Vulgate editions, the Vulgate readings still oppose the *Received Text* readings, with a few exceptions, in that a few RT readings are found in the Vulgates of the Reformation. However the Vulgate editions of the 20th, removed these TR readings! But, as a whole, the 16th century Vulgate edition was regarded as agreeing strongly with *Vaticanus*. The printed Greek edition in use today by many Papists is the Nestle[26] Greek edition, which agrees often with *Vaticanus*.

LATIN VULGATE READINGS; This term ought to be used for readings which occur in Vulgate MSS, but which do not occur in the Old Latin. The oft-repeated claim that the *Johannine Comma* is a Latin Vulgate reading, is misleading, since it is an Old Latin reading, which was *transmitted by* (not derived from) Vulgate MSS. It also remained in Old Latin MSS whose longevity extented up to the 13th century.

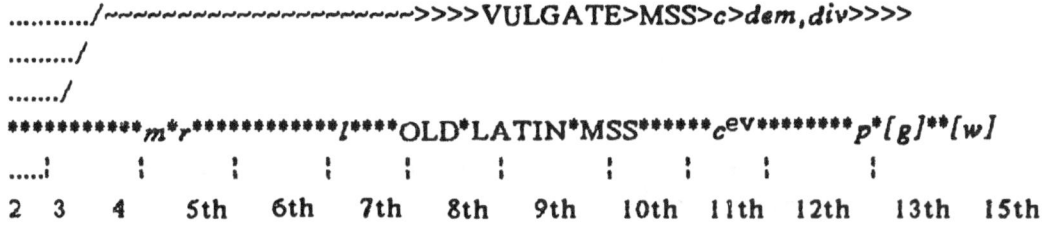

OLD LATIN MSS: This term, an update of the former "Old Italic", denotes the Latin MSS predating Jerome. They have been designated with letters. In the diagram above, apart from *g* and *w*, there are codes for seven MSS shown. All seven of these Latin MSS contain the *Johannine Comma*. (*g*, written in Bohemia, has an Old Latin text only in Acts

---

21. Metzger. *Early Versions of the New Testament*, 346.
22. Ibid.
23. Ibid.

and Revelation, and contains Acts 8:37a, 9:5, and 15:34. *w* contains Acts. Both *g* and *w* have a "remarkable feature" of longevity, respectively, into the 13th and 15th century).

What is the significance of the Old Latin? Today, the discovery of Greek papyri have superseded the role of the Old Latin MSS. However, in Appendix 8 of this paper, it is shown in detail, that for evaluation of 1 John 5:7-8, the Greek papyri are defective (cannot be checked) for that verse. Tischendorf expressed the importance of the Old Latin thus:

> The text of the old Italic is substantially that which Tertullian, about the end of the second century, and the Latin translator of Irenaeus still earlier, made use of. If we had any Greek text of the second century, [and today we do not for 1 John 5:7-8] to compare with this old Italic version, we should then be able to arrive at the original Greek text at that time in use. We should be able to approach very nearly to the original text which came from the Apostle's hands, since it is certain that the text of the second century must resemble more closely that of the first than any later text can be supported to. K. Tischendorf *When Were Our Gospels Written?* (London: Religious Tract Society, 1866) 114.

Do the Old Latin MSS correspond to the *Vaticanus,* the *Sianiticus,* the *Textus Receptus* or to the 𝔐? In other words, which of 5 groups is able to claim the Old Latin MSS for their views, the 19th century mta, the 20th century mta, the 19th century MTA, the 20th century MTA, or the RTa? Miller (19th cent. MTA), claimed the Old Latin for the "traditional text", another term for 𝔐. Tischendorf (20th cent. mta), claimed it for Codex Aleph.

Edward Miller:
> The best of the Old Latin Versions. . .were made two hundred years before those two manuscripts [Aleph and B], and . . .support the Traditional Texts.[24]

K. Tischendorf:
> Such a manuscript is before us in the Sinaitic copy, which more than any other is in closet agreement with the old Italic version.[25]

Who was correct? Miller or Tischendorf? Neither! Considering one text type, they were both wrong. The 20th century mta say there are doubtful cases whether a MS is Old Latin or Vulgate and call them "mixed texts". The 20th century MTA demonstrate a complete

---

24. E. Miller, *Guide to Textual Criticism of the New Testament* (1886) 85.
25. Tischendorf, *When Were our Gospels Written?* 116.

disregard for all Latin MSS, even the Old Latin MSS![26] Yet, Old Latin MSS were translated from Greek copies. It seems premature for the RTa (or anyone) to claim the Old Latin MSS today, since there are still so few. As of 1988, there are less that 30 for the Acts, less than 40 for the Pauline corpus.[27] Scrivener said the Old Latin MSS of his day, "agree remarkably with Cod. D and the Curetonian Syriac", but Kenyon's view (1912) that the extant Old Latin MSS "differ so greatly from one another" is problably the best reply, since some (as Hills showed) are corrupt. However, in spite of the variety, the RTa should be delighted that of so few Old Latin MSS which do contain the 5th chapter of John's First Epistle, at least four of them testify to the *Comma*.

The implications of an undisputed verdict of "spurious" upon the *Comma* leaves the mta, MTA, and the pRT to continue their debate over which MSS are most reliable. Whereas a verdict of "genuine" causes three groups to reluctantly abandon long-held cherished theories on MSS.

It is important to recognize the variety of attacks upon the received text. A popular tactic is to attempt to discredit the entire RT by the so-called interpolation. First they chose to begin with Erasmus. A few words are given about the "origin of the textus receptus." However, this popular "origin" account is misleading. In an aricle published in Kurt Aland's *Studia Evangelica*, K.W. Clark says:

> We should not attribute to Erasmus the creation of a "received text", but only the transmission from a manuscript text already commonly received to a printed form in which this text would continue to prevail for three centuries more.[28]

---

26. Even Hoskier said (after commenting on Bently's intended plans to restore the Greek and Latin) "Since then, comparatively speaking, much has been done as regards Greek MSS., but little as regards the Latin" *The Golden Latin Gospels in the Library of J.Pieront Morgan* (New York: privately printed, 1910).
27. Vööbus *ISBE* 4: 971.
28. *The Gentle Bias and Other Essays*. "The Erasmian Notes in Codex 2." (Leiden: E.J.Brill,1980), 168. Even a century ago, George W. Samson said "It is an unwarranted custom to allude to the text. . .at the era of the Reformation, styled in Latin the "textus receptus," as if it were made up at that time;" *The Text Used for the Revised New Testament Shown to Be Unauthorized.* (1882, Collingswood, NJ: Bible for Today, 1988), 18.

After a few words about Erasmus and his text, they proceed with their case againt the *entire* TR, by focusing upon an alledged "error" (the most evident one being the *Comma*!). Their liberty to dicuss any other possibility of "errors" in the printed TR, surely depends upon the *first error* found within the Received Text. Consequently, this is the basis they build upon. They devote much time and ink on this *one verse*, claiming that it is an *interpolation* (an unjustified insertion of words) from the Latin Vulgate. The accounts tell us, again and again, that the verse came from "the Vulgate" and that from marginal readings, it "crept into" (or "found its way" into) the main Greek text. Therefore, by these planting of doubts, they have implied that the entire RT tradition ought to be under suspicion, since they have labored to establish proof of a claim for the *first* undisputed "error" within that tradition. But their claim continues to be disputed.

One may say that, before one considers the facts, an *initial* arousal of suspicion toward any claim for an "error" (or for any other possible "errors") is understandable as long as a *hasty generalization* is avoided. But often, it is not avoided. Three examples follow, in which this fallacy was not avoided. First, in A.T. Robertson's *An Introduction to the Textual Criticism of the New Testament* (2nd ed.,1928), chapter one is entitled "The Textus Receptus" and is 11 pages in length. About one-third of the article deals with 1 John 5:7-8! Secondly, in 1979, D.A. Carson devoted about 25% of his "Origins of the Textus Receptus" to the *Comma*. Thirdly, in a debate held in 1983, Dr. S. Custer, in his opening rebuttal, declined to refute his opponent's assertions, and changed the issues. He spoke for 9 minutes 32 seconds.[29] In this time, he invested 43.7% (4 minutes 10 seconds) contending that the *Comma* is spurious.

One wonders whether modern authors in their attempt to describe the "origin of the *textus receptus*" are capable of doing so without a tendency to employ the fallacy of *converse accident*, i.e, to hastily generalize the RT as deficient, on account of a half dozen verses, one of them inevitably being the *Johannine Comma*.

-----One reason for this history and bibliography on the famous verse is to provide resources for those who are aware of the recent revival of interest on the views of the MTA and those of the RTa, and who realize that other verses which lack an abundance of Greek MS support, Acts 8:37, Acts 9:5-6, the *Johannine Comma*, etc., will be major factors in deciding which postion to adopt.

Before proceding with the discusssion, another unique feature of the verse must be announced. De Jonge describes it thus, in *Erasmi Opera Omnia*, IX-2: 257 note 505, elaborating on "codex" as it appears in the context of Erasmus' discussion.

---

29. The time-keeper intended to give each of the four debaters 10 minutes for their opening comments. After Dr. Quorello spoke, 13 seconds of silence (except for some light laughter in the audience) followed. If these 13 are added, then we may say the timekeeper called "time" on Custer after 9 minutes 45 seconds. However, the point is that from my cassette copy, Custer's opening comments lasted 9 min 32 sec.

The Codex Vaticanus *par excellence*, now Gr. 1209, B in N.T. textual criticism. This is the very first time that this highly important ms. is appealed to for critical purposes. On 18 June 1521 Paul Bombasius, the secretary of the cardinal Lorenzo Pucci at Rome, sent a letter to Er. containing a copy of I *Ioh*.4,1-3, and 5, 7-11 from the Cod. Vatic.(Ep. 1213). In his *Annot.* on *I Ioh*.Er. stated in 1522 that the *Comma* was missing from the Cod. Vat. ..

The significance of mentioning this, is that serveral books claim that Erasmus had neither access nor knowledge of any minority texts readings from uncials or from anywhere.

The MTA, pRT, and the RTa all have high esteem for the bulk of MSS known as 𝔐. But since the release of Codex B and the discovery of Codex aleph and certain papyri, most scholars in this modern day are mta, and regard 𝔐 as inferior. This claim was sufficiently disproved by MTA such as Burgon,[30] Scrivener,[31] Hoskier [32] in the late 1800s but their works have been generally ignored and forgotten, until recently.[33]
An interesting series of events took place. In 1934 Edward F. Hills graduated summa cum laude from Yale University. He obtained an A.B. in classics. In 1946 he obtained his Th.D. from Harvard Divinity School. His contributions were discussed in a thesis [34] by Theodore P. Letis. Dr. Hills was influencial upon Wilbur N. Pickering, who obtained his masters in Greek exegesis.

The development of interest in the 𝔐 and the TR is noted by the the following new organizations, dissertations, books, and reprints:

year	stand	title of organization or book
1831	TR	Trinitarian Bible Society
1950	TR	*God Wrote Only One Bible* J.J. Ray.
1951	𝔐	"Critical Examination of the H-W Textual Theory" by Alfred Martin
1956	TR	*The King James Version Defended* E.F. Hills.
1968	𝔐	*Contr. of John W. Burgon to NT Text Crit.* W. Pickering.
1971	TR	"Which Bible? Society" was founded by D.O.Fuller.
1971	TR/𝔐	*Which Bible?* (included essay by Burgon et al.)

---

30. *The Revision Revised (1883)*
31. *A Plain Introduction to Textual Criticism of the New Testament, 4th ed. (1894)*
32. *Codex B and Its Allies (1914)*
33. These are available from 900 Park Ave. Collingswood, NJ 08108
34. *The Contribution of Edward Freer Hills to the Revival of the Ecclesiastical Text*. Journey Magazine (Nov-Dec 1987) published by Grace Orthodox Presbyterian Church of Lynchburg, VA, reports on page 4 "Rumor has it that Rushdoony considers this work so significant that a whole issue of *The Journal of Reconstruction* will be given over to Letis' output next year."

1976	TR	*The Greek Text Underlying the English A.V. of 1611* (by TBS)
1977	MT	*Identity of the New Testament* Dr. Wilbur N. Pickering
1978	TR	Nov: "Dean Burgon Society" (DBS) founded by Dr. D.A. Waite
1981	MT	Mar: Burgon's *Revision Revised (1883)* reprinted by DBS
1982	MT	*Greek Text According to the Majority Text* published by Nelson
1983	MT	May: Burgon's *Last Twelve Verses of Mark (1871)* reprinted by DBS
1983	MT	Sep: Burgon's/Miller's *Tradition Text of...Gospels* reprinted by DBS
1983	MT	Sep: Burgon's/Miller's *Causes of Corruption (1896)* reprinted by DBS
1984	MT	*The Byzantine Text and NT Textual Criticism.* H. Sturz.
1985	MT	Jan: Scrivener's *Plain Introduction to Text. Crit.* reprinted by DBS
1988	TR	Jan: "Institute for Reformation Biblical Studies" founded
1988	MT	Dec: "Majority Text Society" founded by Dr. Pickering
1988	MT	TBS officer shifted his position[35] from RTa to MTA.
1989	pRT	"Christian Liturature World" Journal founded by J.Green
1989	mta	Nov 15: "Great Christian Books [36]" advertises Burgon!
1990	MT	Burgon's *Unholy Hands on the Bible* [37] appears on the market.

Soon after *Identity of the New Testament Text* was on the market, one reviewer was so shocked that he began his review of Pickering's book with:

> "The Textus Receptus is as dead as Queen Ann," A.T. Robertson used to say. But if that judgment is accurate, Queen Ann must be experiencing something of a resurrection. Certainly there is a revival of interest in the Greek Textus Receptus (TR) today, and at just such a time as most scholars were convinced on its "death" and "burial".[38]

In his published reply, Pickering made it clear to his reviewer that he is an MTA, not a RTa.

---

35. D.A. Waite, *Answer to Andrew Brown of the Trinitarian Bible Society*, Bible For Today, CS-1561 #1 & #2, Jan 2, 1988, cassettes. In April 1990, the TBS reported Mr. A.J. Brown's termination from the Society.

36. This major book distributor (formerly called Puritan Reformed) is noted for its promotion of books by mta editors (esp. NIVs and NIV aids). This Nov 15 issue was of special interest since it advertised not only a book by an MTA (Burgon), and one with MTA/RTa contributors (Letis: *The Majority Text...*), page 6; but even a book by an exclusive RTa (Hill's 4th ed. of *The King James Version Debate*, page 6!)

37. GCB advertised *"Unholy Hands on the Bible, vol. 1.* John Burgon" on its back cover of the Nov 15, 1989 issue. This hardbound book, published by Sovereign Grace Trust Fund, was released in 1990. A sampling of the multitude of errors introduced by its editor, J.P. Green, Sr., was provided in an article "Whose Unholy Hands on What?" See (1990: ROBINSON)

38. See *Journal of Evangelical Theological Society*, xx, (December 1977) 377-381.

Despite the fact that all these new societies with RTa and MTA have formed, and that all these Burgon reprints were made, some seminaries, and some classics departments in universities, still have never heard of Burgon. But how are Burgon and the MTA relevant to the debate over the *Comma*, which is regarded as part of the RT? As already mentioned, the RT view recognizes most of its text is supported by a majority of Greek MSS. If indeed we are at the start of a revival toward the majority text, and if modern scholars will finally stop quoting Metzger's commentary or his handbook as the last word on every textual issue, and will *begin* to study (with discernment as a Baptist) Nolan, and Hills, (after gaining a familiarity with Burgon, Scrivener, and Hoskier), then the time is ripe to draw their attention to the evidence in favor of non-majority Greek readings such as the *Comma Johanneum*.

In a paper entitled *Demystifying the Controversy Over the Textus Receptus and the King James Version of the Bible*, the authors, Douglas S. Chinn and Robert C. Newman write on p.7

> One of the authors (DSC) asked Wilber N. Pickering...how he
> resolved the problem of minority text readings in the KJV with his majority text thesis. In a letter dated January 19, 1978, he answered stating, "The status of I John 5:7, etc. will be resolved in due time."

The implication of a undisputed verdict of "authentic" upon the verse would imply a conclusion that even the mta will be pleased to hear, viz., that the majority of Greek MSS which contain I John chap 5, are slightly defective in that area of verse 7. Such a conclusion is not even conceivable to some, and thus they have shifted to the pRT.

Though there is no dispute that the number of Greek manuscripts which contain the passage is very few, the current popular belief that it "is absent from the manuscripts of all ancient versions (Syriac, Coptic, Armenian, Ethiopic, Arabic, Slavonic)..." (Metzger, 1975) is misleading, for one may refer to a statement by Scrivener

> ...scarely any Armenien codex exhibits it, and only a few recent Slavonic copies, the margin of a Moscow editon of 1663 being the first to represent it.[39]

In the attack upon the majority text, the mta often indicate that it is a serious error to over-emphasize the quantity of Greek MSS, at the expense of neglecting the quality. Thus, it is tragic that these mta commit the same error with an continual emphasis that the *Johannine Comma* does not have a bulk of Greek MSS supporting it. Because of the lack of *Greek* MS support, an editor wrote.

---

39. *A Plain Introduction to the Textual Criticism of the New Testament*, 4th ed., p.403.

There is hardly a passage in all literature more demonstrably spurious.[40]

But if that were true, why have there been, and why are there so many defenders of the *Comma* (as shown in appendix one)? The debate ought to be of further interest today, when one considers the statement of an authority in the classics (1908: Sandys) concerning Richard Porson and his *Letters to Travis*, in which "he proved the spuriousness" of the disputed text. If Porson proved its spuriousness back in 1790, we would expect widespread acceptance of his refutation, and no further debate. Indeed, over a hundred years ago, a commentator (1880: Kitto) described this passage as "once contested but now rejected". If that is the case, we ought to expect no further discussion on this passage after 1880 and certainly no further published discussion. But has the discussion ceased?

At this point consider that three of the following four alternative views were discussed by one of the most scholarly defenders of the RT [41]

1. The Naturalist Critical View   = mta   >liberals
2. The High Anglican View   = MTA   >Anglicans
3. The Orthodox Protestant View   = RTa   >Lutherans, Presbyterians
4. The Inclusive Age View   = RTa   >Waldenses, Lollards, et al.

Even the issue of theological classification is relevant to the discussion of the disputed verse. Within these four views, the respective denominational groups (in very generalized terms) are listed. Hills showed the deficiency of restricting the debate to only the first two viewpoints, neither of which allows for the inclusion of the non-majority RT readings into a standard text. He depicts the theological views of the brilliant MTA scholars (Burgon,

Scrivener, and Miller) to show why they "looked askance" at the RT. Thus the *Comma* was rejected. Hills sets forth the third view to defend Reformation theology, which provides a basis for accepting non-majority RT readings, such as the *Comma*. But if one seeks to defend the *Comma*, it is not necessary to adopt the "Reformation text" view, since a fourth viewpoint exists, whose history begins centuries before the Reformation. The Oxthodox Protestant View has at least three deficiencies.

---

40. *Ellicot's Commentary*, 1959 edition
41. E.F. Hills *The King James Version Defended*, 3rd ed., 1979, p.219.

Firstly, it overlooks the use of a Received Text during the pre- Reformation age. The fourth group includes the neglected medieval age. The third view promotes the term "Reformation Text" not merely to suggest the RT was used in Reformation days, but to DEFEND Reformation theology and to call for a New Reformation. In his defense of the received text, Dr. Hills claimed

> The Defense of the Textus Receptus, therefore, is a necessary part of the defense of Protestantism.[42]

---

42. E.F. Hills, *The King James Version Defended*, 3rd ed., p.193

Secondly, if the *Comma* is genuine, the Oxthodox Protestant position (Reformed and Lutheran) is somewhat deficient. Why? Although the Greek Received Text is that "which represented unimpeachable orthodoxy in the eyes of the Lutherans" [43] of the 17th and 18th centuries, the historic Lutheran position is to reject the *Johannine Comma*. Apart from Calvin and Beza, "other early Reformers and friends of Luther generally rejected the passage" [44]

Thirdly, the Protestant view utilizes the factor of the printing press not to explain how the RT was distributed so widely in printed form, but rather to interpret this distributed printed text as a "restoration" of the true text, almost as if it were not preserved, but lost during the medieval ages. Protestants[45] often view the Middle Ages either as *Christendom* in its infant stage, or as being without the true Gospel, and hence without Christianity. Thus, medieval groups have been slandered by Reformed and Catholic churches as *Donatisten, Stäbler, Catharer, Sacramentschwärmer, Winckler, Wiedertäufer, Kommunisten, and Rottengeister.* [46] Today, they are slandered as "heretics", "schismatics", or "sectarians". This is the old (yet erroneous) historiography that Ludwig Keller labored to kill. Leonard Verduin, who is associated with the Christian Reformed Church, says "There seems to have been some dualistic tendencies among the Albigenses; but it also appears that these dualistic touches led to grave tensions between this variety of heretics, and those whose system revolved about the repudiation of Constantinianism." [47] But Reformed authors [48] portray all of them as holding to the heresy of dualism [49] or

---

43. Reuß. *NSHE* 5:77.
44. See the quotes in this paper listed under (1527: LUTHER), (1888: ABBOT) and (1985: POSSET). Let there be no misunderstanding of the immense contribution Luther made (translation skills, text distribution, etc.) to the German Received Text. But let us beware of the error which J.D. Michaelis, E. Nestle, and others made, i.e., to ignore all Luther's contributions to the Received Text, and instead to exploit Luther's error on 1 John 5:7,, and to quote Luther as if Luther himself were a 4th century Greek uncial.
45. *Why Baptists are not Protestants* by C. E. Tulga, D.D. and *The Reformation, or Protestant Societies not Christian Churches, and Baptists not Protestant* (1855) by John H. Waller, are examples of liturature explaining why Baptists ought not to identify with this name.
46. Leonard Verduin. *The Reformers and Their Stepchildren*. Grand Rapids: Eerdmans, 1964, p.9
47. *The Reformers and Their Stepchildren*, 99.
48. E.g., the Free Presbyterian writer Alan Cairns in *Dictionary of Theological Terms*, (Greenville, SC: J.C. Print, Ltd., 1982), 2.
49. To mention a very interesting third view, Dr. Hauck concurs with Dr. Allix that "the Albigenses were not dualist, but identical with the Waldenses, and he [Allix] contributed much to the upholding of this erroneous view." *Schaff-Herzog*

Docetism. Cairns [50] also errs when he says that Waldensians "knew nothing of the Protestant doctrine of justification." The idea that heretics would use a pure text (the Received Text) is inconceivable to defenders of Reformation theology. Therefore they must employ a form of the word "restore" to describe their views. For example, in one of the (unnumbered) binder pages describing the "Purposes and Goals" of a recently formed RTa society, we find;

> The Reformation was the restoration of the true Gospel. . .It was also the restoratation of. . .the true canon and original language texts.[51]

Protestants have also taught that the Bible was hardly in use during the Middle Ages. But only recently have Protestants begun to admit their error. Johann Michael Reu says:

> We do not, of course, want to conclude from the results established in sections I and II that before the Reformation, the Bible was the most extensively circulated and most widely read book, but only that, together with its related literature, it was much more extensively used than the almost universal popular opinion among Protestants wants to admit, *even today*.[emphasis mine][52]

Dr. Hans Rost says:

> To be sure, however, it is a fabel, that the Bible in Luther's time lay under the bench and had been unknown in the catholic world. Protestant research has long ago abandoned this claim and made the concession, "that as concerns the outward knowledge of the Bible, it had not, at the beginning of the Reformation lain under the bench." (W. Köhler, Katholizismus und Reformation, S. 13). In 1494 Sebastion Brant wrote in his *Narrenschiff*: "All

---

Encyclopedia of Religious Knowledge. 12 vols. (New York & London: Funk and Wagnels, 1908) 1:133. Professor Albert Hauck, Ph.D., D.Th.,D.Jur., the famous church historian of Germany, edited the *Realencyklopädie für protestantische Theologie und Kirche*.

50. *Dict. of Theol. Terms*, 200.

51. This society is the Institute for Reformation Biblical Studies. Having been invited to their first meeting (1988) in Ft. Wayne, IN, I was not only impressed with their discussions, but especially with the zeal of the Lutherans in favor of the *Johannine comma*. The historiography (Baptist) that I hold, differs too sharply with theirs. This difference prevented my further involvement with the IRBS. However, let this be a testimony to all, that despite two contrasting views of history, both parties agree on the text.

52. J.M.Reu, *Luther's German Bible* (Columbus, OH: Lutheran Book Concern, 1934) 55.

the countries are now filled with the Sacred Scriptures" and Janssen can write "The rapid succesion of the printings and the explicit testimonies of the contemporaries indicates a wide diffusion of the translations of the Sacred Scriptures among the people." "The Bible under the bench" is a fabel, which no one can maintain any longer.[53]

Nor can we rely on the Reformation architects even on the determination of the New Testament canon. Metzger elaborates:

> How easily an individual can err in these matters is shown by the untenable judgements of Luther on the Epistles of James, of Jude, to the Hebrews, and the Apocalypse. . . Zwingli's denial of the Biblical character of the Book of Revelation was the result of contemporary controversies.... Subsequently at the Berne disputation (1528), Zwingli declared that this book is not a Biblical book.[54]

A rough illustration of the four views

legend:
/////////// =RT Latin readings (non-majority)
\\\\\\\\\\\ =Byz reading (majority)
xxxxxxxxxx =Received Text
>>>>>>>>>> =RT readings (editions of Greek NT)
.... =gap
@@@@@@@@@@ =minority text

1. minority text view
@@@@\@\\\\\\\\\\\\\\\\\\\\\\\\\\\\\>>>>>>>>>@>@@ true reading = @
1 2 3 4 5 6 7 8 9 10 11 12 13 14 15 16 17 18 19 20
        gap: 1500 yrs

2. majority text view
\\\\\@\@\\\\\\\\\\\\\\\\\\\\\\\\\\\>>>>>>>>>@>@>>\ true reading = \
1 2 3 4 5 6 7 8 9 10 11 12 13 14 15 16 17 18 19 20
     gap   gap

---

53. Hans Rost. *Die Bibel im Mittelalter; Beiträge zur Geschichte und Bibliographie der Bibel*. (Augsburg: Kommisions Verlag M. Seitz, 1939)
54. B.M. Metzger, *The Canon of the New Testament*. (Oxford: Clarendon Press, 1987), 273

3. Reformation view
xxxx\\@\@\\\\\\\\\\\\\\\\\\\\\\\\\\\\\>>>>>>>>>>@>@>@> true reading = >
1 2 3 4 5 6 7 8 9 10 11 12 13 14 15 16 17 18 19 20
      gap: 1000 years

4. Inclusive Age view
xx//@x@//x\\x//x\\x//x//x\\x//x>>>>>>>>>@x@x@x true reading = x (or \+/)
1 2 3 4 5 6 7 8 9 10 11 12 13 14 15 16 17 18 19 20
      gap: minimal

Reformers and non-Reformers assisted with the promotion of Greek editions of the RT, but the impression is given, that a text with RT non-majority readings (in any language) was unknown during the medieval ages, when we are told the Gospel and Christianity did not exist. However, this proposed fourth view does allow for these non-majority readings (which were *kept pure in all ages*) in Latin, French, German, etc. without slandering medieval Christianity.

This background information on theological views was necessary to explain some of the current factors involved in the debate. Centuries ago, other theological views that affected one's view against the genuineness of the verse include Sabellianism, and Arianism. Today Unitarianism persists. The Harvard scholar Ezra Abbot described the *Johannine Comma* as a "gross interpolation", but his bias is immediately understood, once we recognize that he was a Unitarian.

In the early drafts of this paper, no mention was made to the historical importance of the Greek Received Text for Baptists. Theology was kept separate from the textual issue. But as we ruminate about the past, we note that Lutheran, Reformed, and Baptist theologians of the 16th, 17th, and 18th centuries, all agreed upon the Received Text. Hence, a mere possession (without proper application) of the correct text does not suffice. However, as Baptists, we cannot properly apply the text, when we still do not agree which Greek text is correct.

As a result of the popular view that "theology is irrelevant to the identity of the text", many authors involved in the textual debate do not want their views labeled as "dogmatic" or "theological." Thus, they remain quiet about their denominational views.

Sturz said the Burgon-Hills position rests on a "theological and dogmatic basis." Metzger, an ordained minister, has criticized Burgon's views as "theological and speculative." After denouncing theological presuppositions, they resort to their own presuppositions, which many do not agree with, to engage in research in an alleged "neutral" fashion.

As Baptists, we believe that a Scriptural theology results in Baptist distinctives, missionary work, revivals, evangelism, personal pursuit of holiness, even the doctrine of Bible Preservation, and above all, the Soveignty of God. Generally speaking, all these duties and doctrines comprise a "theology" that is "irrevelant" to a critic who is supposedly "neutral." They may cry out "We don't follow your theology. We follow only the manuscripts." This claim appears objective, and scientific. But the fact that MSS today are still largely ingored, reveals that the critics are yet bound by their presuppositions.

Johann S. Semler tried to separate theology. "One of Semler's most important theses was his distinction between theology and religion. By means of this distinction he created free course for this criticism and thereby liberated scientific research from the theological odium, his purpose being to grapple with the Christian faith itself."[55]

But Semler "soon felt a profound disinclination toward all manner of pietism, only by degrees, however..." In his later days "he busied himself with natural sciences, alchemy, mystical theosophy, and freemasonry."

While the major theme of this paper is a discussion of 1 John 5:7-8, an attempt is being made to contribute toward a resolution of four deficiencies among Baptists.

1. Often, we Baptists will either rejoice over the Doctrines of Grace, and then argue in defense of an <u>ever-changing</u> Greek text, or we will argue for a <u>forever-settled</u> Word of God and then misunderstand Particular Baptists as being "anti-missionary."
2. Today, many Baptist are not even familiar with the term "Particular Baptist", although nearly every book on Baptist history begins with a section on "General Baptists" and "Particular Baptists" and defines the terms.
3. Despite occassional claims of revival of interest among ourselves in Baptist History, it seems that there is still widespread disinterest and lack of knowledge of our own Baptist heritage amoung us.
4. Baptists, beginning around 1850, have placed excessive confidence in scholarship from non-Baptists. At times we have accepted their views without any question, and thus have been led into grievous error.

Two noteable exceptions demonstrate that non-Baptists works, are not always to be discarded: The 2nd London Confession (1689): based upon a Presbyterian document. The Authorized Version (KJV): largely the work of Anglicans, and yet "Most English-speaking Baptist families have three or more copies of that one translation,. . . Most Baptist preachers still preach from the King James Version."[56]

---

55. Carl Mirbt. *NSHE*,10:355.
56. Bush & Nettles, *Baptists and the Bible*, 406.

These are exceptions from the 17th century, where we have no cause to regret. But in the 18th and 19th century, it was especially regretable that many Baptists adopted rationalistic principles from the non-Baptists.

It should be explained, that so-called Anabaptists (of the 16th), and Baptists (of the 17th, and 18th centuries), did not have the textual debate among themselves as we do today. They used the Greek *Textus Receptus*. For this reason, there have seldom been Baptists (if any) in these centuries, who tampered with the text and won the currently coveted title "textual critic."[57] The term, carries the concept of a scholar who zealously searches the globe for neglected MSS to be compared to the Greek TR, which he believes is in desparate need of "restoration". But, with that definition, it is a blessing that we have practically no Baptist texual critics of the 17th and 18th centuries. Thus, most of the quotations in this paper, will necessarily be from non-Baptists; not to endorse them, but to acknowledge that the context of the history of textual criticism is largely non-Baptist and secular, to discerningly use their findings to build a stronger case for trust in the RT, and to trace the development of textual criticism from those engaged in it, and to show where and how Baptists began to depart from their heritage.

-----It is grievous that in 1980 Bush and Nettles could publish *Baptists and the Bible*, and within 450 pages could find no space to explicitly mention the "Greek Received Text." But Robert J. Barnett has properly said that this Greek text "which was preserved pure and authentic to the generation of our 17th century [Baptist] forefathers was the Greek Textus Receptus from which our King James Version was translated." [58]

Some may ask "Why bother with secular history?" B.R. White replies:

> The reason for facing this question as students of Baptist History is, in essence, very simple: secular society provided at least 95 per cent of the context in which any man, any congregation, or any institution in Baptist History which we decide to study actually lived.[59]

---

57. Two examples: In May 1990, Gary Hudson announced he had two scholarly works "by a man who holds an academic Ph.D in Textual Criticism". In Oct 1990, J.P. Green, Sr. proudly spoke of Peter J. Johnston as "a first-rate textual critic." *SGT Perspective* (1990). Both Mr. Hudson and Mr. Green profess to be Baptists. Apparently, laymen are expected to sigh with relief whenever an article by a textual critic comes into their neighborhood, to correct their TR. The wise laymen will discern that "textual correcter of the TR" is a more explicit term.
58. *Word of God on Trial* (Wyoming, MI: Paris Press, 1981) 7.
59. Barrington R. White "Why Bother with History?" *Baptist History and Heritage*, IV, No.2 (July 1969) 78-88.

B.R. White continues in a later paragraph:

> We cannot avoid knowing that Baptists are influenced by the generation in which they live, by the country in which they live and by the politics of the class to which they belong-let us recognize these facts![60]

If it is only secular institutions which are collecting MSS, and being selective (careless/forgetful?) to reveal certain MSS, it calls for caution. Likewise if we depend upon ecumenical institutions to collect and catalog MSS, and if their ulterior motive is ecumenism at all costs, we ought to begin questioning their textual notes.

Is church history often neglected by textual critics? Kurt Aland says:

> The evidence of church history, an area largely if not completely ignored by textual critics, is decisive at this point.[61]

Above all, this paper is an attempt to deal with the disputed passage of 1 John 5:7-8 from a Baptist historiography. Selected incidents of church history (esp. Baptist history) have been interwoven into a chronological bibliography. The standard form was modified to include page numbers and often to omit names of individual printers/publishers.

It is not without reason that the *Comma* has been displayed so often throught this work. E.F. Hills has said:

> God must do more than merely preserve the inspired original New Testament text. He must preserve it in a public way. . .in such a manner that all the world may know where it is and what it is. . .not secretely, not hidden away. . .but openly before the eyes of all men through the continuous usage of His Church.[62]

Harry Sturz objected "To assert what of necessity lies upon God would seem to go too far. . ." and "Why must God do so?"[63] A suggested improvement upon the important statement by Hills, is to replace each occurrence of "must" with "did". Thus we have : God did do more. . .He did preserve it in a public way. (etc.) Why? "that all the world may know where it is and what it is."

-----The following bibliography is positioned after selected citations relevant to the debate. Orme provided a bibliography in 1830, and the last entry of T.H.Horne's

---

60. Ibid.
61. *The Text of the New Testament.* 52.
62. *King James Version Defended* (1956) 29.
63. *The Byzantine Text Type and NT Textual Criticism.* (Nashville: Thomas Nelson, 1984) 42.

listing is 1852. It appears that over a 100 years have passed and Horne's list has yet to be updated. In this update the items were re-arranged in chronological order. For that reason, quotes from selected church "fathers," which form the substance of much of the debate, were placed before the actual bibliography. The bibliographic items (until 1852) which were not included in Horne's list, are indicated with an asterik (*). By no means is the list complete. Others will be added in an new edition, as they are obtained. The dates and citations for the church "fathers" are those employed in 1982 by Raymond Brown, as indicated by "per RB." (Professor Brown does not regard the *Comma* as authentic). Elsewhere, only the date of the recorded death of the father is given. Thus the date of the writing is prior to that given.

Latin quotations (as well as German) have occasionally been included throughout this paper for the encouragement of students to study these languages.

> . . .the Latin language has remained a mark of the educated man throughout the centuries, although since World War II the popularity of classical languages in schools has declined, and a generation of scholars who know no Latin. . .will soon be seen. [64]

A.D. 70   [The fall of Jerusalem]

147-157   [The rulership of bishop Pius I]

According to Mill, Pius I was the first bishop of Rome after Clement, who bears a Latin name. Consequently, Mill felt the Old Latin translation was made prior to A.D. 157.

c. 215   TERTULLIAN. *Adversus Praxean* (25.1; CC 2, 1195), per RB.

> Ita connexus Patris in Filio, et 'Filii' in 'Paracleto' tres efficit cohærentes, alterum ex altero, qui "tres unum sunt," *non unus;* quomodo dictum est, "ego et Pater unum sumus," ad *substantiæ* unitatem, non ad *numeri* singularitatem."

c.220-c.270   [Dominance of the heretical view of Sabellianism]

c.250   CYPRIAN. *De catholicae ecclesiae unitate.* (*Corpus Scriptorum Ecclesiastocorum Latinorum*. vol. III, p.215.)

> Dicit dominus, Ego et pater unum sumus (John x.30), et iterum de Patre, et

---

64. Re.P "Languages of the World: Romance Languages" *Encyclopedia Britannica* (1985) 649.

Filio, et Spiritu Sancto scriptum est, *Et tres unum sunt*[65]

SIGNIFIANCE: Cyprian is regarded as one "who quotes copiously and textually"[66] Further, the interpolation "In Chriso Iesu" does not yet appear.

c.250 CYPRIAN. *Epistle to Jubaianus*.

> Si baptizari quis apud haereticos potuit, utique et remissam peccatorum consequi potuit, -si peccatorum remissam consecutus est, et sanctificatus est, et templum Dei factus est, quaero cujus Dei? Si Creatoris, non potuit, qui in eum non credidit; si Christi, nec hujus fieri potuit templum, qui negat Deum Christum; si Spiritus Sancti, cum tres unum sunt, quomodo Spiritus Sanctus placatus esse ei potest, qui aut Patris aut Filii inimicus est.

303-313 [The Great Persecution]

306-337 [Constantine in Gaul]

311 [First edict of toleration (by Galerius)]

312-337 [Constantine in Italy]

312 [Second edict of toleration (by Milan)]

314 [Council of Arles, on the Donatists, etc.]

315-337 [Constantine in Illyricum]

c.317 ATHANASIUS *de Incarnatione Verbi Dei*

c.318 [Outbreak of Arian controversy]

323-337 [Constantine in the East]

325 [June: Council of Nicaea]

330 [Constantinople founded]

---

65. It is interesting how this is treated in *The Ante-Nicene Fathers; Translation of the Writings of the Fathers down to A.D. 325*. (New York: Charles Scribner's Sons, 1926) 5:423. The translation given is "The Lord says, "I and the Father are one;"[4] and again it is written of the Father, and of the Son, and of the Holy Spirit, "And these three are one."[5]. Footnote 5, reads "I John v.7"

66. F.G. Kenyon. *Textual Criticism of the New Testament* (London: MacMillan) 212.

c.335   [charge against Athanasius]

The charge brought against him was that one of his clergy, Marcarius, broke into the chancel (θυσιαστηριον) of Isohyras and "burned the holy Bibles"[67]

336-337   [Feb-Nov: first exile of Athanasius]

c.337-c.379   [Dominance of the heretical view of Arianism]

339   [Lent-Oct: second exile of Athanasius]

340-381   [Arians held "an unlimited sway over the church"(F. Nolan, p.29)]

341   [Ulfilas was consecrated]

356-362   [Feb 8-Feb 22: third exile of Athanasius]

362   [fourth exile of Athanasius]

365   [fifth exile of Athanasius. His final restoration]

c. 371   EUSEBIUS of Vercelli (?: debated). *De Trinitate.* 7 Books (of 12)

Raymond Brown says:

". . . Books 1-7 written just before 400, and 8-12 at a period with the next 150 years. In Books 1 and 10 (PL 62, 243D, 246B, 297B) the Comma is cited three times."[68]

c. 380   PRISCILLIAN. *Liber Apologeticus.*

(The quote as given by A.E. Brooke from Schepps. Vienna Corpus xviii):

> Sicut Ioannes ait: Tria sunt quae testimonium dicunt in terra: aqua caro et sanguis; et heác tria in unum sunt. et tria sunt quae testimonium dicunt in caelo: pater, uerbum et spiritus; et heác tria unum sunt in Christo Iesu.

Notice the Sabellian interpolation "in Christo Iesu," which effects the meaning so that (as R.Brown said) it "fits Priscillian's theology." It's possible that Priscillian, or another Sabellian added these three words, for "Priscillian seems to have been a

---

67. Socrat. *Hist. Eccl.* book 1. cap xxvii p.64 (as quoted by T.H. Horne (1822) 4: 502
68. *The Anchor Bible; Epistles of John* (New York : Doubleday & Co.,1982), 782.

Sabellian or modalist for whom the three figures in the Trinity were not distinct persons but only modes of the one divine person."[69] Up to this point, we may agree with R. Brown. But rather than claiming an addition of three words, R.Brown errs with his wild claim (made in 1982) that Priscillian inserted the entire *Comma!* His use of the word "many" in the statement "many have surmised that he created it" is an apparent exaggeration. It was Künstle's theory (in 1905), but in 1912, A.E. Brooke had already summarized Babut's refution of Künstle's theory. See summary under (1909: BABUT). A.E. Brooke was not listed in R. Brown's bibliography! Yet Brooke concluded this summary with "It is far more probable that both Priscillian and his opponents found the gloss in the text of Bibles."[70]

383 ["Last overtures of Theodosius to the Arians."[71]]

c. 390? JEROME [prologue to the Canonical Epistles]

Wilhelm Sirlets (1514-1585) commented:

"So that no one distorts the word of Jerome, we provide the text here:
> si ab interpretibus fideliter in latinum eloquium verterentur nec ambiguitatem legentibus facerent nec sermonum sese varietas impugnaret, illo praecipue loco, ubi de trinitatis unitate in prima joannis espistola positum legimus, in qua etiam , trium tantummodo vocabula hoc est aquae, sanguinis et spiritus in ipsa sua editione ponentes et patris verbique ac spiritus testimonium omittentes, in quo maxime et fides catholica roboratur, et patris et filii et spirtus sancti una divinitatis substantia comprobatur.

Erasmus said that Jerome merley expresses the assumption that this passage of several is forged. Judge for yourself whether the words ab infidelibus translatoribus multum erratum esse a fidei veritate comperimus express only an assumption. The sense is so clear that I regard it superficial to write more about it. Jerome said that irresponsible translators left out this testimony. He said this in order that it may be understood that formerly it occurred in the Greek codicies. We may conclude that in his time the Greek books were not yet tampered with at this passage."

-----He continues:

"But people object it is entirely improbable that this passage is corrupted since Cyril, who lived 1100 years before us, never quoted the same, but only the words *tres sunt qui testimonium dant, spiritus, aqua et sanguis*. I don't deny that Cyril cited only this verse. I add further that even Gregory of Nazianzus, who lived before Cyril and has a greater reputation, cites only these words as did Pope Leo

---

69. R.Brown *Anchor Bible; Epistles of John*, Appendix IV,
70. A.E.Brooke, *Critical and Exegetical Commentary on the Johannine Epistles* (Edinburgh: T & T.Clark, 1912) 160.
71. H.M.Gwatkin *The Arian Controversy* (London: Longmans, Green & Co, 1914) "Chronological Table" 169-171.

in a letter to Flavius. But upon that fact, we cannot infer that the passage *tres sunt qui testimonium dant in caelo* etc. was unknown to them. Not only Jerome argues for the Johannine origin, but also Athanasius, patriarch of Alexandria . . ."[72]

c. 450   (North African author). *Contra Varimadum*.

"The Comma is cited in 1.5 (CC 90, 20-21)" [73]

c. 450   *De divinis Scripturis suie Speculum*. [dated c. 5th century]

The reading from this Latin MS, also known as *m*, is here provided by A.E. Brooke (1912):

> Quoniam (quia C) tres sunt qui testimonium dicunt in terra, spiritus aqua et sanguis: et hii tres unum sunt in Christo Iesu, et tres sunt qui testimonium dicunt in caelo, pater, uerbum et spiritus: et hii tres unum sunt.

A.D. 484   The *Johannine Comma* was "invoked at Carthage" says R. Brown.
It was invoked when the "bishops of North Africa confessed their faith before Huneric the Vandal (Victor of Vita, *Historia persecutionis Africanae Prov*. 2.82 [3.11]; CSEL 7,60]"

c. 485   VICTOR VITENSIS. (c.430-?). *Historia persecutionis Africanae Provinciae*. (2.82 in CSEL 7, 60; 3.11 in PL 58, 227C), per RB.

> "Et ut adhuc luce clarius unius divinitatis esse cum Patre et Filio Spiritum Sanctum doceamus, *Johannis Evangelistæ testimonio comprobatur:* ait namque, "Tres sunt qui testimonium perhibent in cælo, Pater, Verbum, et Spiritus Sanctus, et hi tres unum sunt.

c. 500   *Codex Freisingensis* [dated to the 5th or 6th century]

Fragnemts of this MS, known today as *r* (or Beuron 64), were discovered by Johann A. Schmeller (1785-1852). With additional fragments, Leopold Ziegler published these in Marburg, 1876. The reading here is provided by A.E. Brooke, with legible letters in capitals:

> QM TR es sunt qui testificantur IN TERRA· SPs ET AQUA ET SAnguis et tres sunt qui tesTIFICANTUR IN CAELO PaTER Et uerbum et s̄p̄s̄ s̄c̄s̄ et hi TRES UNUM SUNT· SI TEST. . .

---

72. According to: H. Höpfl *Kardinal Wilhelm Sirlets Annotationen zum Neuen Testament* (Freiburg im Breisgau: Herdersche Verlag, 1908) 65-66.
73. *Anchor Bible; Epistles of John*, 782.

c. 527   FULGENTIUS. *Responsio contra Arianos* (Ad 10; CC 91, 93), per RB.

R. Brown records that Fulgentius uses "Word" instead of "Son" in this work, but in another work, *Contra Fabianum* (Frag. 21.4; CC 91A, 797), he uses "Son".

c. 527   FULGENTIUS. *De Trinitate* (1.4.1; CC 91A, 636), per RB.

In this century ". . . the Comma was known as the work of John the apostle as we hear from Fulgentius, the bishop of Ruspe in North Africa."

pre 550   JEROME? *Prologue to the Catholic Epistles*. "Preseverd in the Codex Fuldensis (PL 29, 827-31)." per RB.

> *Sed tu, virgo Christi, Eustochium, dum a me impensius Scriptura veritatem inquiris, meam quodammodo senectutem invidorum dentibus corrodendam exponis, qui me falsarium corruptoremque sacrarum pronunciant Scipturarum.*

According to R. Brown "The *Prologue* states that the *Comma* is genuine but has been omitted by unfaithful translators." Orme (p.7) says that Father Jean Martianai (1647-1717) "hath fully proved in his edition of Jerom's version" that the Prologue is not by Jerome, but "is the work of a forger." Orme says Nolan and Burgess have argued for its authenticity. Oxlee attempted to refute their claims.

c.570   A quote from *Complexionn. in Epistt. Paulinn.* by Cassiodorus
Testificanture "in terra" tria mysteria, "aqua, sanguis et spiritus," quæ in passione Domini leguntur impleta; "in cælo autem Pater, et Filius, et Spiritus," et hi tres unus est Deus."

A.D. 546   *Codex Fuldensis*

The *Comma* does not appear in *Fuldensis*. Based on the view that "the oldest are the best" *Codex Fuldensis* is regarded as one of the oldest of the Vulgate MSS, and thus, among the best. But since thousands of Latin MSS remain unexamined, no one has verified this. A footnote in the appendix of Orme's *Memoirs of the Controversy* says that it is remarkable that Cava and Speculum, the two oldest Latin manuscripts containing the *Comma* "support also the spurious Epistle of Paul to the Laodiceans."

But *Codex Fuldensis* also contains this Laodicean Epistle! [74]

c. 550   FACUNDUS of Hermiane. *Pro Defensione Trium Capitulorum ad Iustinianum* (1.3.9; CC 90A, 12; also inferior MSS of Bede) per RB.

Facundus, says R. Brown, reads I John as saying, "There are three who give testimony *on earth*"

c. 583   CASSIODORUS. *In Epistolam S. Joannis ad Parthos.* (10.5.1; PL 70, 1373A) per RB.

"In Italy Cassiodorus (d. *ca.*583) cited the Comma in his commentary. . ."[75] Brown also says that Cassiodorus employs "Son" in place of "Word".

589   ["Visigoths abandon Arianism"[76]]

599   ["Lombards abandon Arianism"[77]]

c. 636   ISIDORE of Seville. *Testimonia diviae Scripturae.* 2 [PL 83, 1203C] per RB.

According to R. Brown, Isidore of Seville "shows knowledge of the Comma" in this work.

c. 638   [Moslems destroyed the library in Caesarea]

The library is said to have contained 30,000 volumes, and is said to have been used by Origen, Pamphilius, Eusebius, and Jerome. Today, no one knows how many Greek MSS of the NT were in the library.

c. 650   [The León palimpsest] [dated to 7th century]

It appears that this is the one referred to with the letter "*l*" (*Codex Pal. Legionensis*) today. The reading provided by A.E. Brooke (as quoted by S. Berger in *History of the Vulgate*):

---

74. Scrivener, *Plain Introduction.* 3rd ed. p. 353. In *Canon of the New Testament* (Oxford: Clarondon Press, 1987), p.239 Metzger says this Laodecian Epistle is present in more than a hundred MSS of the Vulgate, "in all eighteen German Bibles printed prior to Luther's translation," as well as "manuscripts of early Albigensian, Bohemian, English, and Flemish versions". The Tepl Codex contains this epistle as well as the *Comma*.
75. *Anchor Bible; Epistles of John,* 783.
76. Gwatkin *The Arian Controversy,* 171.
77. Ibid.

> *quoniam* tres sunt qui *testimonium dant in terra* sps et *aqua et sanguis et tres sunt* qui tes*timonium dicunt in cælo p*ater *et verbum et sps scs et hi tres unum* sunt *in xpo ihu...*

Note the earthly witnesses precede the heavenly ones.

c. 700   JAQUB of Edessa. A Syriac commentary *On the Holy (Eucharistic) Mysteries*. Translation into English provided by Raymond Brown:

> The soul and the body and the mind which are sanctified through three holy things: through water and blood and Spirit, and through the Father and the Son and the Spirit.

Brown says "No clear knowledge of the Comma appears among the great church writers in Syriac, although a debate has arisen about Jaqub of Eddesa (d.708)."[78] It is interesting to note that a new debate has arisen, since so many textual critics on the 19th century claimed victory, and assured us that there exists no more debate about the "spurious" verse.

c. 716   *Codex Amiantinus* presented to the Pope.

Scrivener dated *Amiantinus* at "about A.D. 541" and the comment from Schaff (1883) is hackneyed that it "is the oldest and best MS." But Kenyon (1912) says it "must have been written quite early in the eighth century"[79] and it was given as a present to Pope Gregory in 716. Kenyon (1912), Metzger (1977), and others, say that *Amiantinus* is the "best authority exant" of the Latin Vulgate. Yet, over 300 years passed since the completion of Jerome's Vulgate. According to de Levante, it does not contain Acts 8:37, 9:5-6, 15:34, 18:4, 24:7, 28:29. Nor does it contain the *Comma*.

c. 735   [The year of the decease of the Venerable Bede]

C. Jenkins[80] reported in 1942 that a new manuscript used by Bede was discovered. This manuscript contained the *Comma*. It is noteworthy that E.J. Epp says that "Bede in the early eighth century use either E or a precisely simililar manuscript [81] since Kenyon (1912) also said of the Greek manuscript E that "it is practically certain that it was used by Bede in his commentaries on the Acts." Kenyon says that E "is the earliest MS. . . containing Acts viii. 37 (the confession of faith

---

78. *The Anchor Bible; Epistles of John*, 778.
79. Kenyon, *Textual Criticism of the New Testament*. (London: MacMillan, 1912) 225.
80. See (1942: Jenkins, C.) in this paper.
81. *Theological Tendency of Codex Beza Cantabrigiensis in Acts* (Cambridge: University Press, 1966) 32.

demanded by Philipp of the eunuch before baptism)"[82]

c. 750   harl[2] [Latin MS dated to the 8th century]

Scrivener says it contains "all the Epistles (that to the Colossians following 2 Thess., and 1 John v.7 -Jude being crowded on one leaf)" and that it is "a text much mixed with the Old Latin."

c. 850   The *Ulmensis* manscript. [dated 9th cent.]

quia tres sunt qui testimonium dant s̄p̄ē et aqua et sanguis, et tres unum sunt. Sicut in caelo tres sunt pater verbum et s̄p̄ē, et tres unum sunt.

c. 923   [Latin MS of the Cathedral of Leon.]

This is designated as *leon*[1] by Scrivener, who dates it in the time of Ordogno II. (913-923). He says it "is a specimen of the Visigoth miniscule, and contains 1 John v.7,8 in a varied form."

c. 930   [Latin MS in the church of S. Isidore in Leon.]

Scrivener designated this MS as *leon*[2]. He says "1 John v. 7,8 is here found only in the margin." *leon*[1] and *leon*[2] are catagorized by Scrivener as MSS "which contain a text wherein the Old Latin was gradually being replaced by the Vulgate."[83]

A.D. 988   [*Codex Toletanus*: Latin MS]

E.A. Lowe says he does not accept the view that this Latin MS "in all its parts is a product of the 10th century. Parts manifestly go back to an older period."[84] But due to a subscription in the MS, he say it may have been completed in 988. The MS is of interest to us because it contains Acts 8:37a, 8:37b, 9:5, 9:6, and the *Comma*. The vagueness of the sigla "it" (for Itala) used by NA[26] for the Old Latin support for Acts 8:37 and 9:5-6 prevents readers from knowing exactly which Old Latin MS supports a verse.[85]

c.1120   [An exposition of the Apostle's Creed]

---

82. Kenyon *Textual Criticism of the New Testament* 102
83. *Plain Introduction*. 3rd ed, p. 356.
84. Elias Avery Lowe "On the Date of the Codex Toletanus" *Revue Bénédictine* xxx (1923) 271.
85. In these examples from Acts, it was necessary to resort to Scrivener (1883) and Epp (1966).

"There is an exposition of the Apostle's Creed used by the Waldenses and Albigenses, in which they quote, I John v.7, in defense of the Trinity, and they defend all the doctrines now found in that summary except descending into hell and believing in the holy catholic church."[86]

> We must believe in God the Father Almighty, the Creator of heaven and earth; the which God is one Trinity, as it is written in the law: 'Hear O Israel, the Lord thy God is one.' And Isaiah: 'I am the Lord, and there is none else; neither is there any God besides me.' And St. Paul, in the fourth of the Ephesians: 'One Lord, one faith, one baptism, one God and Father of all.' And St. John: 'There are three that bear witnes in heaven: the Father, the Son, and the Holy Ghost; and these three are one.'" [87]

c.1150   *Codex Demidovianus* [Old Latin: MS dated to the 12th century.]

Since it contains the *Comma*, and even Act 8:37[88], this MS would be extremely interesting to examine further. However Metzger reported in 1977 "its present location is unknown."[89]

The Nestle tradition from 1927 (the year in which the Nestle editions began to provide MS evidence in the notes), show that NS^{12} NS^{15} NS^{16} NA^{21} NA^{23} NA^{24} NA^{25} and NA^{26} failed to mention this manuscript in their notes, tables, anywhere in the Greek edition.

c.1150   *Codex Divionensis* [Old Latin: dated to the 12th century.]

The UBS^3(1975) and UBS^3 corrected (1983) recorded in the critical notes, that this MS contained the *Comma*. But evidently, it never appeared in the Nestle editions. I have checked NS^{12} NS^{15} NS^{16} NA^{21} NA^{23} NA^{24} NA^{25} and NA^{26}. Each one failed to mention this manuscript evidence in their notes.

c.1150   *Codex Colbertinus* [dated to the 12th century.]

Metzger says "The manuscript was written in Languedoc, where *the use of the Old Latin*, prepared a thousand years earlier, *lingered on long after other parts had adopted Jerome's Vulgate*."[90] [emphasis mine]. In the Gospels, "c" has an Old Latin text. The UBS Greek NT reports that Colbertinus contains the *Comma*.

---

86. Adam Blair, *History of the Waldenses* (Edinburgh: Adam Black Publ., 1832) I:220. Credit is due to Dr. Ken Johnson of Ft. Collins, CO, who informed me of this quote.
87. Ibid., p.523 Appendix vi.
88. See *Plain Introduction*, 3rd, p.615
89. *Early Versions of the N.T.* 312?
90. *Early Versions of the New Testament*. 313.

NS¹² NS¹⁵ NS¹⁶ NA²¹ NA²³ NA²⁴ NA²⁵ and NA²⁶ have failed to mention this manuscript evidence in their notes.

c.1170   [here] French translation made by Waldenses

"of the two old versions which have been published in French, two were made by the Waldenses; vid. Le Long *Bibl. Sacr.* Tom. I. p. 313"⁹¹;lm+5)
Bibliorum libri quidam (imprimis Novum Testamentum in linguam vernacula, sc. Gallicam translati à Stephano de Ansa (*vel* de Emsa) Sacerdote Lugdunensi, studio & impensis Petri Valdensis, post annum 1170 aut 1180.

c.1180   [or here] [French translation made by Waldenses]

1215   *Acts of the Lateran Council.*
A quote from this Latin document:(as given by T.H. Horne)

Quemadmodum in Canonicâ Joannis epistolâ legitur, Qui tres sunt qui testimonium dant in Cælo, Pater Verbum et Spiritus Sanctus: et hi tres unum sunt. Statimque subjungitur, Et tres sunt qui testimonium dant in terra, Spiritus aqua et sanguis: et tres unum sunt. Sicut in codicibus quibusdam, (scil. Latinis) invenitur.

"These Acts were translated into Greek, and sent to the Greek churches, in the hope of promoting a union with the Latin, which was one of the subjects of debate in this Lateran council."⁹²

1218   [convention of Italian and Ultramontane Waldenses]

c.1230   [Passau Anonymous. *Rescriptum Heresiarcharum Lombardie ad Pauperes de Lugduno, qui sunt in Alemania*]

In 1875 this was a newly discovered genuine Waldensian document. W. Preger discusses it in *Beiträge zur Geschichte der Waldensier im Mittelalter* (1875).

1231   [The Synod at Trier]

"The earliest mention of heretical translations in German occurs in an account of a synod for the suppresion of heresy at Trier in 1231; the offending books were immediately confiscated. It is certain that such *translations*, from which the heretics drew their religious inspiration, were *current in Germany* in the the thirteenth century, for the

---

91. F. Nolan, *Inquiry into the Integrity of the Greek Vulgate or Received Text.* xviii.
92. Horne, *An Introduction to the Critical Study and Knowledge of the Holy Scriptures,* 2nd ed. (London: for T.Cadel in the Strand, 1821) 505.

sect was both *numerous* and *influencial*."[93] [emphasis mine]

1248   [The Waldenses flourished in Languedoc]

Referring to Waldenses, "In the Franche Comte, Provence, and Languedoc, however, they were so numerous in 1248 that Count John of Burgundy deemed himself able to cope with them only by means of the Inquisition."[94]

c.1250   *Codex Montfortianus* [dated 13th cent. by Clarke]

ὅτι τρεῖς εἰσὶν οἱ μαρτυποῦντες ἐν τῷ οὐρανῷ, _ πατήρ, _ λόγος, καὶ _ /πνα ἅγιον/, καὶ οὗτοι οἱ τρεῖς ἕν εἰσι [8] καὶ τρεῖς εἰσι οἱ μαρτυροῦντες ἐν τῇ γῇ, _ πνα, _ _ ὕδωρ, καὶ αἷμα _ _ _ _ _ _ _ εἰ τὴν μαρτυπίαν τῶν ἀνθρώπων λαμβάνομεν,

variations from common received text:

[v.7] omissions: ὁ, ὁ, τὸ;   transposition: /ἅγιον πνεῦμα/
[v.8] omissions: τὸ, καὶ τὸ, τὸ and καὶ οἱ τρεῖς εἰς τὸ ἕν εἰσιν.

The reading here is given according to the careful facsimilie provided by Adam Clarke in vol 6, p. 1972 of his *Commentary*. In his 3rd edition of *Plain Introduction*, Scrivener says Clarke's reasons for the dating of this MS to the 13th century are "marvelously unsound" but he doesn't explain why.[95] Scrivener also says of the *Britannicus*, that "there is the fullest reason to believe that the Cod. Montfortianus is the copy referred to (*see below*, Chap. ix)." But when the reader turns to Chap ix, p. 653, he finds no explanation provided. Scrivener merely repeats himself: "and notwithstanding the discrepancy of reading in ver. 8, there can be little doubt of the identity of his [Erasmus'] "Codex Britannicus" with Montfort's.

The "discrepancy of reading in ver. 8" is an entire clause of seven words! How can these two MSS be the same one?

...*Britannicus*   καὶ οἱ τρεῖς εἰς τὸ ἕν εἰσιν.
Montfortianus _ _ _ _ _ _ _ .

Thus Forster said (in 1867) "it cannot possibly be the same with the Codex Britannicus."[96]

---

93. W.B. Lockwood "Vernacular Scriptures in Germany and the Low Countries Before 1500" *Cambridge History of the Bible* (Cambridge: Univ. Press, 1969) 2: 427.
94. Alberto Clot. "Waldenses". *NSHE* 12:242.
95. An evaluation of the debate Clarke vs. Michaelis & Marsh is beyond the scope of this paper. But readers are encouraged to read it in Clarke's *Commentary*.
96. *A New Plea for the Authenticity of the Text of the Three Heavenly Witnesses*. 126. (1867)

c.1250   *Codex Perpinianus* [dated to the 13th century]

The reading from the *Comma* as given in *Journal of Theological Studies* xii (1911) 528.

> Quia tres sunt: qui testimonium dant in terra. Sp̄s. aqua. et sanguis. Et hii tres: unum sunt in xp̄o iħu. Et tres sunt qui testimonium dant in celo. Pater. uerbum. sp̄s sc̄s. Et hii tres: unum sunt.

This MS was discovered by S. Berger in 1895. Note the variation "in xp̄o iħu" in the *Comma*. p is also interesting, for its orthographical forms "prove that p was copied from a MS not later that the sixth century before words began to be divided."[97] Further, p contains Acts 8:37, 9:5-6, 10:6, 10:21, 15:34 as well as 1 John 5:7-8.

1303   [The king of Armenia, Haitho or Haithom, lived 1224-1270.]

> As 1 John v.7 is quoted by a synod held as Sis in Armenia thirty-seven years after the death of Haithom, it was deemed pretty certain that it had been brought into the text by that king...[98]

c.1350   [The *Augsburger Bibelhandschrift* (2° Cod 3)]

This MS is the oldest complete German New Testament.[99]

> wan drei sint dr da geziuchnüsse gebent in d' erden d' geist wass' uñ bluet vnd dis drei sint ainz vnd frie sint di da geziuchnüsse gebent ī dem hiṁel. det vat' d' sun od' daz word. vñ d' hilige geist und dis drie sint ainez.[100]

This reading is unique in that it reads neither "son" nor "Word" exclusively, but rather "the son or the word".

c.1350   *Codex Ottobonianus* at the Vatican (Greg 629)

---

97. E.S. Buchanan "An Old Latin Text of the Catholic Epistles" *Journal of Theological Studies* xii(1911) 497.
98. Horne/Tregelles, *Introduction to the Critical Study*, 11th ed., 312.
99. For further reading on this MS refer to these dissertations: Max Bisewski's *Die Mittelhochdeutsche Übersetzung des Perikopenbuchs, der Apokalypse, und der Katholischen Briefe in der Augsburger Handschrift* (Greifswald: Univ Greifswald, 1908) [115 pp]; and Kurt Zimmermann's *Die Mittelhochdeutsche Apostelgeschichte in der Ausburger Handschrift* (Greifswald: Univ Greifswald, 1908) [84 pp].
100. The reading is taken from microfilm of selected readings purchased from the Staats- und Stadtbibliothek in Augsburg and received on Jan 23, 1991. (The expected reading "sun" has a strange stroke after the "s")

Formerly known as Act.162 [dated to the 14th century (per NA²⁶)]

> 7) ὅτι τρεῖς εἰσὶν οἱ μαρτυροῦντες {ἀπὸ τοῦ οὐρανοῦ}, _ Πατήρ, _Λόγος, καὶ _ πνεῦμα ἅγιον. (8) καὶ ____ οἱ τρεῖς {εἰς το} ἕν εἰσι. καὶ τρεῖς εἰσιν οἱ μαρτυροῦντες {επι της γης}, τὸ πνεῦμα, __ τὸ ὕδωρ, καὶ τὸ αἷμα· __ _

Variations from the common received text:
ἐν > ἀπὸ; ἐν > ἐπὶ   2 dative phrases made into genitive: τοῦ οὐρανοῦ, της γης
12 words omitted: (7) ὁ ὁ τὸ (8) οὗτοι, καὶ, and the final clause: καὶ οἱ τρεῖς εἰς τὸ ἕν εἰσιν
swapped: πνεῦμα ἅγιον

A contrast with the Complutensian Polyglott:

629:(7) πατήρ ___ λόγος... _ πνεῦμα ἅγιον (8)...εἰσι
CPG:(7) πατήρ καὶ λόγος... τὸ ἅγιον πνεῦμα (8)...εἰσιν

Scriveners say it has "a Latin column in the post of honour on the left, and the Greek column on the right" and claims that "the omission of the article in ver.7, while it stands in ver. 8 in 162, proves that the disputed clause was interpolated (probably from its parallel Latin) by one who was very ill acquainted with Greek."[101] Perhaps he is referring to (7) πνεῦμα and (8) τὸ πνεῦμα. It's hard to "prove" anything from the omission of this one article. When Dr. Dobbin noted an article and word missing from Erasmus' description of *Britannicus*, he said they are "clearly typographical errors"[102] One says proof of interpolation. Another says typos. One can only speculate. Besides, Latin has no articles, definite or indefinite. How then does he explain all the articles in verse 8? Further, he not only said "on the whole 162 best suits the Complutensian"[103] but he also admitted that for the Complutenian "we must emphatically deny that on the whole the Latin Vulgate had an appreciable effect upon the Greek.[104]

1377   [May: Pope Gregory issued 5 Papal bulls against Wycliffe]

c.1380   [Wycliffe attacked the doctrine of transubstantiation]

c.1380   WYCLIFFE, John. *The Holy Bible...in the Earliest English Versions made from the Latin Vulgate by John Wycliffe and his Followers*. ed. by Forshall and Madden.

> For thre ben, that ziuen witnessing in heuen, the Fadir, the Word, *or Sone*, and the Hooly Goost; and thes thre ben oon. And thre ben, that ziuen witnessing in

---

101. Scrivener. *Plain Introduction*, 3rd ed. p. 649.
102. *The Codex Montfortianus: A Collation*, 10.
103. Ibid.
104. Ibid. p.427.

erthe, the spirit, watir, and blood; and thes thre ben oon.

It is easy to be misled by the Wycliffe Bible, for Wycliffe's doctrine deviated somewhat from official Roman Catholic doctrine. For this deviation, he is still associated with the Lollards today. However "His associations with Lollardy remain in doubt. The Lollards hailed him as their inspiration and endorsed his anticlericalism, but for his part, Wyclif could scarcely have stomached their social and economic programs."[105] Today, Wycliffe is hailed as the "Morning Star of the Reformation", even though readings from his Bible differ sharply from those of the Reformation Bibles. Before providing sample verses, note how Rev. Hugh Pope was initially misled. In 1926 he said, without even checking the Wycliffe version

> From this it is clear that the Wycliffite Bibles, i.e., those which emanated from him or his followers, were distincly heretical, as indeed the whole story supposes.[106]

Some selected verses from the Forshall-Madden ed. of the Wycliffe Bible: Math 5:44 "bless them that curse you" (omitted), Math 6:13 "For thine is the kingdom and the power and the glory, for ever" (omitted), John 8:59b "going through the midst of them, and so passed by" (omitted) Acts 16:7, Rom 8:21, and Eph 4:24 are similar to the Revised Version (1881) and 1 Tim 3:16 reads "that thing that was schewid in fleisch".

Within 20 years this of condemnation by Hugh Pope (d. 1946) of Wycliffe's version, he decided to finally investigate its readings, which caused him to rapidly correct himself. Hugh Pope's altered opinion is thus:

> Yet there is nothing heretical in the Wycliffite versions. Hence, unlike Tyndale's New Testament, the version itself was never condemned either by the English bishops or by the Holy See.[107]

Wycliffites are also called Lollards. The Lollards are of interest to Baptists since even C.H. Spurgeon said "It is also certain many of the Lollards, perhaps the majority of them, strongly opposed infant baptism."[108] And Frederick Nolan has said that 1 John 5:7-8, "easily made its way into Wicklef's translation, through the Lollards, who were disciples of the Waldenses"[109]

---

105. *NCE* 14: 1051.
106. *The Catholic Student's Aids to the Study of the Bible* 248-52.
107. *English Versions of the Bible*, enlarged by S. Bullough (St. Louis & London: B. Herder, 1952) 86. Rev. Pope, upon this discovery, takes delight in showing examples in chapter 17, how the Wycliffe Bible agrees with the Rheims-Douay, and the ERV of 1881.
108. Charles Spurgeon "Review of J.M. Cramp's Baptist History" *Sword and Trowel* (August 1868)
109. *An Inquiry into the Integrety of the Greek Vulgate or Received Text of the New Testament.* (London: printed for F.C. and Rivington, 1815).

But we, as Baptists, ought to be cautious of these statements, for though we may admire his anticlericalism, Wycliffe continued to attend Mass[110] and "his death, which followed a stroke suffered while hearing Mass, is scarcely noticed by the chronicles."[111]

What then does the presence of Act 8:37, 1 John 5:7-8, etc. in Wycliffe's Bible indicate? It indicates (as we will be reassured with an entry under (1582: MARTIN, Gregory)) that there was no debate among "good Catholics" or heretical Catholics, over these verses.

1388   *Cabinet des Manuscripts*, vol. III.

In this volume, "Deslie has published the general catalog of the Library of the University of Paris, of the year 1388."[112]
The "library possessed at that time 33 complete Bibles, 18 libri legales (the Pentateuch), 15 libri historialies (historical books of the Bible), 28 psalteria glossata, 17 libri sapentiales (The Wisdom of Solomon and Ecclesiasticus), 24 books of the Prophets, 42 Gospels with glosses, 15 Pauline Epistles, 38 other Epistles, Acts and Revelation, 5 libri glossati mixti"[113] etc.

1386   [University of Heidelberg was founded][114]

c.1389   HUTTLE, Max, ed. *Der Codex Teplensis enthalend Die Schrift des Newen Geyeuges*. (Augsburg-München: Literarischen Institute von Dr. Max Huttle, 1884) The *Comma* is located in "dritte theil," p. 20

The book of Acts in the Tepl Codex was consulted by A.C. Clark (1933) and E.J. Epp (1966). Presumably, we may excuse them for not informing us that its Epistle to John contains the *Comma*. But this neglect from the Greek editions (at least the 9th and 10th) of A. Merk is inexcusable. For in these editions, the Tepl is listed in the forward pages as one of the MSS consulted. But the Tepl is NOT listed in the notes of Merk under 1 John 5:7-8.[115] It is noteworthy that Merk lists the Tepl amidst the *codices veteris versionis latinae*, i.e., the Old Latin MSS. This is testimony that Merk recognized the Tepl as a MS

---

110. "he ascribed justification in the presence of God to sanctification and good works, and did not deny all merit to the latter. Justification through faith alone was not within his view" *NSHE* 12: 464.
111. *NCE* 14: 1051.
112. J.M. Reu. *Luther's German Bible* (Columbus,OH: Lutheran Book Concern, 1934) 56.
113. Ibid.
114. "Originally there were four faculties; theology, law, philosophy, and art." *Ency Americana* 14: 69. Its official name is Ruprecht-Karl-Universität, after its founder Ruprecht I (1309-1390).
115. To my knowlegde, no scholarly work in print has ever acknowledged the inclusion of the *Comma* in the Tepl.

based on a non-Vulgate text. "Athough this ms. is listed by Merk among its Old Latin mss. it is written in Middle High German. (See. . .) Textually the ms. is close to w (58)."[116] But Latin MS w is dated to the 15th century, while the German Tepl is dated to the 14th! Had this been reversed, the German MS would be regarded with less value. But as it is, the Tepl MS (in Acts) actually predates a pre-Jerome text, w, which is a non-Vulgate MS with a "remarkable longevity" into the 15th century!

Wir ist Jhesus Krist der da kumt /⁷ durch das wasser/ und durch das plut/ nit allayn in wasser/ wan un wasser/ und im plut. Und der Geist ist/ der da bezeught/ das Krist ist di Warheit. Wan drey sint/ di gebend gezeug ⁸im himel, der Vater/ das Wort/ und der heilige Geist/ und dise drei sent ain/ ⁹und drey sint/ de geben gezeug ¹⁰uns der erden Geist/ wasser/ und plut, und dese drey sint ain.

Some sources provide "c. 1400" for the date. Recently in 1971, H.J. Frede of the VLI said "*vor* 1389". The superscript numbers in the reading are part of the printed text, and were placed for marginal notes.

---

116. J.K. Elliot, "Old Latin MSS in NT Editions", *A Survey of Manuscripts Used in Editions of the Greek New Testament* (New York: E.J.Brill, 1987) 280.

SIGNIFICANCE of the Tepl Codex:

Once again, the Tepl actually predates a pre-Jerome text from a non-Vulgate MS, w, which has "Old Latin readings in Acts and Catholic epistles",[117] has a remarkable longevity into the 15th century. This indicates German MSS ought not to be dismissed as mere copies of Latin Vulgate MSS. Second, how can the Papists claim the Tepl? They cannot, for it is non-vulgate. Third, the *Comma* is not inverted. The following Tepl readings, rejected by the mta, and rejected by the MTA, exclusively support the Received Text. In other words, in these passages, which are disputed by the mta, MTA, and RTa, the Tepl, together with the ancient testimony of Old Latin MSS supports readings of the Authorized Version.

blank = not checked for defective nature;   * = defective

	tep	c	l	p	r	t	w	gig	h	m	tol	idem	D/E	sy
Act 8:37a.	tep		l	p	r	t	w	gig			tol	idem	E	sy[h*]
Act 8:37b.	tep		l	p	r	t	w	–		m	tol	idem	E	
Act 9:5	tep			p			w	gig	h		tol			
Act 9:6	tep			p			w	–	h		tol			sy[ph]
Act 15:34	tep	c	l	*			w	gig						sy[h*]
1 Joh 5:7	tep	c	l	p	r					m	tol	idem	div	

However, the Tepl MS, as a whole, does not correspond exactly to the RT, for it has additions to the RT. Three examples follow:

	tep	c	l	p	r	t	w	gig	h	m	tol	idem	D	sy
Act 18:4		ck					w	gig	h				D	sy[hm]
Act 19:14.	tep						w						D	sy[hm]
Act 28:31.	tep			p			w			m		idem		sy[h]

This is mentioned here in anticipation of future exploitation of these facts. We may expect the following objection from opponents of the RT: "Since there are additions to the RT in the Tepl, then the distinctive RT readings are also additions." But the Tepl is not necessarily a representative of every German manuscript of the 14th century. Nor are the scant number of Old Latin MSS extant today necessarily representative of all Latin MSS of the 2nd century. What do these non-TR additions, based on some Old Latin MSS, indicate? In contrast to the heretical omissions of Codex B and its allies, which dishonor the name of Christ, and minimize testimony of His divinity, it is suggested here that the nature of some Old Latin interpolations, (e.g., Acts 18:4, Acts 19:14) indicates that the Old Latin MS tradition, "devotes greater attention to the person of Jesus. This is evident in the frequency with which the fullest form of the name (or better, title), ὁ κύριος

---

117. Metzger, *Early Versions*, 304.

Ἰησοῦς Χπριστός, is found deeply rooted in the early 'Western' tradition". And it also "indicates that the 'name of the Lord Jesus Christ' was of special importance for the D text"[118] which is noted for its agreement with several Old Latin readings. The RTa perhaps do not yet have perfect copies of the RT in the Old Latin. But neither do the mta nor the MTA. A second point to mention, is that these interpolations (from the few MSS which contained them) dropped out at some point prior to the days of the *Textus Receptus*. We may speak of "longevity" of non-TR interpolations which appear in the Tepl, as well as providential preservation of genuine TR readings, which also appear in the Tepl.

1394 [funeral of Queen Anne of Bohemia]

Wycliffe is reported to have complained "that since it was allowable for the Queen of England (Anne of Bohemia) to have copies of the Gospels in their languages, Bohemian, German, and Latin, and that to dub her a heretic on that account was simply diabolical stupidity, so ought the English to defend the right to read it in their own tongue"[119]

c.1400 PAUES, Anna C., ed. *A Fourteenth Century English Biblical Version*. 1904, AMS Reprint 1974. Cambridge: University Press. 41.

QUOTE from 1 John 5:7-8 of this version: (note: þ = th)
    For þer beþ þre þat beueþ wytnesse in hefne, þe Fader, & þe Sone, & þe Holy Spyryt: & þese þre beþ on. & þer beþ þre þat beueþ wytnesse in erþe, þe Spyrit, & blod, & watyr: & þese þre beþ on.

1403 [strife in Bohemia over control of the Prague University]

Emperor Wenceslaus arranged that the Czechs outvoted the Saxon, Bavarian, and Polish parties. "Soon afterwards Huss was appointed rector of the university, and the Germans, disgusted, quitted Charles [IV] in a body and founded the University of Leipzig."[120]

1409 [Leipzig University was founded][121]

c.1414 *La Nobla Leyczon* [a Waldensian document]

---

118. E.J. Epp *Theological Tendency of Codex Beza. . .in Acts* (Cambridge: Univ Press, 1966) 62-63.
119. *De triplice vinculo amoris*, quoted by John Huss against Stokes;cf. Ussher, *Historia dogmatica*, in turn quoted by H. Pope (1952) 69.
120. *Ency Americana* 22:504.
121. As of 1990, it had 12,000 students from the DDR, and 1,500 foreign students. In 1953 the name was changed to Karl-Marx-Universität.

A quote from this longest and most important poem (dated 1414)[122] of Waldensian literature:

> Ben ha mil e cent ancz compli entierament,
> Que fo scripta l'ora, car sen al derier temps.
>
> A thousand and [four][123] hundred years have been entirely accomplished since it was written that we are in the last time.[124]

1466 [G01]: pre-Lutheran German Bible; (Strassburg: Johann Mentel)

> Wann drey seind die gebent gezeúg auf der erde, der geist, wasser, vnd blůt, vnd dise drey seind ein. Vnd drey seind die gebent gezeúg im himel, der vatter, das wort, vnd der heilig geist: vnd dise drey seind ein.

1470 [G02]: pre-Lutheran German Bible; (Strassburg: H.Eggestein)

(This is was not available in Tübingen nor in Leipzig)

1475 Catalog of the Vatican Library in Rome

Vercellone (1860) said that Codex B is listed in this catalog. The claim was repeated by Scrivener and Gregory. But Dr. F. Spiro verified that it is not listed in the reprint by E.Müntz and P. Fabre ***La Bibliothèque du Vatican au xve siècle***,(1887), and informed F.G.Kenyon, who says it is listed in the 1481 catalog.

1475 [G03]: pre-Lutheran German Bible; (Augsburg: Jocudus Pflanzmann)

> Wañ drey seind die gebẽ gezeűg auff dez erd, der gaysst wasser vnd blůt,

---

122. The date is taken from ***Waldenser im Hochmittelalter und die Folgen bis heute; Katalog des Waldensermuseums Zimmer 1 im Henri-Arnaud-Haus Ötisheim- Schönenberg*** ed. by the Deutschen Waldenservereingigung e.V. p. 26.

123. The Baptist scholar, A.H. Newman, reported that a MS of the ***Noble Lesson*** from Samuel Morland's collection "was found to have originally read 1400 years instead of 1100, the term for ***four***, partially erased, being still visible." ***Baptist Quarterly Review*** VII(1885) 307.

124. A.H. Newman, in his article "Early Waldenses" (1885) said the mention of "Vaudes" and the supposed early date of the poem "has seemed to furnish the strongest support for the modern Waldensian claim, that the Waldenses existed from primitive times, and that before Peter Waldo began to teach (about 1170) they already bore the name "Vaudes."

vnd dise drey seind eī Vnd drey seind die gebēt gezeůg im hímel, der vater, das wort, vnd der heilig gaíst, vn̄ dise drey seind ein.

1476 [G04]: pre-Lutheran German Bible; (Augsburg: Günther Zainer)

wan̄ drey seind die da gebent gezeugknuß auff der erde, d' geyst, das wasser, vn̄ dz blůt, vnd dise drey seind eins. Vnd drey seind die da gebent gezeugknuß im himel. Der vatter, das wort, vnd der heylig geist vnd dise drey seind eyns. Ob wir auffnemen...

1476 [G05]: pre-Lutheran German Bible; (Nuremberg: Johannes Sensenschmidt & Andreas Frisner), p.xcv

wān dry sind die da gebēt gezugknusz vff o erde der geyst, das wasser, vnd das plůt, und dise dry sind eins. Un̄ dry sind die da gebent gezugknusz im himel Der vatter, das wort, vn̄ der heylig geyst, vnnd dise dry sind eins. Ob wir uffnemen...

The words "Monasterÿ Wemgartensis AniGis" are written in the Tübingen copy. On the inside of the front cover, one finds the words "De hac Editione Vid. D. Panzer ..."

1477 [G06]; pre-Lutheran German Bible: (Augsburg: Günther Zainer)

wan̄ drei seind die do gebent gezeůgknuß auff d'erd, d'geyst, dz wasser vn̄ dz plůt, vn̄ dise drei sind eins. Vn̄ drei seind die do gebent zeůgknuB ī himel. Der vater dz wort vn̄ d' heylig geyst, vnd dise drei seind eins. Ob wir aufnemē...

1477   [Count Eberhard of Bart of Württemberg founded Tübingen Univ.]

"The case was the same in Tuebingen, where Count Eberhard had stipulated in the original charter that three doctors should devote their time to the Sacred Books and to theological literature."[125]

1477 [G07]; pre-Lutheran German Bible: (Augsburg: Anton Sorg)

---

125. Heinrich Hermelink, *Die theologische Fakultät in Tübingen vor der Reformation. 1477-1534* (Tübingen: J.C.B. Mohr, 1906) 41, as quoted in J.M. Reu. *Luther's German Bible* (Columbus, OH: Lutheran Book Concern, 1934) 58-59. The German (from Hermelink) reads "Auch die Doktoren erläuterten die Bücher der Sentenzen und die Schriften des alten und neuen Testaments (*quorum tres sacris theologie libris atque scripturis intenderent* heißt es in der Stiftungsurkunde der Grafen Eberhard)."

> wañ drey seind die da gebent gezeügk-nuß auff dez erde, der geyst, das wasser, vnd das blùt vnd dise drey semd eins. Vñ drey semd die da gebent gezeügknuß im hymel.Der vater, das wort, vnd der heylig geyst und dise drey seind eins. Ob wir auffnemen. . .

In the copy in Tübingen, the verse is underlined in light red.

1478 *Kölner Bible.* (a pre-Lutheran Low-German Bible)

> 7. wente dre sint de dar gheuen ghetuchnisse in dem hemmel. de vadeer. dat word. vnde de hillighe gheyst. vnde desse dre sint een. 8. Vnde dre sint de dar gheuen ghetuchnisse vp der erden. de gheyst. dat water. vnde dat bloed. vnde desse dre sint een.[126]

1480 [G08]: pre-Lutheran German Bible: (Augsburg: Anton Sorg)

> wann dreÿ seind die do gebent gezeügknůþ aff o erd. der geÿst das wasser und das plůt. uñ dise dreÿ seynd eÿns. Uñ drey seind die do gebēt zeügknůſk im himel. Der vater dz wort uñ d heilig geist. uñ dise drei seind eins Ob wir auffnemē. . .

1481 Catalog of the Vatican Library

Codex B is listed in this catalog. Kenyon says the MS "entered the Vatican between 1475 and 1481".[127]

1483 [G09]; pre-Lutheran German Bible: (Nuremberg: Anton Koberger)

> wañ drey sind, Sy da geben gezewgknuß auff der erde, der geyst, dz wasser, und daz blut, und dise drey sind eins. Und drey sind die da geben gezewgknuß im̃ hymel. Der vater. das wort, vñ der heylig geyst, vñ dise drey seind eins. Ob wir aufnemen. . .

1485 [G10]: pre-Lutheran German Bible; (Strassburg: Johann Reinhard de Grüningen)

> Wann drey seind, die da geben gezewgknuß auff der erd, d' geist das wasser, vnd das Blut, vnnd dise drey seind eins. Unnd drey sind dye da geBen gezewgknuß imm hymel. Der vatter das wort, vnd der heilig geist, vnd dyse drey seind eins, oB wir auffnemen. . .

---

126. The reading is provided in *Die Niederdeutschen Bibelfrühdrucke*, ed. by Gerhard Ising (Berlin: Akademie-Verlag, 1976) 6: 623.
127. *Textual Criticism of the Bible* 77.

1490 [G12]: pre-Lutheran German Bible: (Augsburg: Johann Schönsperger)

> wann drey sind, die da geben gezeugknüß auff der erde, der geyst, das wasser, vnnd auch dz blůtt, vnnd dise drey sind eyns. Umd drey sind die da geben gezeügknub iṁ hymmel. Der vater, das wortt, vnnd der heylige geyst, vñ dise drey sind eins. Ob wir auffnemen. . .

1494 BRANT, Sebastion. *Narrenschiff*

This is the book containing Brant's testimony that all the lands are filled with holy writings (the Scriptures, Fathers, other books).

1514 *Bibia Poliglota Biblia sacra, hebraice, chaldaice et graece, cum tribus interpretationibus latinus*. Faks. der Ausgabe 1514-1517 (Madrid: Univ. Complutense, 1983-1984).

In 1964, Bruce Metzger referred to Deno J.Geanakolplos, who provided clues to say that with Stunica, D. Ducas was another editor, as if everyone in the 20th century forgot who all the editors were. As Tynan said there were "seven to eight editors". It appears that everyone did forget. But Dr. de Levante, in 1876, said "This is called the Complutensian Polyglot, and its chief promoter and patron was Cardinal Ximenes. The following learned men were employed in the undertaking:- Ælius Antonius Nebrissensis, Demetrius Ducas, Ferdinandus Picianus, Lopez de Stunica, Alfonsus de Xamora, Paulus Coronellus, and Johannes de Vergera, a physician of Alcala"[128] The Complutensian reading in 1 John 5:7-8 follows:

> 7) ότι τρείς εισίν οι μαρτυρούντες εν τω ουρανώ, ο πατήρ,{καὶ} ο λογος, και το αγιον πνευμα. (8) και ..... οι τρεις {εις το} εν εισί. και τρείς εισιν οι μαρτυρούντες {επι της γης}, το πνευμα, και το ύδωρ, και το αίμα. ___

> Variations from the common received text:
> 8 words omitted, 3 words added, 1 substitution ἐν > επι, 2 dative case words changed to genitive

omissions: the word: οὗτοι, & the clause: καὶ οἱ τρεῖς εἰς τὸ ἓν εἰσιν
additions: καὶ and εἰς το

Dr. Dobbin, in his *The Codex Montfortianus: A Collation* (1854) compared 4 readings: the Complutensis, the Montfort, Erasmus 3rd, and Stephanus 3rd. In this

---

128. Edward Riches de Levante *The Hexaglot Bible*. . . (London: Dickinson & Higham, 1876) b.

comparison he copied the Complutensis wrong, and on p. 10 he has πνευμα αγιον instead of αγιον πνευμα as it should be.

The Complutensian note for 1 John 5:7f as given by H.T. Armfield, *The Three Witnesses; The Disputed Text in St. John: Considerations New and Old* (pp. 67-68)

> St. Thomas in his exposition of the second decretal upon the Supreme Trinity and the Catholic faith, in treating the following passage against Abbot Joachem-viz., "There are Three who bear witness in heaven, Father, Word, and Holy Ghost," says as follows:
>
>> "And in order to teach the Unity of the Three Persons, there is subjoined, 'And these Three are One' "
>
> -which indeed is said on account of their unity of essence. But Joachim, minded to take this perversely, tried to fasten its authority upon a unity of love and consent. For there is added in the same passage:
>
>> "And there are three that bear witness on earth -Spirit, Water, and Blood."
>
> And in some books there is added: "And these Three are One." This, however, is not contained in the true copies: but it is said to have been added by the Arian heretics, in order to pervert the true understanding of the foregoing authority about the unity in essence of the Three Persons. Thus far St. Thomas in the place cited above."

1516   [Balthasar Hübmaier became pastor in the cathedral in Regensburg]

1516   ERASMUS, D. *Novum Testmentum Græcum.* [first ed.]

[7] ὅτι τρεῖς εἰσὶν οἱ μαρτυροῦντες __ __ _____, _ _____, _ _____ ___ _
. _____ [8] __ _____ __ _____ __ _____ __ _____ __ _____
, τὸ πνεῦμα, καὶ τὸ ὕδωρ, καὶ τὸ αἷμα· καὶ οἱ τρεῖς εἰς ἕν εἰσιν.

The mta often say this edition was done by Erasmus in haste. Reference is made to his words ...*praecipitatum fuit verius quam editum.* However, K.W. Clark disagrees: "It is not clear that Erasmus meant that he had been careless or negligent in preparing the text. The context suggests that he was dissatisfied with the haste and pressure of the printer. In any case, typographical errors are not properly to be attributed to Erasmus."[129]

1519   ERASMUS, D. *Novum Testmentus Græcum.* [2nd ed.]

Didbin[130], in 1827, says it was the 2nd ed., in which the *Comma* first appeared. Nearly all other accounts indicate it was the 3rd.

[7] ὅτι τρεῖς εἰσὶν οἱ μαρτυροῦντες .. .., ..., ..., ... [8] ... .
.. .., τὸ πνεῦμα, καὶ τὸ ὕδωρ, καὶ τὸ αἷμα·
καὶ οἱ τρεῖς εἰς ἕν εἰσιν.

1519   ERASMUS, Desiderus. [Nov 1: Letter to Jan Slechta]

See appendix #8 for excerpts from this reply from Erasmus, who speaks favorably of the Bohemian Brethren. Jan Slechta was a citizen of Bohemia.

[1520?]   *Codex Britannicus*

The placement here in the year 1520 is likely in error, since it is the date assigned to the *Montfort.* So until evidence arrives, we have no idea of the date or of the location of *Britannicus.*

---

129. *The Gentile Bias and Other Essays,* p. 167.
130. *Introduction to the Greek and Latin Classics,* 4th ed. (London: printed for Harding & Lepard, G.B. Whittaker, 1827) 109.

How the *Comma* may have appeared in it:

[7] ὅτι τρεῖς εἰσὶν οἱ μαρτυροῦντες ἐν τῷ οὐρανῷ, _ Πατήρ, _ Λόγος, καὶ _ πνα [___]. [8] καὶ οὗτοι οἱ τρεῖς ἕν εἰσι. καὶ τρεῖς εἰσιν [_] μαρτυροῦντες ἐν τῇ γῇ, τὸ πνα, _ τὸ ὕδωρ, καὶ _ αἷμα· καὶ οἱ τρεῖς εἰς τὸ ἕν εἰσι ει την μαρτυριαν των α'νῶν λαμβάνομεν. . .

Suggested differences from *Montfortianus*:

.Brit πνα _____ ... _ μαρτυροῦντες
Mont πνα ἅγιον ... οἱ μαρτυροῦντες

..Brit τὸ πνα, τὸ ὕδωρ, καὶ αἷμα· καὶ οἱ τρεῖς εἰς τὸ ἕν εἰσι ει την μαρτυριαν
Mont _ πνα, _ ὕδωρ, καὶ αἷμα· ___ __ _____ ___ __ __ _____ ει την μαρτυριαν

The *Montfortianus* omits 9 words:

Did *Britannicus* have the articles (τὸ πνα, τὸ ὕδωρ) or not (πνα, ὕδωρ)? The description of Dr. Dobbin implies "no." That of Scrivener implies "yes." Dr. Dobbin did compare the reading for *Britannicus* as provided in Erasmus' *Apologia ad Jacobum Stunicam* (Paris: 1522) as given by the "last volume of the Basle edition of Erasmus' Works, pp. 238-296,"[131] Dr. Dobbin was honest enough to admit that it agrees with the Montfort "except in the omission of the word ἅγιον, and of the article οἱ before μαρτυρουντες. . ."[132] Aha! And how does he explain that? He claims they "are clearly typographical errors, because they are *not* wanting in his third edition of the Greek Testament. . ." Forster said that Bishops Marsh "labours hard to identify the Codex Britannicus used by Erasmus, with the Codex Monfortianus." Clarke and Scrivener followed Marsh. Scrivener, referring to this as *Montfortianus* (Evan.61, Act.34), points to verse 8 and says "162. -τὸ *ter* 34." He is saying the third article of verse 8 is missing. So we assume that τὸ *prim. et secund.* of verse 8 are present in the MS Scrivener is describing. But these two articles before "spirit" and "water" (τὸ πνα, τὸ ὕδωρ) are not in the MS which Adam Clarke calls "*Codex Montfortii*, or *Codex Dubliniensis*, cited by Erasmus, under the title *Codex Britannicus*." Clarke's MS reads "πνα, υδωρ", without articles. Why didn't Scrivener mention these two other omissions of τὸ in his MS? Did he overlook them? Unlikely. More likely, they were not omitted in *Britannicus*.

Some will object, and say that the use of the Latin abreviation *ter* of the quote

---

131. Dobbin, *The Codex Montfortianus: A Collation*...(London: Bagster, 1854) 10.
132. Ibid.

"162. -τὸ *ter* 34" means all three, not only the third article. But the context of Scrivener's use of *prim. et secund.* shows that he is not employing the sense of cardinal numbers, but that of ordinal numbers. Besides, Erasmus noted the last clause καὶ οἱ τρεῖς εἰς τὸ ἕν εἰσι was in Britannicus. This clause in not in *Montifortianus*.

Scrivener says it was first known in 1519-22. Gregory says it was written in Oxford in 1520. But no one really knows, since the Montfort is not the *Britannicus*. Scrivener did not agree with Alford's speculation that Erasmus tampered with "the very few MSS. which he collated." But Scrivener admits "I never saw the Basle manuscripts."[133]

1520   LEE, Edward. *Annotationes in Annotationes Novi Testamenti Desiderii Erasmi.* Paris: G. de Gourmont for D. Resch. [February]

QUOTE from de Jonge's introduction to *Apologia Respondens ad ea qvae Iacobvs Lopis Stvnica...* (p.11) concerning this work of Lee:
> ...Lee did not refrain from accusing Erasmus of Arianism (*inter alia*) on account of his leaving out *1 Ioh. 5,7b-8a* from his Greek and Latin text), Pelagianism and other heresies.

(De Jonge says this work "contained 243 notes on Erasmus' first edition of the New testament...and 25 on the second edition.")

1520   ERASMUS, Desiderus. *Apologia invectivis Lei (Opuscula 236-303).* Antwerp: Michaël Hillen [early March], Cologne: reprint by Eucharius Cervicornus [late March]

1520   ERASMUS, Desiderus. *Responsio ad annotationes Lei.* (LB IX 123-200) [April]

1520   ERASMUS, Desiderus. *Liber tertius quo respondet reliquis annotationibus Ed. Lei.* (LB IX 199-284) [May]

This was the work in which Erasmus defended his omission of 1 John 5:7b-8a. A portion of his lengthy argument follows, as quoted from Orme,p. 4. The first point of Erasmus was that only such words (without the *Comma*) occur in the Greek and he continues:

> 2. "That this passage is so cited by Cyril in the 14th book of his *Thesaurus*,

---

133. *Plain Introduction*, 3rd. ed. p.433.

and that an othodox father, as he was, would infallibly have cited the whole passage, against the Arians, if he has found it in any copies in his time.

3. "That the same may be said of Augustin, who also cites it thus against Maximinus the Arian. . .

4. "That Beda cites the passage in the same manner as Augustin.

1520   ZUÑIGA, Diego López. *Annotations contra Erasmum Roterodamum in defensionem tralationis Novi* A.G. Brocario. [Jun or Aug]

De Jonge points out that this work had begun in 1516, but was delayed, has 115 pages containing 212 notes on Erasmus' NT. Zuñiga tried to demonstrate the superiority of the Vulgate.

1521   [Balthasar Hübmaier began preaching in Waldshut in Breisgau]

Hübmaier was still a Catholic at this time.

1521   [June 18] Bombasius sent two passages from Codex B to Erasmus]

Reviewing the past, neither the 1st edition (1516), nor the second edition (1519) of Erasmus contained the *Comma*. In 1521, Paulus Bombasius finally located the neglected Codex B in the Vaticanan Library, and informed Erasmus "I found it with difficulty."[134] In June, he sent readings from 1 Joh 4:1-3 and 1 Joh 5:7-11 to Erasmus.[135] Upon examination he noted that Vaticanus omitted the *Comma*. But this was not enough to persuade him. The inclusion by Erasmus of the *Comma* in all his subsequent editions, prove that he rejected the Vaticanus reading.

1521   ERASMUS, Desiderus. *Apologia respondens ad ea quae Iacobus Lopis Stunica taxaverat in prima duntaxat Novi Testamenti aeditione* (ASD IX-2 58-267) Louvain: Dirk Martens. [Oct.]

QUOTE from article (de Jonge, 1983), concerning this work by Erasmus:

> In the course of the work Erasmus began obviously to weary of it; from *Philemon* up to and including *Revelation* his paragraphs are considerably shorter than in the preceding part of the work (with the exception of his long excursus on *1 Ioh. 5,7-8*)

---

134. C.H. Turner. *Early Printed Editions of the Greek Testament*, p. 22.
135. *Erasmi Opera Omnia*, IX-2: 257 n505.

1521   GERBEL, Nicholas. ed. *Novum Testamentum Graece*. Hagenoae: Thomas Anshelmus. [left side of p.257 in Ga I 33, Tübingen copy.]

Gerbell, "Erasmus' one time assistant in the production of the *editio princeps*, had pleaded as long ago as September 1515 for an edition small enought to be carried about."[136] Gerbell did not include the *Comma*. Gerbel sent Luther a copy. Upon its arrival at the Wartburg, Luther expressed his delight by refering to Gerbel's editions as his "best man". He had also referred to his copy of the Erasmus 1519 edition as *uxor*, his "wife."[137]

1521   A French Bible printed at Lyons, France, which Frederick Nolan had obtained. Commenting on this verse he remarks "(1) It *differs* from the Latin Vulgate; as it reads "le filz" for "verbum" (2) It *agrees* with this reading with the ancient Confession of Faith used by the Waldenses..."

> Trois choses sont qui donnent tesmoing au ciel, le pere le filz et le sainct esperit, et ces trois sont une chose. Et trois choses qui donnent tesmoing en terre, esperit eaue et sang

1522   ZUÑIGA, Diego López. *Erasmi Roterodami blasphemiae et impietates*. [April] [54 pages]

1522   ERASMUS, Desiderus. *Apologia adversus libellum Iacobi Stunicae cui titulum fecit Blasphemiae et empietates Erasmi*. [June] [52 pages]

1522   ERASMUS, Desiderus. *Novvm Testamentvm Omne, Tertio iam ac diligentius ab Erasmo Roterodamo recogintum, non solum ad Græcum veritatem, uerumetiam ad multorum utrisqe linguæ codicum, eorumɛß ueterum simul & emendatorū fidem, postremo ad probatissimorum autorum citationem, emēdationem & interpretationem, unà cum Annotatinibus recognitis, ac magna accessione locupletatis, quæ lectorem do ceant, quid qua ratione mutatum sit. Quisquis igitur amas ueram Theologiam, lege, cognosce, ac deinde iudic. Necß statim offendere, si quid mutatum offenderis, sed expēde, num in melius mutatum sit. Nam morbus est, non iudicium, damnare quod non inspexeris. 522.*

---

136. C.H.Turner, *Early Printed Editions of the Greek Testament* 20.
137. J.M.Reu, *Luther's German Bible; An Historical Presentation Together with a Collection of Sources*. (Columbus: Lutheran Book Concern, 1934) 351.

[7] ὅτι τρεῖς εἰσιν οἱ μαρτυροῦντες ἐν τῷ οὐρανῷ, _ Πατήρ, _ Λόγος, καὶ _ /πνεῦμα ἅγιον/. [8] καὶ οὗτοι οἱ τρεῖς ἕν εἰσι. καὶ τρεῖς εἰσιν οἱ μαρτυροῦντες ἐν τῇ γῇ, _ πνεῦμα, καὶ _ ὕδωρ, καὶ _ αἷμα· καὶ οἱ τρεῖς εἰς τὸ ἕν εἰσιν.

Variations from the common received text

6 omissions: [v.7] ὁ, ὁ, ὁ and [v.8] τὸ, τὸ, τὸ
1 transposition: ἅγιον and πνεῦμα are swapped

Note the clause at the end of v. 8:

Erasmus 3rd: καὶ οἱ τρεῖς εἰς τὸ ἕν εἰσιν.
Comp Polygl: ___ __ ____ ___ __ __ ____.
Montfortii : ___ __ ____ ___ __ __ ____.

Where did Erasmus get this last clause? Not from the Complutensian. Nor from the Montfortii. Neither one had the clause! Erasmus said (according to Forster, via Scrivener's *Plain Introd.* 3rd) "*Postremo; Quod Britannicum etiam in terræ testimonio addebat,* καὶ οἱ τριες εἰς τὸ ἕν εἰσιν, *quod non addebatur hic duntaxat in editione Hispaniensi.*" It came from Britannicus. This is why Charles Forster argued (in 1867) that the Montfort Codex "cannot possibly be the same with the Codex Britannicus."

Scrivener offers a "conjecture." He supposes the man who sent the passage to Erasmus "might have broken off after copying the disputed words" from the Britannicus. But this conjecture does not explain the omission of the clause in the Montfort! A facsimilie of the Monfort was carefully made by Adam Clarke, whose hope for accurate copying of the verse was that "it may be said every jot and every tittle belonging to the text are here fairly and faithfully represented; nothing being *added* and nothing being *omitted*." The Montfort reading, which clearly omits the clause, is easily accessible for inspection, in Clarke's Commentary on the Bible.

1522   LUTHER, Martin. *Septembertestament* [reprinted by Kenneth Strand in 1972.]

[7] Denn drey sind die da zeugen... der geyst und das wasser und das blut [8] un die drey sind eynts

J.M. Reu cited a letter in "*Briefe II, 397*" by Luther in which he alluded to his copy of Erasmus's 1519 edition of the Greek N.T. as his "wife", which was the basis for his translation into German. The question ought to be raised "How could Luther, who despised Roman Catholicism, select to use a Greek edition edited by a Roman Catholic?" How could he ever call a Roman Catholic-composed Greek New Testament his "wife"? See appendix 7.

1522   *Novum Jesu Christi Testamentus Graece antiquorum aliquot exemplarium collatione multo quam hactenus emendatius.* Basieae

. . .ἐν τῷ οὐρανῷ, ὁ πατηρ, ὁ λογος, καὶ τὸ ἅγιον πνοῦμα. καὶ οὗτοι οἱ τρεῖς ἕν εἰσι. καὶ τρεῖς εἰσιν οἱ μαρτυρουντες ἐν τῇ γῇ.

1522   [B. Hübmaier was drawn to the doctrines of Luther and Zwingli]

1523   [B. Hübmaier discussed the verses on baptism with Zwingli]

Zwingli later said "Nothing grieves me more than that I am at present obliged to baptize children, for I know it ought not to be done" and further "However, if I terminate it I fear for my prebend."[138]

1523   MÜNTZER, Thomas. *Von der Taufe, wie man die heldet.*

This liturgy for the baptism of infants, though in use in 1523, was printed in 1524. Thomas Müntzer, its author, could not possibly be an Anabaptist.

1523   EMSER, Jerome. *Auβ was Gründ unnd Ursach Luthers Dolmatschung oder das naior testament dem gemeine man villich vorbotten worden sey*

The translation of the title is *On What Ground and for What Cause Luther's Translation of the New Testament Should Justly Be Forbidden to the Common Man.* Leipzig: [completed Sep 21].

1524   EMSER, Jerome. *Annotationes vber Luthers naw Testament gebessert vnd emendirt.*

In English: *Annotations Concerning Luther's New Testament Improved and Emended.* These two works (this and the one directly above) may provide insight into another factor explaining Luther's bias against the verse. J.M. Goeze said in *Continuation of the Comprehensive Defense of the Complutensian Greek New Testament* (1769) "So Luther stood firm as a pillar; and he was so much less moved to take up this verse in his translation, i.e., the screaming was more despised and more bitter, which the Papists and esp. Emser had, for that reason, made against him. These were precisely the reasons which determined the attitude of Bugenhagen.

---

138. L. von Muralt & W. Schmidt *Quellen zur Geschichte der Täufer in der Schweiz* (Zurich: 1952) 184. as transl. by L. Verduin *Anatomy of a Hybrid*, 173.

The attitude of both men in these portions can be used neither for nor against the validity of this scripture-verse." (p. 130).

1524   [Tyndale sailed to Hamburg, Germany]

1524   [Swiss-German New Testaments printed in Zurich]

Why didn't they simply use Luther's edition? In his article "Zur sprachlichen Stellung der Zürcher Bibelübersetzung 1524 bis 1535" *Festschrift für Ingo Reiffenstein zum 60.Geburtstag* (Göppingen: Küummerle, 1988) S. Sonderregger said

> Regard for the Swiss language of the countryside of the time as well as the philological struggle from a translation as clear as possible and one generally understandable have often led to the deviation of Luther's text in the Zurich Bible itself, where people basically followed Luther

1525   [Peasant's War in Münster, Germany] (The relationship between the slander of the Received Text, and the slander of the the Anabaptists[139] involves an exposure of erroneous historiography which remains to be explained in length in a future work.)

1525   [autumn: Tyndale moved to Cologne, Germany]

Here he began printing the New Testament.

1525   [The "Täufertestament" of Zurich]

The citation occurs in the 1983 reprint *Die Froschauer Bibel 1531; Das Buch der Zürcher Kirche* (p. 1364) (Zürich: Theologische Verlag)

1525   [Luther's *Bondage of the Will*] Luther said in section IX *"God foreknows nothing by contingency, but that He foresees, purposes, and does all things according to His immutable, eternal and infallible will.* By this thunderbolt, "Free-will" is thrown prostrate and utterly dashed to pieces."

---

139. Referring to the old myth of Anabaptists=fanactics C.K. says in *ME* III:779 "No other topic of the Reformation and particularly of the Anabaptists has received as much attention throughout the centuries as the Anabaptists of Münster". Dr. H.S. Bender said in *ME* II:752 "Well into the 19th century the great Anabaptist movement of the 16th century was uncritically identified with the Peasants' War of 1525 and the events in Münster"

1526   [Tyndale was betrayed and he fled to Worms, Germany]

He also began printing here. In the city of Worms in 1524, "Anabaptism found a favorable soil."[140]

1526   TYNDALE, William, ed. *The Newe Testament*. 1989 reprint, Milford, OH: John the Baptist Printing Ministry, 304.

February: "The first English New Testament published and the first from the original Greek" (modern spelling by John W. Sawyer).

> For there are three which bear record in heaven, the Father, the word, and the Holy Ghost: and these three are one. And there are three which bear record in earth, the Spirit, and water, and blood: and these three are one.

(Because of Tyndale's importance, various denominations have sought to claim him. Some have said that he was Reformed (Van Bruggen), Lutheran (Egan, Cargill, et al.), Baptist (J.Davis), or Puritan (Knappen) in his theology. But Donald D. Smeaton demonstrated that Wycliffite/Lollard themes abounded in his theology. Yet he properly avoided reductionism and concluded "I do not claim that Tyndale was "only" a Lollard." [141]) Be that as it may, Tyndale believed in unconditional election. In his *An Answer to Sir Thomas More's Dialogue*, he wrote "Why doth God open one man's eyes and not another's? Paul (Rom ix) forbiddeth to ask why: for it is too deep for man's capacity. God we see is honored thereby, and His mercy set out and the more seen in the vessels of mercy. But the popish. . .set up free-will with the heathen philosophers, and say that a man's free will is the cause why God chooseth one and not another, contrary unto all the Scripture." Parker Society reprint, 1850, p. 191 (as quoted in Ian Murray's *The Forgotten Spurgeon*.)

1526   [Apr 6: Hübmaier recants his forced recantation]

Hübmaier entered the pulpit and "began to read his recantation in a broken, weak and quivering voice, until his heart choked his utterance and he broke down. He swayed to and fro before his audience. . . when suddenly the unseen hand of God was put forth to bind him up, and . . .he filled the sanctuary with the shout that 'Infant baptism is not of God, and men must be baptized by faith in Christ!' The crowd . . .burst into tumult. . . Zwingli screamed above the rest." Armitage, *A History of the Baptists* 1:339.

1526   [Jakob Kautz "jointed the Anabaptists".] See (1529: KAUTZ).

---

140. *NSHE* 6:301.
141. *Lollard Themes in the Reformation Theology of William Tyndale*. (Sixteenth Century Journal Publishers: Kirksville, Missouri, 1986), 251.

1527 [January: Hans Denk and Ludwig Haetzer came to Worms]

In Worms, they published their translation of the Old Testament prophets *Alle Propheten nach Hebräischer sprach verteutscht* (Worms: Peter Schöffer). By 1528 or 1529 Kautz became acquainted with the printer, Peter Schöffer.

1527 ERASMUS, Desiderus: *Novum Testamentum* [4th edition]

This edition also contained the *Comma*. According to Roland Bainton, Erasmus defended his restoration of the verse! Bainton cites p. 679 of this fourth edition. Bainton said "His own defense was that the verse was in the Vulgate and must therefore have been in the Greek text used by Jerome."[142]

1527 LUTHER, Martin, *Luther's Work* (St. Louis: Concordia Publishing House) 30:316

> The Greek books do not have these words, but this verse seems to have been inserted by the Catholics because of the Arians, yet not aptly, for whenever John speaks about the witnesses, he speaks about those on earth, not about those in heaven.
>
> Martin Luther, Oct 30, 1527

1527 Luther, Martin, *Weimare Ausgabe* 48:688, 15-20 (No.7101)

> "There are three who give testimony," etc. (1 John 5). Why is this locus not translated in the German translation? He responded: I and others believe that it is sort of added, that it is added by some ignoramus. We do not want, however, to translate it because of the word "testimony," because in heaven there will be no need for a testimony . . .as it is written: "we will see God face to face." There the Trinity will declare Himself.

From a recent article (1985: POSSET) three other sources were mentioned which reveal Luther's thoughts on the verse. The following quote is from the notes of Luther's "graduate student", Georg Röer.

---

142. *Erasmus of Christendom*. (NY: Charles Scribener's Sons, 1969) 137.

Weimare Ausgabe 20:780, 21-781,2

"For there are three." This locus the Greek codices do not have. It seems that it was inserted ineptly by the eagerness of ancient theologians against Arius, if one looks at the analogy of faith. Where God is seen, there is no need for a testimony, but here it is needed, here we have it in the word, and we do not want to have it any other way, since there is no testimony in heaven and no faith, which are of this life. Therefore, we leave out this text. Also the subsequent text ridicules this verse. And I can make fun of it easily because there is no more inept locus for the Trinity.

Concerning this above quote, Posset declared "This is the most precise stenogram of Luther's lecture on the *Comma Johanneum*. Essentially, Luther said the same as in the *Table Talk* and in S [scholia] and P [notes by Probst]."

1527 [B. Hübmaier was arrested and sent to Vienna]

He was then cast into the dungeons of the castle of Gritsenstein.

1528 [March 10: Hübmaier was burned at the stake.]

1529 KAUTZ, Jakob. (ed.) [A complete German Bible]

"In the same year, 1529, Kautz published the first complete German Bible *based on the original text*, five years before Luther's Bible" [143] [emphasis mine]

Kautz was imprisoned with Reublin. "Kautz and Reublin now drew up a statement of their faith; they knew only adult baptism; infant baptism was not in accord with Christ's command;"[144] Because Kautz was an Anabaptist, this ought to be of great interest to all Baptists. But why has Kautz been forgotten today? Who could dare say that Kautz did not use a Greek Received Text?

1529 [Apr 13: Letter of Erasmus; his highest respect for the Anabaptists]

Roland Bainton, a history professor from Yale, said Erasmus "had the highest respect for the Anabaptists"[145] and provides this translation of a letter of April 13, from Erasmus to his friend Ber:

An Anabaptist has just experienced the fate of John the Baptist, except that

---

143. *ME* 3: 160.
144. *ME* 3: 160.
145. *Erasmus of Christendom*, 260.

the one was decapitated, the other burned. Although this sect is of all the most hated by the princes because of anarchy and community of goods, these people have no temple, they establish no kingdom, they defend themselves by no violence and they are said to have many among them much more sincere in morals than others, though what can be sincere if the integrity of the faith is corrupted?[146]

1530 [January: in Antwerp. Tyndale printed the Pentateuch]

1531 [Tyndale translated Jonah and retranslated Genesis]

1531 BULLINGER, Heinrich. *Von dem unverschampten fräfel, ergerlichem verwyrren unnd unwarhaftem leeren der selbsgesandten Widertäuffern, vier gespräch Bücher, zu verwarnenn den einfalten.*

There are non-Baptists even today, who believe the Anabaptists, by way of Conrad Grebel, had it roots with the radical Thomas Müntzer. "Even Bullinger himself says not a word about a personal contact between Grebel and Münster in his two books against the Anabaptists written in 1530 and 1560."[147]

[1531 FRANCK, Sebastion. *Chronica, Zeytbuch vnd geschychtbibel*]

R.F says this book "was written in 1530-31, when Anabaptism had been just a few year in existence, and was slandered everywhere" *ME* I:587
C.K. says "For Anabaptism Sebastian Frank is of lasting importance" *ME* II: 366.

1531 FROSCHAUER, Christof. *Die ganze Bibel der ursprüngliche Ebraischen und Griechischen waarheit nach/auffs aller treüwlicßest verteücschet.* 1983 Reprint. Zürich: Theologischer Verlag. ccciiii.

This Bible was printed in Zürich, which many regard as "the birthplace of the Anabaptist movement"[148]

> dañ deer geyst ist die warheyt. Dañ drey sind die zeugnuß gebend im himel: Der vater das wort unnd der heylig geyst und die drey dienend in

---

146. *Erasmi Epistolae*, VIII, 2149. 40-41 ed. P.S. and Mrs. Allen (as provided by Bainton)
147. H.S.Bender *Conrad Grebel 1498-1526 Founder of the Swiss Brethren* (Goshen, IN: Mennonite Historical Society, 1950). 114. On p. 258 Bender gives the year as 1531, which agrees with the *ME*.
148. See article "Zürich" in *ME* 4:1042.

eins. Unnd drey sind die da zeügend auff erden...

There are the 1524 and the 1525 editions[149] of the Swiss-German New Testament. Thus, the *Comma* was included in that time period.

"Among the people, especially the Anabaptists, the first editions of the Froschaurer Bibles and Testaments were greatly loved."[150]

1533   SEPULVEDA, Juan Ginez (November: letter to Erasmus).

Sepulveda, a Spanish humanist and historian, was in Rome at this time. Delitzsch says that on Nov 1st, he wrote to Erasmas "that in his edition of the New Testament he had followed a diversely corrupt text."[151] Kenyon say of Codex Vaticanus "A few readings from it were supplied to Erasmus by his correspondent Sepulveda, but too late for use in his editions of the New Testament."[152] In this claim, Kenyon made two serious errors. It was not "too late", because Erasmus' 5th edition appeared in 1535. Nor was it merely "a few readings", for in this letter, Sepulveda furnished Erasmus "with 365 readings as a convincing argument in support of his statements"[153] that Codex Vaticanus is "a weighty proof of excellence with the Latin version" (multum convenit cum vetere nostrâ tranlatione) against the common Greek text..."[emphasis mine].

1534   COLINAEUS, Simon. *Novum Testamentum*. Paris:

On p. 535 of *A Companion to the Greek Testament*, Philip Schaff proudly displays a "Fac-simile of page containing 1 John v.7." showing how Colinaeus omitted the *Comma*. With reference to Colinaeus, C.H. Turner says "He ejected the *Comma Iohanneum*, being the last editor to do so till the English Presbyterian Mace or Macey in 1729."[154]

T.H.L. Parker refers to Beza's *Responsio*, in which Beza denounced this Greek edition of Colinaeus: "For I have found many things in it emended on sheer

---

149. See that table in the back of this reprinted Bible (p. 1364) "*Übersicht: Froschauer- Bibeldrucke 1524-1531*" The 1525 editions is also called the "Täufertestament"!
150. A. FL. "Froschaure Bibles and Testaments" *ME* 2:415.
151. F. Delitzsch, *Studien zur Entstehungsgeschichte der Polyglottenbibel des Cardinals Ximenes* (Leipzig: Druck von A. Edelmann, 1871) 13.
152. Kenyon. *Textual Criticism of the New Testament* (London: MacMillan, 1912) 78.
153. See "Codex Vaticanus 1209" in Scrivener's *Plain Introduction*, 3rd ed., p. 105
154. *Early Printed Editions of the Greek Testament*. 25.

conjecture by someone who was in other respects most learned in the Greek tongue."[155]

Anabaptists, Lutherans, and many others rejected the edition of Colinaeus, which fell into oblivion. It "had no influence on the history of the text, and it was first by Mill and then again by Griesbach that it was rescued from oblivion"[156]

The question arises again: What printed Greek text were our Baptist forefathers using? They used the TR. Some will say: Ah! But "they had no other optional available to them!"[157] But T.H.L. Parker said "even in the sixteenth century an alternative to the *textus receptus*" existed, and he referred to the edition of Colinaeus.

1534   [Tyndale completed his second translation of the NT]

   (For there are three which bear record in heaven, the father, the word, and the holy ghost. And these three are one). For there are three which bear record (in earth:) the spirit, and water, and blood: and these three are one.[158]

1534   [Tyndale was betrayed by Henry Phillips]

1535   ERASMUS, Desiderus. *Novum Testamentum*. [5th ed.]

This edition is noteworthy, because not only had Erasmus received the few aformention passages sent to him from Bombasius, but he now had the Sepulveda's 365 readings from Codex Vaticanus where it differered from the Received Text. Since the 5th edition of Erasmus "differs very little from the fourth as regards the text"[159] it is safe to assume Erasmus rejected every last reading from Sepulvada's list.

Also in this 5th edition, the *Comma* appears for the the third time in an edition by Erasmus. Since there is no evidence for the oft-repeated claim that Erasmus

---

155. *Responsio* as translated by T.H.L. Parker in *Calvin's Commentaries*.(Grand Rapids: Eerdmans, 1971) 101.
156. C.H.Turner *Early Printed Editions of the Greek N.T.* 25-26.
157. This is D.A. Carson's view. *King James Version Debate*, 55 n.16
158. *Tyndale's New Testament translated from the Greek by William Tyndale in 1534 in a modern-spelling edition by* David Daniell (New Haven & London: Yale Univ. Press, 1989) 341.
159. Scrivener, *Plain Introduction*, 3rd ed. p. 433.

made a "promise", it raises the question again, "Why did he continue to include it, having written against it fifteen years ago, in 1520?" Because he changed his views prior to 1527, perhaps as early as 1522.

1535 [Tyndale was imprisoned for 7 months of this year at Vilvorde]

1536 [Oct 6: Tyndale: imprisoned for 9 more months, then burned at the stake.]

1539 CRUMWELL. *The Great Bible*. prologue by CRANMER

> This Jesus Christ is he that came by water and bloud, not by water onely, but by water and bloud. And it is the sprete that beareth wytnes, because the Sprete is trueth. (For ther are thre which beare recorde in heaven, the father, the worde, and the wholy goost. And these thre are one), and ther are thre which beare recorde (in erth) the sprete,

1546? Mazarin Bible. (The *Editio Princeps* of the Latin Bible.) Mainz: Gutenberg (or) Fust and Schoeffer.

According to Adam Clarke, it contains the *Comma* and reads as follows

> Quoniam tres sunt qui testimonium dant in cælo, Pater, Verbum, et Siritus Sanctus, et hii tres unum sunt. Et tres sunt qui testimonium dant in terra. Spiritus, aqua, et sanquis, et tres unum sunt.

Kenyon gives the date of 1546. C.H. Turner says the *terminus ad quem* is supplied by a rubricator's note in a copy dated August 24, 1456.

1550 BUGENHAGEN, Johannes, *Exposition Jonae*

1550   ESTIENNE, Robert. *Greek New Testament*. 3rd ed.

[7] ὅτι τρεῖς εἰσὶν οἱ μαρτυροῦντες † ἐν τῷ οὐρανῷ) ὁ Πατήρ, ὁ Λόγος, καὶ τὸ ἅγιον πνεῦμα. [8] καὶ οὗτοι οἱ τρεῖς ἕν εἰσι. καὶ τρεῖς εἰσιν οἱ μαρτυροῦντες ἐν τῇ γῇ, τὸ πνεῦμα, καὶ τὸ ὕδωρ, καὶ τὸ αἷμα· καὶ οἱ τρεῖς εἰς τὸ ἕν εἰσιν.

Stephens (or Estienne) included the *Comma*, but marked the words ἐν τῷ οὐρανῷ as wanting in seven MSS. The words marked off by †...) indicate the extent of the omission. Opponents of the *Comma*, say that the semicircle was erroneously placed, i.e., that it was meant to be put after ἐν τῇ γῇ. Of these seven MSS, 4 were borrowed from the Royal Library at Paris. The account by Orme continues that Le Long found these four in 1720, and noted that each one omitted the entire *Comma*. Marsh claimed in 1793 that he found a fifth MS in the Cambridge Library, ιγ, used by Stephanus. His claim is cogent. But it also omitted the *Comma*. In 1866, there were 188 MSS containing the General Epistles. Rev. A.W. Grafton reported a century ago by, that none of the 188 MSS of the General Epistles omit only those three designated words.

1550   CALVIN, John. *Calvin's Commentary; St. John 11-21 and First John*. trans. T.H.L. Parker.   London: Oliver and Boyd, 1961. p.303.

> *There are three that bear witness in heaven*. Some omit the whole of this verse. Jerome thinks it happened through malice rather than error, and that only among Latins. But, since even the Greek MSS do not agree, I hardly dare assert anything. But because the passage reads better with the clause added and I see that it is found in the best and most approved copies (*codicibus*), I also readily embrace it.

1553   *Novum Jesus Christi Testamentum Graecum, collatis non paucis vererande fidei exemplaribus, accuratissma nunc lima editum*. Basilaea: p. 663

. . .ἐν τῷ ορανῷ, ὁ πατὴρ, ὁ λόγος, καὶ τὸ ἅγι πνοῦμα. και ὅτι οἱ τρεῖς ἕν εἰσι. καὶ τρεῖς εἰσι οἱ μαρτυροῦντες ἐν τῷ γῇ.

1555   WIDMANSTADT, Johann Albrecht. . . .*Liber Sacrosancti Evangelii*. . .*characteribus & lingua Syra*. . . Vienna:

This was the first printed Syriac edition. Today scholars say there are over 475 Syriac MSS (350+ Peshitta; 125 Harclean; et al.) Widmanstadt omitted the *Comma*, but he only used 2 MSS, one of them being provided by a legate to Pope Julius III.

The translators of the King James Bible knew of this Syriac edition.

So the *Syrian* translation of the New Testament is in most learned mens

Libraries, of *Widminstadius* his setting forth.[160]

But the KJV translators rejected Widmanstadt's judgment in 1 John 5:7-8.

1556   BEZA, Theodore. *Novum Testamentum*

The preface to the Rheims NT (1582) gave 10 reasons why "We translate the old vulgar Latin text, not the common Greeke text"[161] Beza, in his edition of 1556, accordingly omitted from Luke 3:36, "the son of Cain", which codex D omits. For reason #9, the Catholic writer of the preface seized this opportunity to say that the "Adversaries themselves, namely Beza, preferre" the Vulgate to the Greek, and "sometime go so wide from the Greek. . .For example, *Luc.* 3.36. they have put the words, 'The sonne of Cainan,' which he wittingly and wilfully left out:"[162]

1556   STEPHANI, Oliva Roberti. *Novvm D. N. Iesv Christi testamentum. Latinè olim à Veteri interrete, nunc denuo à Theodoro Beza versum; cum eiusdem annotationibus, in quibus ratio interretationis redditur.*318.

> 7 Nam tres sunt qui testificantur in cælo, Pater, Sermo, & Spiritus sanctus; & hi tres vnum sunt. 8 Et tres sunt qui testificātur in terra,

An excerpt from the notes: "Non legit tamen Vetus interpres, nec Cyrillus, nec Augustinus, nec Beda; sed legit Hieronymus, legit Erasmus in Britānico codice, & in Complutensi editione. Legimus & in nonnullis Roberti nostri veteribus libris. Non convenit tamen in omnibus inter istos codices. Nam Britannicus legit sine articulis πατήρ, λόγος, και πνεῦμα. In nostris verò legebantur articuli, & præterea etiam additum erat Sancti epitheton Spiritui, ut ab eo distingueretur cuius sit mentio in sequenti versiculo, quique in terra collocatur."

1560   BULLINGER, Heinrich. *Der Widertäufferen Ursprung.*

This was his second book against the Anabaptists. In his third book (1572) he suggested a connection between the Anabaptist Conrad Grebel and the radical Thomas Müntzer. "But in 1560, Bullinger did not venture as yet to suggest such a direct connection."[163]

---

160. *The Translators to the Reader. Preface to the King James Version 1611*, ed. by Goodspeed. (Chicago, 1935). Text above is as quoted by Metzger.
161. "Preface to the Rheims New Testament, 1582" as quoted by Hugh Pope in *English Versions of the Bible* (St.Louis & London: B. Herder, 1952) Appendix 1, p. 621.
162. Ibid. p.623.
163. H.S. Bender *Conrad Grebel 1498-1526 Founder of the Swiss Brethren* (Goshen, IN: Mennonite Historical Society, 1950) 115.

1560   *The Biestkens Bible/ Dooperbibel.*

Referring to Erasmus, the *Mennonite Encyclopedia* says:

> It was due to his idea that I John 5:7 (the text on the Trinity) was spurious, that this verse was omitted from the older Anabaptist translations and was enclosed in parentheses in the later Biestkens Bible (*q.v.*)[164]

This view of Erasmus was his *initial* idea which he later changed. The *ME* also says "the Dutch Anabaptists were deeply influenced by Erasmus."

1560   *The Geneva Bible; A Facsimilie of the 1560 edition* (Madison, Milwaukee, & London: University of Wisconsin Press, 1969)

> For there are thre, which beare recorde in heauen, the Father, the Worde, and the holie Goſt: and these thre are one.

1562   [College of Douay founded by William Allen (1532-94)]

The English College was located in Douay, a city in northern France. It was founded to train Catholic priests. Due to "religious wars in the Netherlands" the college was moved to Rheims in 1578. Rev. Hugh Pope says "The English Colleges of Rheims and Douay were not Jesuit foundations"[165] however its first chancellor, Richard Smith (1500-1563) "actively supported Mary's persecution of the Protestants" *NCE*, 13: 305

1564   ΤΗΣ ΚΑΙΝΗΣ ΔΙΑΘΗΚΗΣ ΑΠΑΝΤΑ. Lipsiae:

> . . .ὅτι τπεῖς εἰσιν οἱ μαρτυροῦντες ἐν τῷ οὐπανῷ, ὁ πατηρ, ὁ λόγος, καὶ τὸ ἅγιον πνεῦμα. καὶ οὗτοι οἱ τρεῖς † ἕν εἰσι. καὶ τρεῖς εἰσιν οἱ μαρτυροῦντες ἐν τῇ γῇ.

1566   *Novum Jesu Christi domini nostri Testamentum. Additis summis rerum et sententiarum, quae singulis capitubus continentur.* Tiguri:

> ὅτι τρεῖς εἰσιν οἱ μαρτυροῦν τες [ἐν τῷ οὐρανῷ] ὁ πατὴρ, ὁ λόγος, καὶ τὸ ἅγιον πνεῦμα. καὶ οὗτοι οἱ τρεῖς ⊕ ἕν εἰσι.

1568   [edition of Luther's Bible with a blank space at I John 5:7]

---

164. C.Neff & H.S. Bender, "Erasmus" *ME* 2:239
165. *English Versions of the Bible*, enlarged by S. Bullough (St. Louis & London: B. Herder, 1952) 277.

Only 23 years after Luther published the last edition in his lifetime, this edition was printed in Heidelberg, in which the "publisher very conscientiously had left a free space in Luther's text in this position . . ."[166]

1569   TREMELLIUS, Emanuel. *Grammatica Chaldaea Et Syra...* Geneva:

A quote (as provided by R. Borger) from Tremellius on his Syriac translation:
> But because it was omitted not only in the printed version, but also in the manuscript Heidelberg codex, nor was read in all the old Greek codicies, I did not dare to insert it into the text. So in order that there might not be a disturbance of the verses and so that their numbers may correspond to the numbers on the verses on the Greek text, I have passed from the sixth to the eighth verse.

Most modern accounts only say that Tremellius put the *Comma* into a margin. But they, as well as Scrivener (1883), Metzger (1977) et al. do not mention the "blank space." However the Harvard scholar Ezra Abbot does mention it. From a footnote of the appendix of the 1866 edition of Orme's *Memoirs*, we read "Tremellius, in his edition of the Peshitto published in 1569, left a blank space for it in the text, and placed *his own translation of it into Syriac* in a note;"[167] Now, there are questions to ask, if he regarded it as spurious:

(1). Why did he take time to translate it?
(2). Why did he put it into the margin?
(3). Why did he hesitate to cause a "disturbance of the verses"?
(4). Why did he leave a "blank space" for it?

How often is "blank space" provided for the *Comma*, in any English translation of modern days? The four questions alone indicate that Tremellius must have had doubts. His actions are not in accord with his words. Perhaps, with a blank space, he wanted not only to retain the correspondence with numbers[168] but to ensure that a future Syriac editor would not overlook this spot. (Moderns editors do not hesitate over a "disturbance of the verses". They merely split verse 7 in half)

---

166. Eberhard Nestle, *Vom Textus Receptus des Griechischen Neuen Testaments* (Barmen: Wupperthaler Traktat-Gesellschaft, 1903), 38.
167. *Memoirs*, 204.
168. Some (if not most) Greek editions prior to 1569, (e.g.,1522 Basileae, 1553 Basileae, 1564 Lipsiae, 1566 Tiguri) had no numbering of verses.

1572   BULLINGER, Heinrich. *Reformationsgeschichte.*

In this book, Dr. Bender reports that Bullinger asserted that Conrad Grebel and the other Zurich Anabaptists "went down to Griessen and drew their ideas from Müntzer in person."[169] But Bender says this was "fifty years after the supposed events had happened." Bender further says: "In his excellent monograph, *Das Zwinglibild und die Züricherischen Reformationschroniken* (1929), Jacob Berchtold has proved that Bullinger's history of written with a bias."

1574   *Novum Jesu Christi D.N. Testatmentum.* Antwerp: C. Plantini.

ὅτι τρεῖς εἰσιν οἱ μαρτυροῦντες ἐν τῷ οὐρανῷ, ὁ πατὴρ, κ, ὁ λόγος, κ το ἅγιον πνευμα, οἱ τρεῖς εἰς τὸ ἕν εἰσιν. καὶ τρεῖς εἰσιν οἱ μαρτυροῦντες οπι τῆς γῆς

1578   [College at Douay moved to Rheims]

1581   [The *Johannine Comma* first appeared in a Luther edition.] Opinions vary as to the date: Panzer (1574), Nestle (1575), Klose (1582), Ricki (1593). According to *Werke. Kritische Gesamtausgabe. Die Deutsche Bible*, vol 7, 629, 10-14 (via Greeven) it was 1581.

Significance:

If Greeven is correct, about 36 years elapsed, from Luther's last edition, until the *Comma* was restored in the Luther edition. However, we know that it was included even earlier in the Swiss-German Bible used in Zurich, Switzerland, which included it in 1524 or 1525.[170] The duration of the gap in the Luther Bible is nearly 60 years without the *Comma* (from Luther's first N.T. of 1522 to 1581). But in Zurich, the gap may be 1 year (if its first appearance was in the 1525 edition), or there may be no gap (if it was in the first Swiss-German edition of the NT: 1524)!

```
------------------------------------xxxxxxxxxxxxxxxxxxxxxxxxxx
:              :              :
1522 25 30 35 40 45 50 55 60 65 70 75 81


---------xxxxxxxxxxxxxxxxxxxxxxxxxxxxxxxxxxxxxxxxxxxxxxxxxxxx
.................:
.................1531
```

---

169. *Conrad Grebel 1498-1526 Founder of the Swiss Brethren*, 115.
170. The *Comma* is clearly in the complete (OT+NT) *Zürcher Bibel* of 1531. It is a matter of which edition of the Swiss NT portion was used.

1582   MARTIN, Gregory. *The Rheims New Testament.*

Gregory Martin was one of the readers of Divinity at the English College of Rheims.

1582   MARTIN, Gregory. *A Discovery of the Manifold Corruptions of the Holie Scriptures by the Heretikes of our daies, specially the English Sectaries, and of their foule dealing herein, by partial and false translations, to the advantage of their heresies, in their English Bibles used and authorised since the time of the Schisme.* Rhemes: Iohn Fogny (1973 Reprint; Menston, Yorkshire: Scholars Press).

The following passage from page ii(b) of the preface is interesting:

> An other vvay is, to alter the very original text of the holy Scripture, by adding, taking away or changing it here and there for their purpose. So did the Arians in sundrie places, and the Nestoriās in the first epistle of S. Iohn, and especially Marcion. . .

But Martin deals with only two verses from 1 John, namely, 1 John 5:3, and 1 John 5:21. In the corresponding pages (42 & 178), he refered neither to Arians nor to Nestorians.

Martin labors to expose every possible fault with the Protestant versions. Yet in the "brief table" of Scripture verses, Acts 8:37, Acts 9: 5,6, 1 John 5:7-8, and other non-majority readings are not listed! But why should they? Both Papists and Protestants were agreed on these verses.

1583   FULKE, William. *A Defense of the Sincere and True Translations of the Holie Scriptures into the English Tong, against the manifold cavils, frivolous quarrels, and impudent slaunders of Gregorie Martin.*

Similar to Martin's index, Fulke's extensive "Index of Texts of Scripture" does not include Acts 8:37, 9:5-6, 1 John 5: 7-8, etc. since there existed no dispute over these verses.

1588   WITHER, George. *A View of the Marginal Notes of the Popish New Testament translated into English by the fugitive Papists resiant at Rhemes in France.* London:

1588   BULKELEY, Edward. *An Answere to ten frivolous and foolish reasons set doun by the Rhemish Jesuits and Papists in their Preface before the New Testament by them lately translated into English, which have mooved them to forsake the originall fountaine of the Greek, wherein the Spirit of God did indite the Gospell, and the holy Apostles did write it, to follow the stream of the Latin translation translated we know not when nor by whom. With a Discoverie of many great Corruptions and Faultes in the said English Translation set out at Rhemes.* London:

1589   FULKE, William. *The Text of the New Testament of Jesus Christ, translated out of the vulgar Latine by the Papists of the traiterous Seminarie at Rhemes.* London:

1596   [A German edition after Luther's lifetime.]

On page 25 of his 408-page book *Historie der deutschen Bibelübersetzung D. Martin Lutheri von dem Jahr 1517 an bis 1534* (published in 1772) J.M. Goeze claims that this edition "has the passage 1 John 5:7, but with smaller script."

1599   [A German edition after Luther's lifetime.]

Goeze reported (p. 25) that this edition "has the passage 1 John 5:7, but with Latin letters."

1600   HUTTER, Elias. *Novvm Testamentum dni; nri Iesu. Christi. Syriacè, ebraicè, græcè, latinè, germanicè, bohemicè, italicè, hispanciè, gallicè, anglicè, danicè, polincè.* Nürnberg:

(The Göttingen professor, Dr. Borger said in 1987: "The omission of the Comma Johanneum according to Hutter is an immense error and in no way to be excused. For this somewhat daring statement he refers to Jerome. However, the Prologue of the seventh canonical epistle (Wordsworth and White III, p. 230f.) is obviously not from Jerome.")

Metzger, the scholar whom (since the 1960's) liberals, evangelicals, and even fundamentalists have regarded as the "last word" on all textual matters, does not mention the inclusion of the *Comma* in the Syriac section of Hutter's polyglott in his *A Textual Commentary on the Greek New Testament*. Nor is Hutter's polyglott mentioned in Metzger's *Early Versions of the New Testament*.

Scrivener in his 1883 edition of *Plain Introduction*, page 615, says Hutter included the Epistle to the Laodecians, as well as Acts 8:37, in his Syriac portion.

1601 *Nouum Iesu Christi Dn. nostri Testamentum ut ex Bibiotheca Regia anno 1550 per Robert Stephanus excusum fuit.* Francofurti:

ὅτι τρεῖς οἱ μαρτυροῦντες ἐν τῷ ουρανῷ ὁ πατὴρ, ὁ λόγος, καὶ τὸ ἅγιον πνευμα. καὶ οὗτοι οἱ τρεῖς ἕν εἰσι. καὶ τρεῖς εἰσιν μαρτυροῦντες ἐν τῇ γῇ

1602 HUTTER, Elias. *Novum Testamentum Harmonicum Ebraicè, Græcè, Latinè, & Germanicè.* Noribergæ:

7. ὅτι τρεῖς εἰσιν οἱ μαρτυροῦντες ἐν τῷ οὐρανῷ, ὁ πατὴρ, καὶ ὁ λόγος, καὶ τὸ ἅγιον πνευμα. καὶ οὗτοι οἱ τρεῖς ἕν εἰσι. 8. καὶ τρεῖς εἰσιν οἱ μαρτυροῦντες ἐν τῇ γῇ

1602 CARTWRIGHT, Thomas. *The Answere to the Preface of the Rhemish Testament.* Edinburgh: [213 pp.]

1607 HUNNII, Ægidii. *Oper um Latinorvm. Continens Articulos Christianæ Religionis sacræ fundamentis extructos.* . .Tomus primus. Witebergæ: 79.

1608 HUNNII, Ægidii. *Oper um Latinorvm. Continens potissimum Commentarios in Evangelium S. Matthæ & B. Iohannis.* III: 1034.

Hunnii devotes an entire page of tiny print in expounding the verse of the heavenly witnesses.

1609 *Novvm Testamentvm Graece cum vulgata interpretatione Latina Graeci contextus lineis inserta.* Avreliae Allobrogvm

Quoniam tres sunt *illi testantes* in caelo, Pater, & Verbum &
ὅτι τρεῖς εἰσιν οἱ μαρτυροῦντες ἐν τῳ οὐρανῳ, πατηρ και λογος

sanctus Spiritus. & tres *in* vnum sunt. Et tres sunt *illi*
τὸ ἅγιον πνεῦμα, καὶ οἱ τρεῖς εἰς τὸ ἕν εἰσι. καὶ τρεῖς εἰσιν

testantes in terra.
οἱ μαρτυροῦντες ἐπι της γης

1611   *The Authorized Version* [first edition]

Lightfoot said its "language is not the language of the age in which the translators lived, but in its grand simplicity stands out in contrast to the ornate and often affected diction of the liturature of the time."[171]

The executive director of the New King James Version (1979), admitted that the old AV "still remains the most widely-sold English Bible of North America."[172]

1611   *The Authorized Version*. [second edition]

Dr. E.F. Hills says two editions[173] were published in 1611. Another source says "Three distinct editions appeared in 1611. . ."[174]

Daniel Wallace asked: "Second, why do majority text advocates count only *Greek* manuscripts? Is is because inclusion of the Latin Vulgate with more that 8000 extant copies would destroy their theory?" [175]

On the one hand, some object "But why aren't you consulting the Vulgate MSS?" Then, on the other hand, they object "But the *Comma* was taken from the Vulgate!" M. W. Holmes, referring to Dr. Edward F. Hills, claimed:

> Hills argues for the very wording of the TR, including the places where it follows the Vulgate against all known Greek manuscripts. In his opinion, it was part of God's providence that these Vulgate readings should enter the TR, there to be available to the translators of the KJV!

M.W. Holmes cannot conceive of trusting "the very wording of the TR" nor "the translators of the KJV", because in his opinion the original text is lost, and its RECOVERY must still be sought. As he said in 1983 (after over 400 years of labor by editors of the printed Greek text) "much work towards the recovery of the original text yet remains to be done."[176]

---

171. *On a Fresh Revision of the English New Testament*, pp.212, 299 as quoted in *English Versions of the Bible* (1952) p.322.
172. Arthur Farstad, *The New King James in the Great Tradition* (Nashville, TN: Thom. Nelson, 1989) 24.
173. *The King James Version Defended* 4th ed, p. 217.
174. *Old Bibles*, J.H. Dore (1876; 2nd ed. 1888) is the source provided by Huge Pope.
175. "Some Second Thoughts on the Majority Text" *Bibliotheca Sacra*, (Jul-Sep 1989) 270-290.
176. Michael W. Holmes, "The 'Majority text debate': new form of an old issue" *Themelios*. 2 (1983) 19.

1611   *The Authorized Version* [third edition]

S.C. Malan, in his *Vindication of the AV,* said that once the AV is replaced, the "unbroken associations of two centuries and a half...would perish forever." (p. iii). But he said this 1856. Thus, today, over 100 years later, Baptists who study from the AV now have 3.5 centuries of "unbroken associations", and know that what they read is identical to what J. Gill, A. Fuller, W. Carey, etc. read in their Bibles. These Baptist forefathers knew its language ought not be an irreverent colloquial language. They would agree with Malan that "the style of the BIBLE ought to be more solomn, and it ought to speak with more gravity, than that of any other book in the language." (*Vindication of the AV*, 228).

1613   King James Bible [1613 edition]

> 7 For there are three that beare record in heauen, the Father, the Word, and the holy Ghost, and these three are one.
> 8 And there are three that beare witnesse in earth, the Spirit, and the Water, and the Blood, and these three agree in one.

1618   CARTWRIGHT, Thomas. *A Confutation of the Rhemists Translation, Glosses and Annotations on the New Testament so farre as they containe manifeste Impieties, Heresies, Idolatries, Superstitions, Prophanesse, Treasons, Slanders, Falsehodds, and other Evills.*

1629   *King James Version.*

Dr. E.F. Hills says this edition was subjected to a "minor revision". The *Comma* is retained.

1636   *States-General Bible* (Dutch translation).

This was based upon the expert opinion of the Synod of Dort
The reading from this translation

"welche auf Gutachten des Dordrechtischen Synodi Anno 1618. und 1619 und auf Befehl der H Herrn. General Staten, durch 6. Sprach-kundige Theologos, Reformirter Parthey, ausgefertigt, und Anno 1636"

is taken from column 5 of the *Biblia Pentapla* (title as given on outside binding) of 1710. (For actual title, see entry under A.D. 1710, in which 4 High Germans bibles are compared to this translation.)

> 7.Want drie zijnder die getungen in den Hemel, de Vader, het Woort, ende de Heylige Geest. ende dese drie zijn een. 8. Ende drie zijnder die getuygen op de Aerde

Jakob Van Bruggen said "the State-General translation can be considered the last, most ripe fruit of Reformation translation work in Europe."[177]

1637   CANNE, John. [Reference Bible: "first English Bible that had marginal references throughout" (*Bapt Encycl*, 180)] Amsterdam:

"The text is that of the Authorized Version"[178]

1638   BOIS, John, et al. (eds.) *The King James Bible*. Cambridge:

The editors made improvements, but they did not omit the *Comma* nor any other verses.

1639   *Novum Testamentum ex utraque regia, aliisque optimis editionibus summo studio expressum.* Amsterdam: Joannis Janssonii

> 7 ὅτι τρεῖς εἰσιν οἱ μαρτυροῦντες ἐν τῷ οὐρανῷ, ὁ Πατὴρ, ὁ Λόγος, καὶ τὸ ἅγιον Πνεῦμα, καὶ οὗτοι οἱ τρεῖς ἕν εἰσι.
> 8 Καὶ τρεῖς εἰσιν οἱ μαρτυροῦντες ἐν τῇ γῇ

1640   [The first president of Harvard is appointed.]

Henry Dunster (1609-1659), was appointed as Harvard's first president. He served for 14 years as president, and was forced to resign "on account of his antipedobaptist views." Because he was outspoken against infant baptism "he was indicted by the grand jury and sentenced to a public admonition; and later was presented to their body for failure to baptize one of his children."[179]

1644   *A Confession of Faith of Seven Congregations or Churches of Christ in London, which are commonly (but unjustly) called ANABAPTISTS*

1647   BIDDLE, John. *Twelve Questions or Arguments drawn out of Scripture, wher in the commonly received Opinion touching the Deity of the Holy Spirit is clearly and fully refuted.*

1647   [Sep 6: The *Twelve Questions* were "ordered to be burnt by the hangman as being blasphemous"[180]]

1648   [May 2: An ordinance was passed to assign the death penalty to those who

---

177. *The Future of the Bible* 49.
178. *English Versions of the Bible* (St. Louis & London: B. Herder Book Co., 1952) 512.
179. *NSHE* IV: 31.
180. *DNB* 5:14.

denied the Trinity.]

1648   BIDDLE, John. *The Testimonies of Irenæus, Justin Martyr, Tertullian, Novationus, Theophilus, Origen. . .concerning that One God and the Persons of the Trinity, with observations on the same.*

"Upon the publication of the 'Testimonies' the assembly of divines sitting at Westminster made their apeal to the parliment that he [Biddle] might suffer death."[181]

1653   BIDDLE, John. "An Exposition of 1 John 5.7" *The Apostolical and True Opinion concerning the Holy Trinity, Revived and Asserted. . .*(see appendix 3)

1653   [The Slavonic version: 1 Jo V.7 :"it is in the edition of 1653"]

According to R. Porson, Mr. Poletika believes the verse was inserted here "during the lifetime of Nicon." *Letters to Travis*, xi.

1655 * SELDON, John. *De Synediis & Praefecturis Iuridicis Veterum Ebraeorum.* 3 vols. Londoni:

[1656   This is the date of the one Armenian MS, of the 18 used by Zohrab.] Tregelles/Horne in *An Intro. to Critical Study*, 11th ed., provide this quote from Dr. Rieu:

> Out of *eighteen* MSS. used by Zohrab, only *one*, written A.D. 1656, has this passage as in the Stephanic Greek text.

Since when does a process of "counting New Testament manuscripts, rather than weighing them"[182] determine a true reading? Only one has it? Wonderful! Today, this *one* Armnian MS has been conveniently forgotten by the modern accounts.

1656 * COTTON, John. *A Practical Commentary or an Expostion with Observations, Reasons, and Vses upon The First Epistle Generall of John.* London:

John Cotton commented on the meaning of the *Comma*, but he gave no indication that it was being disputed.

1657   WALTON, Brian. *Biblia Sacra Polyglotta.* (1964 Reprint, Graz, Austria:

---

181. *DNB* 5:15.
182. These are the words Metzger used in *Canon of the New Testament*, p.267, as he reveals his attitude toward J.W. Burgon and the MTA.

Akademische Druck- U. Verlagsanstalt). 5: 922-923.

The Gospels appear in six languages. All remaining books in the *tomus quintus*, are provided in five: Greek, Latin, Peshito-Syriac, Æthiopic, and Arabic. The *Comma* appears in his Greek (Stephanus 1550), and in his Latin (Versio Vulgata Latina). His "Latin Vulgate" for 1 John 5:7-8a reading is:

> Quoniam tres sunt, qui testimoinum dant in cælo; Pater, Verbum, & Spiritus sanctus: & hi tres unum sunt. Et tres sunt, qui testimonium dant in terra:

1658   CURCELLAE, Stephani. *Novum Testamentum In quo dilgentius quam unquam antea Variantes Lectiones tam ex-manuscripriptis quam impressis codicibus collecta. Parallela Scripturae Loca annotata sunt, Studio & labore Stephani Curcellae.*

7. ὅτι τρεῖς εἰσιν οἱ μαρτυροῦντες [ἐν τῷ οὐρανῷ, ὁ Πατὴρ, ὁ Λόγος, καὶ τὸ ἅγιον Πνεῦμα. καὶ οὗτοι οἱ τρεῖς * ἕν εἰσί.
8. καὶ τρεῖς εἰσιν οἱ μαρτυροῦντες ἐν τῇ γῇ]

> v. 7,8. verba inclusa his duobus [] uncinulis, desiderantur in multis veteribus codicibus Græcis & Latinis; ut & versione Syriaca, Arabica, & Æthiopica; non agnoscuntur à multis Patribus; & desunt in quibusdam vetustis impressionibus. v. 7. εἰς τὸ ἕν εἰσι. v.8. deficiunt ultima.

1659   OWEN, John. *Considerations on the Biblia Polyglotta.*

For a profitable treatment of the debate with Walton see "John Owen *Versus* Brian Walton: A Reformed Response to the Birth of Text Criticism" by T.P. Letis in *The Majority Text; Essays and Reviews in the Continuing Debate* (Grand Rapids: Institute for Biblical Textual Studies, 1987)

1659   WALTON, Brian. *The Considerator considered.*[183]

1659-1689 * *Puritan Sermons 1659-1689; Being the Morning Exercises at Cripplegate, St. Giles in the fields, and in Southwark by seventy-five Ministers of the Gospel.* 6 vols. (Wheaton, IL: Richard Owen Roberts, 1981).

In vol 3, p. 611, the sermon by Rev. David Clarkson is entitled "What advantage may we expect from Christ's prayer for union with himself, and the blessings relating to it?" In vol. 5, p. 54, the sermon by Rev. Benjamin Needler, B.C.L., is entitled "The Trinity Proved by Scripture". Also in vol. 5, p. 516, Rev. Thomas

---

183. The titles are provided by Scrivener in *Plain Introduction* 3rd ed., 446.

Case, A.M., concluded his sermon on 2 Timothy 1:3. All three pastors include the *Johannine Comma*, as authentic words of Scripture.[184]

1660 *Nouum Testamentum Accessit Prologvs in Epistolas S. Apostoli Pauli, ex antiquissimo MSC. Secunda Editio.* Argentorati

7. ὅτι τρεῖς εἰσιν οἱ μαρτυροῦντες ἐν τῷ οὐρανῷ, ὁ πατὴρ, ὁ λόγος, καὶ τὸ ἅγιον πνευμα. καὶ οὗτοι οἱ τρεῖς ἕν εἰσι.
8. καὶ τρεῖς εἰσιν οἱ μαρτυροῦντες ἐν τῇ γῇ

1664 Aegidius GUTBIER. *Lexicon Syricum concerdatntiale, omnes N.T. Syriaci...*

Dr. G.Benson complained[185] that Gutbier, and after him, Schaaf inserted the *Comma* into their Syriac editions. He says they "boldly, without any apology, and without any mark of distinction, inserted Tremellius his translation into the text." Both the Gutbier and Schaaf editions of the Syriac included Acts 8:37.

1666 * *Biblia Armena juxt versionem LXX. interpretum, jussu Jacobi Characteri Armenorum ProtoβPartiarchæ adornata et edita studio Oskan Wartabied (id est) Episcopo Zuschuaran in Armenia de Domination Persica, juvante Salomone de Leon ejus Diacono. Amstelodami æra Armenorum 11155. Christ 1666.*

This was the first printed Armenian Bible. The synod of Armenian bishops in 1662, selected Uscan for the task. He went to Rome for 15 months, and onwards to Amsterdam where it was printed. It contains the *Comma*.

1669 * SAND, Christopher. *Nucleus Historia Ecclesiasticae; cui praefixus...* Cosmopoli:

1675 *Novum Testamentum cum Distinctione versiculorum qui omnes Novi Testamenti voces continent.* Ultrajecti

7. ὅτι τρεῖς εἰσιν οἱ μαρτυροῦντες ἐν τῷ οὐρανῷ, ὁ Πατὴρ, ὁ Λόγος, καὶ τὸ ἅγιον Πνευμα. καὶ οὗτοι οἱ τρεῖς ἕν εἰσι.
8. καὶ τρεῖς εἰσιν οἱ μαρτυροῦντες ἐν τῇ γῇ

---

184. It would be an interesting research project to examine in detail the treatment given to the *Comma* by the Puritans.
185. Orme, *Memoirs*, p.46. Benson was a Socinian.

1675   SPENER, Philipp Jackob. *Pia Desideria*.

This work, by the founder of Lutheran pietism, resulted in a revival in Germany. It was another spiritual revival that occurred during the reign of the German Received Text. For an example of Spener's application of the *Comma*, see (1689: SPENER).

"Spener was writing at a time when virtually all citizens were baptized (as infants) and therefore (according to Lutheran doctrine) believed to be regenerate."[186] "But Spener would not have people imagine that baptism was enough."

1678   *The Orthodox Creed* of the Baptists

In the Baptist Creed the 66 books of the Bible are listed "as they appear in the King James Version."[187]

1678   GRANTHAM, Thomas. *Christianismus Primitivus*.

Grantham, "a Lincolnshire man, was for many years the principal minister among the General Baptists."[188] Gantham is quoted as saying:

> I conceive it abundantly satisfactory, that the Copies of the Sacred Oracles. . .have no corrupt Doctrine in them.

Although not as elequent or as precise as John Owen's statements of 1659, Grantham also did not base his trust upon invisible unattainable autographs, but upon trustworthy "Copies."

Bush and Nettles also say the Papists attacked the accuracy of Protestant Bibles, and Grantham "countered their accusations by demonstrating that the Protestant translations were far superior to the Rhemist, or Roman Catholic, translation; for the Protestants used Greek and Hebrew as the source, while the Roman Catholics use the Latin Vulgate."[189]

---

186. A.N.S.Lane. "Conversion: a comparison of Calvin and Spener" *Themelios* 13 (Oct/Nov 1987) 19.
187. Bush & Nettles, *Baptists and the Bible*, (Chicago: Moody, 1980) 38.
188. Ibid.
189. *Baptists and the Bible*, 41. Note: On p. 407, Bush/Nettles speak of "the text of any good translation (King James, NASB, NIV, and so forth." But the NASB and NIV have omissions similar to the Rhemist versions!

1681 [edition of Luther's Bible from Bach's personal library [190]]

1685 [revocation of the Edict of Nantes]

Many Protestants fled France. Pierre Allix settled in England. Peter Malan (grandfather of C.H.A. Malan) settled in Geneva.

1688 WARD, Thomas. *Errata of the Protestant Bible; or the Truth of the English Translations examined in a Treatise shewing some of the Errors that are to be found in the English Translations of the Sacred Scriptures*. . .

E. Ryan (1808), Richard Grier (1812), J.Browne (1859) and others responded to Ward. John Milner (1841) responded to Grier's attacks.

1688 * TURRETIN, Francois. *The Doctrine of Scripture*. Grand Rapids: Baker Book House, 1981 reprint

> The statement that. . .the Greek [manuscripts] of the New [Testament] have become defective is false, and the passages which are offered in proof of this by our adversaries cannot demonstrate it. Not the pericope of adultery (John 8). . .Not the saying in 1 Jn 5:7, although formerly some called it into question, and heretics do so today.

1689 SIMON, Richard. "Critique du Passage de l'Epistre I. de S. Jean, chap.V.v.7" *Histoire Critique de Texte du Nouveau Testament*. Rotterdam: 203-218. (Reprinted in Frankfurt, 1968, by Minerva Gmbh.)

1689 * ALLIX, Peter. *The Judgment of the Ancient Jewish Church Against the Unitarians in the Controversy upon the Holy Trinity and the Divinity of Our Blessed Saviour*. 1821 Reprint. Oxford: Clarendon Press. 80.

(In the *DNB*, W.G.Blaike says that Allix "was especially distinguished in the study of Hebrew and Syriac, and worked at a new [French] translation". Professor Albert Hauck describes Allix thus: "The fame of his learning was so great that both Oxford and Cambridge conferred the degree of doctor upon him." [191] The following quote suggests that Allix regarded the *Comma* as authentic.)

---

190. In the Bach Museum in Leipzig, a 1681 German edition of Luther's Bible is displayed. The label near the exhibit reads: "Diese Bibel ist eines der wenigen bisher wiederaufgefundenen Büchern aus der Bibliothek Johann Sebastion Bach."
191. *Schaff-Herzog Encyclopedia of Religious Knowledge*. 12 vol. 1908, p. 133.

A quote from p. 80 concerning the three Persons:

> These Persons are called by St. John, 1 John v.7. the Father, the Word, and the Spirit. *There are three*, saith he, *that bear witness in heaven, the Father, the Word, and the Spirit; and these three are one.*

1689 (signators of) *The London Baptist Confession of Faith*

The citation "1 John v.7" is listed with other verses for chapter 2 "God and the Holy Trinity".

It should be of interest that Philip Schaff consulted Dr. Osgood on the differences between this confession and the Westminster (1647). Dr. Kenneth Good says "Both the Reformed Schaff and the Baptist Osgood overlooked the rather glaring differences between the Westminster and the London Confessions, which occupies the very first place in the documents!" Referring to the Baptist signatories, he says "Their first sentence is, "The Holy Scripture is the only sufficient, certain, and infallible rule of all saving Knowledge, Faith, and Obediance." *This does not appear at all in the Westminster Confession, nor does it appear in the Savoy Declaration.*" [192]

Dr. Good also noted a major alteration in section VI. "Where the Reformed said, "The whole counsel of God. . .is either expressly set down in Scripture, or by good and necessary consequence may be deduced from Scripture. . .,"the Baptists said it ". . .is either expressly set down or necessarily contained in the Holy Scripture. . ." The Baptist signatories could vividly recall how the Reformed authorities persecuted them upon deductions "by good and necessary consequence."

1689   SPENER, Jakob Philipp. "Von der H. Dreifaltigkeit: Auff dero Fest." *Kurtze Catechismuspredigten*. 1982 Reprint. Hildesheim & New York: Georg Olms Verlag. 937.

> 1 Joh. 5/7 Drey sind die da zeugen im himmel, der Vatter, das Wort und der H. Geist, und diese drey sind eins: Wo außdrücklich dreyer meldung geschiehet, und doch, daß alle drey GOTT seien, ist darauß zu sehen, weil sie eins sollen seyn, und also, weil der Vatter bekantlich GOTT ist, so müssens die andern auch sein. Matth. 3/16 hat sich solches geheimnuß auch an dem Jordan gezeigt: Da offenbahrte sich GOTT der Vatter in der Stimme, das ist mein lieber Sohn, an dem ich wohlgegallen hab; GOtt der Sohn stunde sichtbarlich in dem Jordan, daß er getaufft würde.

---

192. Kenneth Good, *Are Baptists Reformed?* (Lorain, OH: Regular Baptist Heritage Fellowship, 1986) 108.

1690   SMITH, Thoma. *Dissertatio, in quâ Integritas et αὐθεντία istius celeberrimi loci Epist. Joannis cap. V. v.7 a suppositionis notâ vindicatur.*   Londini: 121-150

1690   SMITH, Thoma. *Defensio superioris Dissertationis contra exceptiones D. Simonii.* Londini: 151-173

1690   LOCKE, John. *Essay Concerning Human Understanding.*

Stillingfleet was alarmed at some passages in this work, which he believed impugned the doctrine of the Trintity. He thus challenged Locke. The debate with Locke lasted from 1696-1699.

1692   [January 20: Le Clerc's letter]

In this letter concerning Newton's treatise on I Jo 5:7, Le Clerc "disclosed his intention of preparing a Latin translation, but Newton contemplated suppressing the work. Le Clerc therefore deposited the MS in the library of the Remonstrants in Amersterdam, and finally in 1754 it was published in an incomplete form in London" 193

1696   STILLINGFLEET, Edward. *Discourse in Vindication of the Doctrine of the Trinity.* [3 pamplets 1696-1697]

According to Dr. Dobbin, Bishop Stillingfleet on page 12 "asserts that the editors of the Complutensian had the use of the English MS. [Codex Montfortianus] when preparing the text of the Polyglot, an assertion evidently without any foundation of fact."[194] The *NSHE* says this work "brought on a controversy with Locke"[195] but the *DNB* says it was in reaction to Locke's essay on human understanding.[196]

1696 * Le CLERC, Jean. *Ars Critica.*

---

193. Bludau "The Comma Johanneum in the Writings of English Critics of the Eighteenth Century: II, *Irish Theological Quartery* (1922), 211.
194. O.T. Dobbin, *The Codex Montfortianus: A Collation*...(London: Samuel Bagster, 1854) 8. He also mentioned that Semler had the same theory.
195. *NSHE* 7:7
196. *DNB* 54:377.

1696 * KETTNER, Friedrich E. *Insignis ac celeberrimi de Trinitate Loci, qui I Jo. V.7 extat, divina autoritas sensus et usus.* Lipsiæ:

1698   ZACAGNI. [a collation of Greek MSS containing the Catholic Epistles]

1699   CURCELLÆ, Stephani. *Novum Testamentum. Editio nova, denue revisa, In qua diligentius quam unquam antea Variantes Lectiones tam ex manuscriptis quàm impressis codicibus collectæ.* Amstelodami:

As in 1658, the *Comma* is surrounded by brackets, and still in the main text. Incidently, Act 8:37 is not bracketed, and in the main text. His note for this reads:

totus hic versus deest in aliquot exemplaribus, & in Syriaca versione.

1703   [W. Whiston succeeded Isaac Newton as professor at Cambridge]

1705   Η' ΚΑΙΝΗ ΔΙΑΘΗΚΗ τοῦ Κυρίου καὶ Σωτῆρες ἡμῶν 'ΙΗΣΟΥ ΞΡΙΣΤΟΥ

7. ὅτι τρεῖς εἶναι ἐκενοι ὅ ιε οἱ μαρτυροῦντες εἰς τ οὐρανὸν, ὁ Πατὴρ, ὁ Λόγος, καὶ τὸ ἅγιον Πνευμα. καὶ οὗτοι οἱ τρεῖς ἕν εἰσι.
καὶ τρεῖς εἰσιν οἱ μαρτυροῦντες ἐν τῇ γῇ

The underlining is not in the text, but indicates difficulty with legibility of the words.

1707   MILL, John. *Novum Testamentum Græcum.* . .

(Mill's edition contained the *Comma*, and his defense of it.) F.H.A. Scrivener said of Mill's edition "During the many years that Mill's N.T. has been my daily companion, my reverence for that diligent and earnest man has been constantly growing;. . .his zeal was unflagging, his treatment of his sacred subject deeply reverential."[197] C.H. Turner described it thus: "There is nothing like it in England: I wonder if there is in any other country. Truly, there were giants in those days."[198]

---

197. *Plain Introduction*, 3rd ed., p. 448.
198. *Early Printed Editions of the Greek Testament* 8 n.1

1708   SCHAAF, Karl. ed., *Lexicon Syricum concordantiale, omnes Novi Testamenti syriaci voces...*

The inclusion of the *Comma* in this Syriac edition by Schaaf is mentioned neither in *Early Versions of the New Testament* nor in *A Textual Commentary on the Greek New Testament* (both by B.M. Metzger). Orme informs us that Dr. Bensen objected to Schaaf's inclusion of the *comma* in this Syriac edition.

Johann Leudsen assisted Schaff up to Luke 18:26. Schaaf completed the remainder alone. This Schaaf-Leudsen edition also contained Act 8:37.

The importance of Karl Schaff, as a Syriac scholar, is indicated by the 20th century author of a Syriac grammar, who referred to Schaff's *Lexixon Syriacum Concodantiale* (1717) as "acknowledged to be the best for the New Testament" [199]

1708   [July: W. Whiston abandoned the doctrine of the Trinity]

William Whiston "wrote to the archbishops in July 1708, informing them that he was entering upon an important inquiry" which "led him to the conclusion that...the accepted doctrine of the Trinity was erroneous."[200]

1708   MONTFAUCON, Bernard de. *Palæographia Græca*, Paris:

This book was referred to frequently in the debate over the date of the Montfort Codex. It was a matter of the double points over the Greek letters ι and υ, as such: ϊ ϋ. When Dr. Orlando Dobbin copied the *Comma* from the Monfort he asserted that he "corrected the dots over the letters, which are altogether wrong in Michaelis."[201]

1710   [Oct 30: Whiston was banished from Cambridge University]

1710   MILL, John. *Novum Testamentum Græcum cum Lectionibus Variantibus MSS Exemplarium, Versionum, Editionum, SS. Patrum et Scriptorum ecclesiasticorum, et in easdem notis accedunt Loca Scripturæ Parallela, Aliaque exegetica.*

---

199. William Jennings, *Lexicon to the Syriac New Testament*. Oxford: Clarondon Press, 1926. 7.
200. *DNB* 51:11.
201. Dobbin, *The Codex Montfortianus: A Collation* (London: Bagster, 1854) 9.

7. Ὅτι τρεῖς εἰσιν οἱ μαρτυροῦντες ἐν τῷ οὐρανῷ,* ὁ Πατὴρ,* ὁ Λόγος, *καὶ τὸ ἅγιον Πνεῦμα. * καὶ οὗτοι οἱ τρεῖς ἕν εἰσι.
8. καὶ τρεῖς εἰσιν οἱ μαρτυροῦντες ἐν τῇ γῇ

The defence and commentary on the verse extends from p. 579 to p. 586.

1710 *Das Neue Testament/ oder Der Neüe Bünd Welchen Gott Durch Jesum Christum mit Uns Menschen gemachet/Und durch dessen Apostel und Lehr Jünger erstlich in Griechischer Sprache schriftlich aufzeichnen lassen. Jetzo Nach den gebräuchlischsten 4. hochdeutschen Ubersetyungen nebst der holländischen.* Wandesbeck bei Hamburg: Herman Heinrich Holle. 799.

The four versions selected (Ulenberg, Luther, Piscator, and Reitz) are the *gebräuchlichsten* (most used) high German versions of the time. The four are then compared to the *Hollandische* translation of 1618, which was based upon the *Gutachen* (expert opinion) of the famous *Dordrechtischen Syodi*, 1618.

C) *Catholische*: Casper Ulenbergius, 1630
L) *Lutherische*: Martin Luther, post-1525
R) *Reformirte*: Johannes Piscator, 1603
N) *Neue Ubersetzung*: Johann Henrich Reitzen, 1703
H) *Hollandische*: Leyden: 1636

C: Dan drey sind die Zeugniß im Himmel: Der Vatter, das Wort, und der Heilige Geist, und diese drey sind eins. 8 Auch sind drey die Zeugniß geben auff der Erden.

L: Denn drey sind, die da zeugen im Himmel: Der Vater, das Wort, und der Heilige Geist, und diese dry sind eins. 8 Und drey sind die da zeugen auff Erden.

R: Dan drey sind, die da zeugen im Himmel, der Vatter, das Wort, und der Heilige Geist; und diese drey sind eins 8 Deßgleichen sind drey die da zeugen auf Erden.

N: Dan drey sind die Zeugniß geben im Himel, der Vatter, das Wort, u. der Heilige Geist, u. diese drey sind eins. 8 U. drey sind die Zeugniß geben auf der Erden.

H: Want drie ziinder die getuygen in den hemel, de Vader, het Woort, ende de Heylige Geest, ende dese drie zijn een 8 Ende drie zijnder die getuygen up de Aerde.

1711 *Novum Testamentum post priores Steh. Curcellæi, tum & DD. Oxoniensium laboresō quibus Parallela Scripturæ Loca. . .Præfatio by Henricus Wetstenius.* Amstelaedami.

7. Ὅτι τρεῖς εἰσιν οἱ μαρτυροῦντες [d] ἐν τῷ οὐρανῷ" ὁ Πατὴρ, ὁ Λόγος, καὶ τὸ ἅγιον Πνεῦμα. καὶ οὗτοι οἱ τρεῖς [e] ἕν εἰσι.

8. καὶ τρεῖς εἰσιν οἱ μαρτυροῦντες ^{f} ἐν τῇ γῇ"

(d) = R.8 s.7. 123. (e)* εἰς τὸ Cp. R.8. Sed= $\tilde{v}$.7 tot. M.R.8. & ab ἐν τῷ οὐρ. usque ἐν τῇ γῇ, incls. A.L.N.2.P.3. Cæs. ¦ 23.34. (f) = M.

R = *Manuscrippta Romana e Biblioth. Barberina*
Cp = *Exemplar Complutense impressum 1514*
M = *Manuscripta Collegii Magdal. Oxon.*
A = *Codex Alexandrinus in Bibliotheca Regis Angliæ*
L = *Evangelia Collegii Lincolniensis Oxon.*
N = *Manuscripta Collegii Novi Oxon.*
P = *Petavii Senat. Paris. Codices.*
Cæs = *Manuscriptum Bibliothecæ Cæsar. Viennens.*

1712   CLARKE, Samuel. *The Scripture Doctrine of the Trinity wherein every text in the New Testament relating to that Doctrine is distinctly considered; and the Divinity of our Blessed Savior according the the Scriptures proved and explained.*

1713   WELLS, Edward. *Remarks on Dr. Clarke's introduction to his Scripture-Doctrine of the Trinity.* Oxford: 32,59.

1713   KETTNER, Frideric Ernest. *Historia Dicti Johannei de Sanctissima Trinitate, 1 Joh. cap. V. vers. 7. per multa secula omissi, seculo V. restituti, et exeunte seculo XVI in versionem vernaculam [i.e., Germanicam D. Lutheri] recepti, una cum Apologia B. Lutheri*   Francofurti et Lipaiæ:

Horne: "This publication was caused by Simon's attack on the disputed clause" and later "Kettner, who reluctantly admits that the preface in question is not the production of Jerome, yet maintains that it is good evidence for the genuineness of the disputed passage in the eighth, ninth, and following centuries!"

1714   CLARKE, Samuel. "Letter to the Rev. Dr. Wells. *Works of Samuel Clark.* 4: 237 ff.

According to Bludau, the letter states that the verse "is not found with certainty in a single one of the Greek originals".

1714 * Le CLERC. [commentary on 1 John]

H.J. de Jonge refers to this work, and comments there is no mention of any promise by Erasmus to insert the verse upon new Greek evidence.

1714   KNIGHT, JAMES. *The Scripture Doctrine of the most holy and undivided Trinity, vindicated from the misrepresentation of Dr. Clarke; to which is prefixed a Letter to the Rev. Dr. by Robert Nelson, Esq.*

Bludau say Knight "relied, for the most part on the Old Latin Version, which, according to Cyprian and Tertullian, was in use in the African Church." Dr. Clarke replied in *A Reply to the Objections of Robert Nelson, Esq* and claimed that Mill proved that the Old Latin did not contain the words.

Today, at least 4 Old Latin MSS (*l, m, p, r*) which DO contain the words, have refuted Mill's "proof." The Beuron Institute regards *dem, div,* and *c* (except for the Gospels in *c*) as Vulgate MSS.

1715   KNIGHT, James. *Defence of the True Scripture Doctrine.*

Bludau says that Knight "admits that this is Mill's view, but remarks that Mill, while holding that the Itala did not have the words originally, yet maintains that Tertullian and Cyprian had corrected their text in accordance with Greek MSS, and that some few copies of this corrected text were in use in some churches.

1715   ROGER, L. (Abbé). *Two Dissertations.* Paris.

The Abbé defended the verses in the first of these dissertations.

1715   *Novum Testamentum Accesserunt Libri Apocryphi ita ut exhibeantur Libri Biblici Græco idiomate scripti, omnes ad fidem probatorum codicum emendate expressi, cum Præfatione Ern. Sal. Cypriani.* Gothæ:

7 Ὅτι τρεῖς εἰσιν οἱ μαρτυποῦντες ἐν τῷ οὐρανῳ, ὁ Πατὴρ, ὁ Λόγος, καὶ τὸ ἅγιον Πνεῦμα, καὶ οὗτοι οἱ τρεῖς ἕν εἰσι.
8 Καὶ τρεῖς εἰσιν οἱ μαρτυποῦντες ἐν τῇ γῇ

1715   EMLYN, Thomas. *A full Enquiry into the original Authority of that Text, 1 John V.7f, containing an Account of Dr. Mill's Evidences from Antiquity for and against its being genuine. With an Examination of his Judgment thereupon.* London:

1717   BENTLEY, Richard. (in a letter of January 1, to an anonymous friend) [Burney-Friedemann. *Bentlei Epistolae.* Lipsiae: 1825. Also *Works of Richard*

Bently, ed. Alex. Dyce, III: 477 ff. London: 1838.

> ...wherein you tell me from common flame, that in my designed edition of the New Testament, I purpose to leave out the verse of St. John's Epistle I chap. 5. v. 7.

1717   BENTLY, Richard. [Inaugural discourse]

Bludau says "Bentley meantime felt how interested was public opinion in the question. . . On taking up the position of Regius Professor of Divinity, May 1st 1717, in his inaugural discourse on I John v. 7, he . . . denied its authenticity, but immediately declared: ' the Trinity stood not in need of such dubious support.' "[202]

1717 * MARTIN, David. *Deux dissertations critiques la première; sur le verset 7. du ch.5 de la Epist. de S. Jean...* Utrect:

(David Martin was pastor of the French Protestant Church at Utrecht.)

1718   EMLYN, Thomas. *An Answer to Mr. Martin's Critical Dissertation on I John V.7., showing the insufficiency of his proofs and the errors of his suppositions by which he attempts to support the authority of that text from supposed MSS.* London:

1719   [Dispute on the Trinity at the Salter's Hall]

"In 1719, when the Salter's Hall conference had made the Trinitarian controversy a burning question among dissenters, Bourn. . .accepted the Clarkean scheme."[203]

1719   MARTIN, David. *An Examination of Mr. Emlyn's answer to the Dissertation.* London:

1719   HARWOOD. *An Examination of Dr. Clarke's Scripture Doctrine of the Trinity.* London:

---

202. Bludau, "The Comma Johanneum in the Writings of English Critics of the Eighteen Century: II" 17 *Irish Theological Quarterly* (1922),
203. *DNB* 6:25. Samuel Bourn (1689-1754) became involved in a controversy with Gill in 1737-39.

1719   MARTIN, David. *A Critical Dissertation upon the seventh Verse of the fifth Chapter of St. John's First Epistle. Wherein the authenticness of this text if fully proved against the objections of Mr. Simon and the modern Arians.* Translated from the French [which was published in 1717.] London:

1720   [March: John Gill, 22, was ordained as a pastor.]

For John Gill's views on 1 John 5:7-8 see (1748: GILL).[204]

1720   EMLYN, Thomas. *A Reply to Mr. Martin's Examination of the Answer to his Dissertation.* London:

Orme: He "was a man ...whose severe and unmerited sufferings, as an Arian, have given considerable celebrity to his name."

1722   MARTIN, David. *The genuineness of 1 John V. 7. demonstrated by Proofs which are beyond all exceptions.* London:

(Martin made use of a Greek MS found in Ireland.)

1722   CALAMY, Edmund. *A Vindication of that celebrated text, 1 John V. 7. from being spurious; and an Explication of it upon the supposition of its being genuine. In four sermons.* London:

Horne erred while referring to him as "Benjamin Calamy" (1642-1686) in item 12 of his list in 1866. Orme was correct using "Edmund Calamy" (1671-1732"). Both Calamys were preachers.

---

204. Baptist historians (Ivimey, Vedder, Armitage, Whitley, Underwood) et al. have unjustly portrayed Gill as a hyper-Calvinist. For a refutation of this long-held myth see Thomas J. Nettles' "John Gill: A correction to modern caricatures and misrepresentations" *By His Grace and for His Glory* (Grand Rapids: Baker, 1986) 84-107.

1722 [Peter Malan settled at Geneva][205]

1722 [SMALBROKE, Richard]. (anonymous for a time). *An Enquiry into the Authority of the Primitive Complutensian Edition of the New Testament, as principally founded on the most ancient Vatican Manuscript; together with some Research of that Manuscript. In order to decide the dispute about 1 John V.7. In a Letter to the Rev. Mr. Archdeacon Bently*. London:

Smalbroke to Bently (as provided by Orme, p. 26):

> On the other hand, if it shall appear from the Vatican MS., when retriev'd, that the Complutensian editors did not insert the disputed passage of St. John from that most ancient copy, but from Latin copies of great antiquity, ...yet agreeably to the method proposed by yourself, Sir, of finding out the genuine Greek text by the concurrence of very ancient Latin copies, that were translated from the most ancient and uncorrupt Greek MSS, I say upon this principle, neither the reputation of the Complutensian edition of the Greek testament, nor the authority of this controverted text in particular, would be affected by such a discovery. For if Stunica and his brethren were persuaded that most, if not all, the Greek MSS. of St. John that are now extant, were corrupted, and that the Latin copies that retain this controverted passage were agreeable to the most ancient uncorrupted Greek copies, and that consequently this passage ought justly to be inserted in that edition, as in fact it was; I do not see why they ought to undergo any censure from yourself, who pay so great a regard to, and lay so mighty a stress upon the ancient Latin copies of the New Testament . . .

1723 PORSON, Richard. *A Second Vindication of Christ's Divinity, or a second Defence of some Queries*. London:

Bludau says "Prof. Porson had declared himself in favour of the verse in 1723."

1724 WHITBY, Daniel. *Examen Variantium Lectionum Johannis Millii, S.T.P in Novum Testamentum*. 405. [No mention of the *Comma*]

1726 CALMET, Augustine. "Dissertatioin sur le Fameux Passage de la première Epitre de Saint Jean, chapitre V.v.7." *Commentaire Littéral*. tom. ix. Paris: 744-752

1727 TAYLOR, Abraham. *The true Scripture Doctrine of the holy and*

---

205. Peter Malan, grandfather of C.H.A. Malan, and great-grandfather of Solomon Malan, had been expelled from France during the revocation of the edict of Nantes.

ever-blessed Trinity stated and defended, in opposition to the Arian.

Taylor argued in defense of the disputed verse.

1729   MACE, Daniel, [anonymously published]. *The New Testament in Greek and English, containing the Original Texts Corrected...* London: 2:934

This is said to be the first edition of the Greek NT published in England, which omits the *Comma*. Metzger says the edition "was either vehemently attacked or quietly ignored." Bludau, referring to the editor as "William Mace," said in 1922, "The editor altered various passages in conformity with the Arian hypothesis."

A quote from D. Mace (as given by Orme):
> The authority upon which any Greek text is founded, is only upon the authority of the Greek fathers, and their authority is founded upon that of the antient [sic] Greek MSS.

Scalin says that in the number of changes he made from the TR, "Mace was conservative." But Bludau quotes S.F. Baumgarten as saying this edition by Mace is "among the most daring attacks ever made by the opponents of the Divinity of Christ and the Trinity"[206]

1730   [Sabellianism spreads among Baptists in England]

1731   GILL, John. *Treatise on the Doctrine of the Trinity.*

1732   TWELLS, Leonard, *A Critical Examination of the late New Testament and Version of the New Testament; wherein the Editor's Corrupt Text, False Version, and fallacious Notes are Detected and Censur'd. In Three Parts. In the Second of which Justice is done to the famous Test of 1 John v. 7* London:

A quote from Dr. Twells, a clergyman of England, (as provided by Orme):

> The disputed passage of 1 John v. 7, has so many marks of genuineness, that if it had not contained a doctrine, to which the disputers of this world have always shown the utmost aversion, its authority had never been called in question.

1734   DAWSON, Thomas. *Disceptio epistololaris de coelestibus testimonus I John v. 7 in qua evincitur authentica istius versiculi.* London:

---

[206] Bludau "The 'Comma Johanneum' in the Writings of English Critics of the Eighteenth Century: II" *Irish Theological Quarterly* 17 (1922) 206.

Dawson favors the claim for authenticity of the passage.

1734   SLOSS, James. *The Doctrine of the Trinity as it is contained in the Scriptures, explained and confirmed, and Objections answered...in eighteen Sermons preached at Nottingham.* London:

This led to a correspondence debate with "Rev. T.P." Orme says there were 78 pages of letters, while Bludau said "The letters cover 27 pages."

1734   BENGEL, Johann Albert. *Novvm Testamentvm Græcvm ita adornatvm vt in testv medvlla editionvm probatarvm retineatvr, atqve in margine ad discernendas lectiones genvinas, ancipites, seqviores, ansa detvr* Stvtgardiæ: 588.

ὅτι τρεῖς εἰσιν οἱ μαρτυροῦντες ° ἐν τῷ οὐρανῷ, ὁ πατὴρ, ὁ λόγος, καὶ τὸ ἅγιον πνεῦμα, καὶ οὗτοι οἱ τρεῖς ἕν εἰσι. καὶ τρεῖς εἰσι οἱ μαρτυροῦντες ἐν τῇ γῇ,

(Concerning Bengel and the *Comma*, Orme says "He thought the evidence afforded by the African Church, and some other considerations, favorable to the passage, and therefore inserted it. . .")

Bengel's notes on 7 passages
Matt 10:8   νεκροὺς ἐγείρετε] pone ante λεπροὺς β [better than TR]
Matt 27:35   βάλλοτες] βαλόντεσ γ [equally good as the TR]
John 3:25   ἰουδαίων] ἰουδαίου δ [inferior to the TR]
Acts 8:37   εἶπε δὲ usq. χριστόν |\ δ π, ἔξεσιν|\γ π χριστόν.] β
Acts 9:5-6 (Bengel omitted these verses from the main text.)
1Tim 3:16   θεὸς] ὅ δ [inferior to the TR]

As a result of his notes on the Greek text, Bengel "was treated as though he were an enemy of the holy Scriptures. So many persons impugned his motives and condemned his edition. . ."[207] E.F. Hills described it thus: "an outcry was raised against Bengel by conservative Christians in Germany."

1736   GEORGIO Christian Sigismund. *Novvm Testamentvm Graecvm ad probatissimorvm codicvm exempla svmma diligentia recognitvm chartarvm ac typporvm elegantia magnifice adornatvm capitvm argvmentis ac locis parallelis cvrativs instrvctvm.* Vvittebergae: 690

Ὅτι τρεῖς εἰσιν οἱ μαρτυροῦντες ἐν τῷ οὐρανῷ, ὁ Πατὴρ, ὁ λόγος, καὶ τὸ ἅγιον Πνεῦμα, καὶ οὗτοι οἱ τρεῖς ἕν εἰσι. καὶ τρεῖς εἰσι οἱ μαρτυροῦντες ἐν τῇ γῇ,

---

207. B.M. Metzger *The Text of the New Testament* (Oxford: Clarondon, 1964) 113.

1739   E.F. (an anti-Trinitarian). *A plain account of the Trinity from Scripture and Reason. . . written by a Gentleman;* London: 25.

E.F. treats 1 John 5:7 as an interpolation.

1739   ZINZENDORF, Nicholas von. [his German translation]

Harold P. Scanlin says that "According to Tregelles. . . Zindendorf, pietist and modern father of the Moravian Church, followed Bengel in his German translation of 1739. However, a personal examination of Matthew shows that Zinzendorf follows Bengel far less frequently than Wesley."

[1740-1742] (Rather than to bypass this age, it was felt that a note should be included here.) These were the years of the magnificent revival known as the Great Awakening. One of the major preachers in this era was Jonathan Edwards. The Yale Professor, John E. Smith, says:
    Edwards used the King James version throughout . . .[208]

The bible of Jonathan Edwards contained the *Johannine Comma.*

(No one doubts the lasting affects upon the souls of men, occurring during the Great Awakening. However, many denominations are calling for a new Reformation, rather than a call for a new world-wide Great Awakening. See appendix three for problems of the Reformation.)

1742 * BENGEL, Johann A. *Gnomen Novi Testamenti.* Grand Rapids: Kregel Publ.

This work was influential upon John Wesley.

1743   [J.S. Semler visited Univ. of Halle and met S.J. Baumgrarten.][209]

1744   [Philadelphia Confession of Faith]

Particular Baptists in the New England states adopted the 1689 London Confession, and added two articles.

1744   SCHOETTGENIUS, Christianus. *Novvm Testamentvm Graecvm. in sectiones divisit, interpvnstiones accvrate osvit, et dispositionem logicam.* Lisiae et Goerlicii: 624.

---

208. *Works of Jonathan Edwards; Vol 2. Religious Affections* (New Haven: Yale University Press, 1959), 82.
209. Siegmund Jakob Baumgarten (1725-1791) "came to form a transition from the Pietism of Spener and Francke to the modern rationalism."*NSHE* 2:79

Ότι τρεῖς εἰσιν οἱ μαρτυροῦντες ἐν τῷ οὐρανῷ, ὁ Πατὴρ, ὁ Λόγος, καὶ τὸ ἅγιον Πνεῦμα, καὶ οὗτοι οἱ τρεῖς ἕν εἰσι. Καὶ τρεῖς εἰσι οἱ μαρτυροῦντες ἐν τῇ γῇ,

1745   WHISTON, William. *Primitive New Testament*. Stamford and London:

According to Scanlin, Whiston "used Claromontanus for the Pauline epistles and Alexandrinus for the Catholic Epistle and Revelation. He also overestimated the antiquity of these uncials, but not as severely as Codex Beza."[210] Due to codex A, he omitted the *Comma*.

1745   WHISTON. *Sacred History of the Old and New Testament*. 5:329.

Bludau informs us that Whiston says that the treatises by Newton on I Tim 3:16 and 1 Jo 5:7 were in the hands of Lord Limmington. "In Nov. 1690 Newton gave the treatise to John Locke; he seems to have been alarmed at the probable consequences of publication". Locke is said to have given the treatise to Le Clerc in Amsterdam.

1748   [Aug: Whiston heard of Gill's ability in the Oriental languages]

"About *August* this year (1748) 'I was informed of one Dr. Gill, a particular or Calvinistic Baptist, of whose skill in the Oriental languages I had heard a great character; so I had the mind to hear him preach;"[211]

1748 * GILL, John. *An Exposition on the New Testament*. 6 vols. (Grand Rapids: Baker Book House, 1980 repr. 6:907-908

In the biography of this profound Particular Baptist scholar and voluminous author (who was made Doctor of Divinity in 1748, by the University of Aberdeen), *A Brief Memoir of the Life and Writings of the Late Rev. John Gill*, John Rippon remarked on p.111: "But how few, in his days, or since, have been able to say, as he, "in self-defence," supposed it necessary to say of himself, that he "had read the *Classics*," and indeed "*Virgil*, at nine years of age?" That he had "read *Logic*, *Rhetoric*, *Ethics*, *Physics*, and *Metaphysics?* The *Greek* and *Roman* historians, *Herodotus*, *Pausanias*, *Livy*, *Sallust*, etc.? *Greek* and *Latin* Fathers of the Christian Church, and Church History? And that he had also read the *Jewish Targums*, the *Misnah*, the two *Talmuds*, Babylonian and Jerusalem: the *Rabbot*, *Midrashim*, *Zohar*, with other writings of the Jews, ancient and modern?" This statement was [made in]...the 42d year of his age..."

---

210. *Technical Papers for the Bible Translator* 39 (1988) 103.
211. Whiston. *Memoirs of the Life and Writings of Mr. William Whiston, Containing Several of his Friends also, and Written by Himself*, (1749)

A quote from page 907:
> As to the old Latin interpreter, it is certain it is to be seen in many Latin manuscripts of an early date, and stands in the Vulgate Latin edition, of the London Polyglot Bible: and the Latin translation, which bears the name of Jerom, has it, and who, in an epistle of his to Eustochium, prefixed to his translation of these canonical epistles, complains of the omission of it by unfaithful interpreters.

1749   GILL, John. *The Divine Right of Infant-Baptism Examined and Disproved*.

This was a reply to Jonathan Dickinson's *A Brief Illustration and Confirmation of the Divine Right of Infanct-Baptism*. (1746).

1750   BENGELII, J. Alberti. *Tractatio de Sinceritate Novi Testamenti Græce de variis Lectionibus Novi Testamenti caute colligendis et dijudicandis*. Halæ Magd.

1751   SABATIER, Petri. *Bibliorum Sacrorum Latinæ Versiones Antiquæ, seu Vetus Italica*. Paris: 977-978. [Rheims (1743), Munich (1976)]

In this work, the *Vulgata Nova* is placed on the inside column, and *Versio Antiqua* is placed beside it, on the outside. The *Comma* appears in both. The reading for the *Versio Antiqua* is:

> [7] 8. ....tres sunt, qui testimonium perhibent in terra : aqua, sanguis, & caro : & hi tres in nobis sunt.
> [8] 7. Et tres sunt, qui testimonium perhibent in cælo : Pater, Verbum, & Spiritus : & ii tres unum sunt.

1751   SEMLERI, Joannis Salomonis. *Vindiciæ plurium præcipuarum Lectionum codicis Græci Novi Testamenti, adversus Whistsonum atque ab eo latas leges criticas*. Hallæ:

In this work Semler argued in defense of the *Comma*. Later, he changed his views as shown by his work *Historical and critical collections, relative to what are called the proof passages in dogmatic theology*. Vol. 1 *on I John v.7* Likewise, Horne and Bloomfield, who once accepted it, later rejected it. Dr. Hales, however, rejected it at first, but years later accepted it!

1752   [S.J. Baumgarten invited Semler to Halle. Semler accepted.]

J.S. Semler was called (by Siegmund Jakob Baumgarten) to Halle as a professor of theology.

1752   WETTSTEIN, Johann Jakob, ed., *Greek New Testament*

QUOTE from Wettstein's remark about Stephen's comment on the verse:
> Secondly, I would observe, that Stephens had not the use of sixteen MSS. of the First Epistle of John, but only of seven. The first copy he made use of was not a MS., but the Complutensian edition of the N.T. The second, which is not the Cambridge MS., contains only the Gospels and the Acts. The third contains only the four Gospels, and is now to be seen in the King's Library, marked 2867. Also the sixth, in the King's Library, No. 2866. The eighth, ditto, 2861. The twelfth, ditto, 2862, and the fourteenth, ditto, 2865. Lastly, the sixteenth is cited by Stephens only in the Revelation.

He also commented on the semi-circles in Stephen's text
> ...so that Stephen's semicircle, which should have been put after the words *in earth* (to mark the whole of what was wanting, as it is put in his Latin editions), was placed after the words *in heaven*, by the fault of the compositors. This Lucas Brugensis had suspected to be the case; but Father Simon, Le Long, and L. Roger have clearly demonstrated it.

He concludes:

> ...that the whole of that verse of the *three heavenly witnesses* was certainly wanting in five of Stephen's MSS. of the Catholic Epistles. As to his two other MSS., as they have never yet been found, there is no determining about them.

1752   de MISSY, César. letters in the *Journal Britannique* VIII & IX

Porson said that de Missy "was bold enough to attack Amelotte's veracity and Martin's understanding. This provoked a nest of hornets. Four anonymous writers fell upon him;" *Letters to Travis*, 19.

1752 * WAGNER, I.E. *Integritas commatis septimi capitis quinti primæ Joannis epistolæ ab impugnationibus naovatoris cuiusdam denuo vindicata.*

Michaelis says this treatise was a defense of the verse. The treatise was directed against him. Michaelis never replied.

1753   GOLDHAGEN, P. Hermanni. *Novum D.N.J.C. Testamentum Græcum cum variantibus lectionibus, quae demonstrant Vulgatam Latinam ipsis è Graecis N.T. codicibus hodienum extantibus authenticam. Editio Catholica Novissim.* Moguntiae.

Ὅτι τρεῖς εἰσιν οἱ μαρτυροῦντες ἐν τῷ οὐρανῷ, ὁ Πατὴρ, καὶ ὁ Λόγος, καὶ τὸ ἅγιον Πνεῦμα, καὶ οὗτοι † οἱ τρεῖς ἕν εἰσι. Καὶ τρεῖς εἰσι οἱ μαρτυροῦντες ἐπὶ τῆς γῆς,

1754   NEWTON, Isaac (Sir). *Two Letters from Sir Isaac Newton to Mr. Le*

Clerc, upon the rreading of the Greek Text 1 John V.7, and 1 Tim. iii. 16 London:

Even Newton, who independently (apart from Leibnitz) formulated the laws of differential calculus, engaged in this debate. But Orme admits his "leanings to Arianism. . . are to be deplored." Bludau says the treatise was written between 1690-1700, but published in 1754.

1755   WESLEY, John. *Explanatory Notes upon the New Testament*.

The following quote concerning the *Comma* is from his second edtion (1757):

> What *Bengelius* has advanced both concerning the Transposition of these two Verses, and the Authority of the controverted Verse, partly in his *Gnomeon*, and partly in his *Apparatus Criticus* will abundantly satisfy any impartial Person.

Bengel ought to be credited for his defense of the *Comma*. However, another question must be asked: Were Bengel's other notes harmless or venomous?

"Wesley had wanted to prepare a New Testament with notes for many years. He finally decided that he could do not better than to adapt Bengel's Gnomon Novi Testamenti, translating, abridging, and adaption Bengel's note for his New Testament. In addition, Wesley prepared a new translation, making, by some reckoning about 12,000 changes in the KJV text. These changes include textual alterations, based on the textual work of Bengel."[212]

1756   BENSON, George. "Dissertation concerning the genuiness of 1 John V. 7,8." *Paraphrase and Notes on the seven Catholic Epistles*. London: 631-646.

1761   ERNESTI, Johann August. *Institutio interpretis Novi Testamenti*.
Ernesti was a philologist and regarded the *Comma* as genuine. This work went through five editions: 1761, 1765, 1775, 1792, and 1809. An English translation appeared in 1832-33. See (1833: ERNESTI) for an English translation of his comment on the *Comma*.

1762   PARIS, Thomas. ed. *The King James Version*. Cambridge:

Spelling, punctuation, and obsolete words were dealt with, in order to modernize the version. Dr. Paris could have omitted the *Comma* and other readings, but no verses were omitted.

---

212. Harold P. Scanlin, "Bible Translation as a Means of Communicating New Testament Textual Criticism to the Public" *The Bible Translator* 39 (1988) Jan. 103.

1763 * BOWYER, William. *Novum Testamentum Graecum ad fidem Graecorum solum Codicum MSS. nunc primum expressum.* London:

C.H. Turner say every editor of the Greek N.T. allowed the *Textus Receptus* to stand unaltered "till Griesbach, with the exeception of a forgotten English scholar, William Boyer, to whose courage Griesbach in the preface to his own second edition does due honor."[213]

1763 * BENGEL, Johann Albert. *Apparatus Criticus ad Novum Testamentum; criseos sacrae compendium, limam supplementum ac fructum exhibens.* Tübingen: 452-482.

Bengel devoted nearly 30 pages to this issue. He argues in favor of the *Johnannine Comma*.

1764   GERHARD, Johann. "Primum argumentum ex Novo Test. pro adstruendo trinitas mysterio deductum" *Locorvm Theologicorvm Exegesin sive vberiorem explicationem qvorvndam articvlorvm religionis Christianæ.* 10th ed. Tübingen: 262.

> sed etiam de solennitate & veritate hujus θεοφανείας, quod vox cælestis delata & publice audita sit ipsius cælestis Patris vox, & quod columba ex aperta illa cæli parte desuper descendens sit ipse Dei Spiritus, quo accommodari potest illud I Joh. V.7 *Tres sunt, qui testimonium dant in cælo. Pater, Verbum & Spiritus,* id est, tres sunt natura divini ac coelstes testes, qui in baptismo Christi visibilibus & externis symbolis sese manifestarunt.

Eberhard Nestle claimed that Gerhard was the last defender of this verse. But he overlooked Goeze.

1764 * SEMLER, Johann Salomo. *Historische und kritische Sammlungen über die sogenannten Beweisstellen in der Dogmatik. Stück 1 über 1 Joh. 5,7.*

1765 * GOEZE, Johann Melchior. *Vertheidigung der Complutensischen Bibel, insonderheit des neuen Testaments, gegen die Wetstenischen und Semlerischen Beschuldigungen. Nebst einem Anhange, in welchem eine völlig unbekant gewordene, in Absicht auf die Hamb. Reform. Geschichte aber höchst merkwürdige Ausgabe des N. Testam. Lutheri, welche zu Hamburg 1523, 8. in niedersächsischer Sprache an das Licht getreten, beschrieben wird.* Hamburg: [130 pp.]

An English translation of the main portion of the title is "Defense of the

---

213. *Early Printed Editions of the Greek Testament,* 8 n1.

Complutensian Bible, esp. the N.T., against the Accusations of Wettstein and Semler." Goeze, a Lutheran pastor, railed against the new ideas of the Age of Enlightenment. "Ramler, Basedow, and Goethe were also rebuked"[214] as well as G. Lessing.

1766   REINECCIO, M. Christian. *Novum Testamentum Græcum as optimas quasque editiones collatum et excusum adjectis nonnullis variantibus lectionibus et notis*. Lipsiæ: 406-7.

Ὅτι τρεῖς εἰσιν οἱ μαρτυροῦντες † ἐν τῷ οὐρανῷ, ὁ Πατὴρ, ὁ Λόγος, καὶ τὸ ἅγιον Πνεῦμα, καὶ οὗτοι οἱ τρεῖς ἕν εἰσι. Καὶ τρεῖς εἰσι οἱ μαρτυροῦντες ἐν τῇ γῇ,

1766 * *J.J. Wetstenii Libelli ad crisin etc. illustr.* Semler.

1766 * SEMLER, Johann. *Genauere Untersuchung der schlechten Beschaffenheit des zu Alcala gedruckten neuen Testaments*.

In English, the title is "A more exact examination of the bad quality of the New Testament printed in Alcala."

1766 * GOEZE, Johann Melchior. *Ausführlichere Verteidigung des Complutensischen griechischen Neuen Testaments, nebst einer Samlung der vernemsten Verschiedenheiten des Grundtextes und der Vulgata desselben mit beygefügten critischen Anmerkungen. Zur Widerlegung des Herrn D. Semlers.* Hamburg: [506 pp.]

1767   SEMLER, Johann Salomo. *Apparatvs ad Liberalem Novi Testamenti Interpretationem*. Halea: 41-42,59-60.

1767 * HOFFMAN. *de prudentia in disquisitione* αὐθεντιας *Dicti, 1 Ioh V, 7 obseuanda*. Wittebergae:

Goeze in his *Continuation of the Comprehensive Defense*. . .(p.136) called upon Kiefer to read this "programma worth reading."

1768   KIEFER. *Gerettet Vermutungen über das Complutische N. Testament, Gegen den Hn. Senior Götz in Hamburg. Hrsg von D. Johann Salomo Semler*.

1769   LESSING, Gotthold Ephraim. *Gotthold Ephraim Lessing's Sämmtliche Schriften* edited by Karl Lachmann. Revised and enlarged by Wendelin von Maltzahn. (Leipzig: G.J Göschen'sche Verlagshandlung, 1857) part one of vol 11: 413.

---

214. *New Century Cyclopedia of Names* (New York: Appleton-Century-Croft, 1954) 2:1773

This is from part IV of the section entitled "Hamburg (1768)." Part IV begins with Lessing's first encounter with Goeze in 1769. After a lengthy paragraph, Lessing refers to the famous dispute:

> Hereupon we spoke on account of his dispute with Semler, in which Goeze is evidently correct. Semler spoke of the Complutensian New Testament without having seen it, and without having examined it. The Spaniards certainly had to have brought manuscripts, and the passage of John had not been translated from the Vulgate. Otherwise, they would certainly have translated ἐν εἰσι, as the Vulgate reads, and not εἰς το ἐν.

1769 * GOEZE, Johann Melchior. *Fortsetzung der Ausführlicheren Vertheidigung des Complutensischen griechischen Neuen Testaments; Nebst einer Samlung der vornehmsten Verschiedenheiten des Grundtextes und der Vulgata deßelben, in liturgischen Stellen, wie auch der vorzugswürdigen Lesarten dieser Ausgabe; Zur Widerlegung des Herrn D. Semlers*. Hamburg: Johan Christian Brandt. a3,117,127-160, 162, 333-340. [472 pp.]

In English, the title of the work [215] is "Continuation of the Comprehensive Defense of the Complutensian Greek New Testament. . ."

Section 29 is "Answer to the 35:40 §. Examination of the position 1 John 5:7. Section 30 is the continuation. Section 31 concerns the Codex Ravianus. Section 32 is "Continuation of the Examination of 1 John 5:7." Section 59 is "Continuation. Mr. K. certainly knows that no more codices will be found, which have 1 John 5:7. His song of triump is being rejected. He has drawn his *facit* from false *datis*."

1769 BLAYNEY, Benjamin, ed. *King James Version* [Oxford edition]

According to one source[216] a sampling of changes from the 1611 include (1611/1769): sister/sisters, told/tell, the Lord/his Lord, law/the law, request/requests, heart/hearts, dwelt/dwell, etc. The claim is that these are alarming "revisions affecting the sense"! Dr. Blayney also updated the spelling, punctuation, and use of italics. He could have omitted the *Comma* and other verses, but no verses are omitted.

1774 * SCHMIDT. *Hist. Antiqua*. [found in Kitto's list]

1774 GRIESBACH, Johann Jakob. *Libri Historici Novi Testamenti Graece pars prior, sistens synopsin Evangeliorvm Mattheai, Marci et Lvcae; Textvm ad fidem*

---

215. The copy I used was borrowed by Universitätsbibliothek Tübingen via Berlin: *Bibliotheka Regina Berolinensi*.
216. Gary R. Hudson. *Revision is no "Myth"*

dodicvm, versionvm et patrvm. Emendavit et lectionis varietatem. Halee: 225-236.

Griesbach must have been impressed with Semler's collection of books.[217]

Ὅτι τρεῖς εἰσιν οἱ μαρτυροῦντες[m] †

---

[m] † ἐν τῷ οὐρανῷ, ὁ Πατὴρ, ὁ Λόγος, καὶ τὸ ἅγιον Πνεῦμα, καὶ οὗτοι οἱ τρεῖς ἕν εἰσι. Καὶ τρεῖς εἰσι οἱ μαρτυροῦντες ἐν τῇ γῇ,

---

Griesbach did not leave the *Comma* in the main text, but placed it in a rectangle. The marking for verse 8 is neglected. Verse 9 begins with Εἰ τὴν μαρτυπρίαν. Acts 8:37 (II,p.97), 9:5,6 (II,p 98) are also removed from the main text.

1776   HARWOOD, E. *The New Testament collated with the most approved lmanuscripts; with select notes in English, critical and explanatory.* London: J.D. Cornish.

On page xi of the preface he refers to his *Third Volume* to explain why he has "in some particular passages discarded the commonly received reading." As the reader would expect, he discarded the *Comma*. He also took the liberty to renumber the verses.

Standard numbering for over two hundred years, 1551 to 1776:

6 [a. first half of verse six]
" [b. second half:] Καὶ τὸ πνεῦμά ἐστι τὸ μαρτυροῦν, ὅτι τὸ πνεῦμά ἐστιν ἡ ἀλήθεια.
7. Ὅτι τρεῖς εἰσιν οἱ μαρτυροῦντες, [ἐν τῷ οὐρανῷ, ὁ Πατὴρ, ὁ Λόγος, καὶ τὸ ἅγιον Πνεῦμα, 8. καὶ οὗτοι οἱ τρεῖς ἕν εἰσι. Καὶ τρεῖς εἰσι οἱ μαρτυροῦντες ἐν τῇ γῇ,] τὸ Πνεῦμα, τὸ ὕδωρ, καὶ τὸ αἷμα, καὶ οἱ τρεῖς εἰς τὸ ἕν εἰσι 9.

---

217. For a listing of Semler's personal library see *Verzeichniß der von dem seligen Herr Doctor und Professor Theologia Johann Salomo Semler hinterlassenen Bücher. . .*(Halle: F.W. Michaelis, 1791)

Harwood's numbering of 1776 (and his accents):

6a. (same)
7. Και το πνευμα εσι το μαρτυρουν, ότι το πνευμα εσιν ἡ αληθεια
8. Ότι τρεις εισιν όι μαρτυπουντες, το Πνευμα το ὑδωρ, και το ἁιμα, και όι τρεις εις το ἑν εισι

Unless the aniti-Trinitarian, Mace,[218] renumbered I John 5 in his 1729 edition, 1776 may be the first time[219] in history, that a Greek edition of the NT edition deviated from the verse enumeration of Stephanus, which had been in use for over 200 years.

1777   GRIESBACH, Johann Jakob. *Novum Testamentum*.

With this edition of Griesbach's, Metzger says it was "the first time in Germany a scholar ventured to abandon the Textus Receptus at many places and to print the text of the New Testament." A copy in Tübingen's Universitätbibliothek is dated 1774.

1780   [Anonymous] *Die drey Briefe des Apostles Johannis übersetzt und erklärt*. Breßlau: 82-83.

1781   FULLER, Andrew. *The Gospel Worthy of All Acceptation*.

Written in this year, but not published until 1785. Fuller's significance is explained in many accounts. One is "The conversion of Andrew Fuller. . .marks an epoch in the history of Particular Baptists"[220] A check of the scriptures employed in this printed sermon reveals that the King James Version was used.

1782 * BOWYER, William. *Critical Conjectures and Observations on the New Testament Collected from Various Authors*.

1784 * TRAVIS, George. "Letters to Edward Gibbon"

---

218. I have not been able to procure the Greek edition by Mace.
219. Edward Reuß counted 584 Greek editions between 1514-1869. The readings displayed in this paper, are from editions of the Greek N.T. in Tübingen, which are only a sample of this amount.
220. A.H. Newman. *NSHE* I: 465.

Archbishop Travis reacted to Gibbon's comment (in *History of the Decline and Fall*, vol.6) on the Johannine verse. Perhaps it was this work, in which Travis rejected the Britannicus = Montfort theory, for Porson said in letter 2 of his *Letters to Travis* "I shall leave the subject of the Codex Britannicus (which is the samewith the Dublin MS. whatever Mr. Travis may say) to another letter." *Letters to Travis*, 36. "Another letter" was letter 6, (p.137). But neither letter 2 nor letter 6 provide proof that they were identical codices.

1785   FULLER, Andrew. *Gospel Worthy of All Acceptation.*

In this year, this book was published "which ultimately led to the formation of the Baptist Missionary Society."[221] It was absolutely proper for Fuller to say "There is no contradition between this peculiarity of design[222] in the death of Christ, and a universal obligation of those who hear the gospel to believe in him, or a universal invitation being addressed to them."[223]

1785   [Herbert Marsh began to study under Michaelis.]

"In 1785, he [H.Marsh] left Cambridge, travelled, studied at Leipzig under J.D. Michaelis, and corresponded with Griesbach on the text of the New Testament." *DNB* 12:1096.

1785 * KNITTEL, Francis. *Neue Kritiken über den berühmten spruch; Drey sind, die da Zeugen im himmel, etc.* Braunschweig:

1786   WOIDE, Carol Godofred. *Novum Testamentum Græcum Codice MS Alexandrino, qui Londini in Bibliotheca Musei Britannici asservatur.*London: Joannis Nichols.

ΟΤΙ ΤΡΕΙC ΕΙC ΕΙCΙΝ ΟΙ ΜΑΡΤΘΡΟΘΝΤΕC, ΤΟ ΠÑΑ ΚΑΙ ΤΟ ΥΔΩΡ ΚΑΙ ΤΟ ΑΙΜΑ, ΚΑΙ ΟΙ ΤΡΕΙΩ ΕΙC ΤΟ ΕΝΕΙCΙΝ

---

221. Nettles, *By His Grace and for His Glory*, 109.
222. What was the "peculiarity of design"? Fuller, "the founder and conductor of the Baptist Missionary Society for twenty-two years" (Ivimey, *History of the English Baptists*, 4:535) said in his *Complete Works* 2:709-10 "That for which I contended was, that Christ had an absolute and determinate design in his death to save some of the human race, and not others;"
223. *Complete Works of Andrew Fuller* ed. by J. Belcher, (Philadelphia: Amer. Bapt. Pub. Soc., 1845) 2:374.

1786   STORR, Gottlob Christian. *Ueber den Zwek der evanglischen Geschichte und der Briefe Johannis*. Tübingen: 226-227.

1786   [W.F. Hezel was called to Gießen as professor of Oriental and Biblical Literature]

Hezel was another defender of the *Comma*. See (1793: HEZEL). Redslob said "as a writer he was uncommonly prolific"[224] He wrote *An Arabic Grammar Made Easier including a Short Arabic Chrestomathy* (1776), *History of the Hebrew Language and Literature* (1776), *A Comprehensive Hebrew Grammar* (1777), *The Consideration of the Syriac and Arabic Languages: 'Syriac Grammar'* (1788). "Also for the classical and new languages, namely the French, he had written a series of handbooks, mostly for practical purposes."[225] *A Comprehensive Greek Grammar including Paradigms* (1795). He wrote many other works including *The Bible of the Old and New Testament with Complete Explanatory Comments* (10 parts, 1780-91).

1788 * GIBBON, Edward. *History of the Decline and Fall of the Roman Empire*, 12 vol. London: 1820 reprint 6:287-288
QUOTE:
> The three witnesss have been established in our Greek Testaments by the prudence of Erasmus; the honest bigotry of the Complutensian editors; the typographical fraud, or error, of Robert Stephens, in the placing a crotchet; and the deliberater falsehood, or stange misapprehension, of Theodore Beza.

1788 * MICHAELIS, Johanne David. *Einleitung in das Neue Testament* Göttingen, 2nd ed.

1789   KNOWLES, Thomas. *Primitive Christianity; or Testimonies from the Writers of the First Four Centuries; to Prove that Jesus Christ was Worschipped, as God, from the Beginning of the Christian Church*. London:

1789   LOFFT, Cappel. *Observations on the First Part of Dr. Knowles' Testimony from the Writers of the First Four Centuries. In a Letter to a Friend*. Bury:

---

224. *ADB* 12:382.
225. Ibid.

1789   VINDEX. [remarks to Porson's comments] Gentleman's Magazine [January]

1789   TOULMIN of Taunton. "An Exhortation to all Christian People, to Refrain from Trinitarian Worship" 54.

This essay is from the section "Six Tracts in Vindication of the Worship of One God" (1794) of the book *Tracts Printed and Published by the Unitarian Society for Promoting Christian Knowledge and the Practice of Virtue.* vol. 1. (London: 1791)

> The words [*in heaven, the Father, the word, and the holy ghost, and these three are one, and ther are three that bear witness in earth*] have never been proved to be in ANY greek manuscript, before the invention of printing; nor were ever cited by any of the numerous writer in the whole arian controversy, concernig the trinity, in the fourth century. In the English bibles in the reign of Henry VIII. and Edward VI. they were printed in a *different character*, to signify their being wanting in the original. See Emlyn's Inquiry. . .and Mr. Capel Lofft's Answer to Dr. Knowles.

1790   BENGEL, Ernest. *Novum Testamentum Græcum manuale, ex iterata recognitione b. Jo. Alb. Bengelii, S.T.D.* 5th edition. Tübingen: Jac.Frid Heerbrandt. 455.

1790   PORSON, Richard. *Letters of Mr. Archdeacon Travis, in Answer to his Defense of the Three Heavenly Witnesses, 1 John V.7.* London:

> I allow you in advance, that a great majority of the Latin MSS. are on your side. Perhaps for one that omits the three heavenly witnesses, forty or fifty may be found that retain them. [p.139]

The view that Britannicus is the same as the Monfort was propounded by Marsh in 1795 but even earlier by Porson [p.117]:

> The conclusions which I draw from these facts are, 1. That the *Codex Britannicus* is the MS. now called Dublinensis or Morfortius 2. That it contained the controverted passage translated in a bungling manner from the modern copies of the Vulgate. For the omission of the final clause of the eighth verse is peculiar to them. 3. That it was probably written in the year 1520, and interpolated in this place for the purpose of deceiving Erasmus.

See the objection to the equating of the two manuscripts under (1867: FORSTER). Forster also says "Porson's charge of interpolation is simply ridiculous." (p. 129)

On page i of his preface, Porson says that it is scarcely necessary to tell the reader "That this MS. after a profound sleep of two centuries, has at last been found in the library of Trinity-college, Dublin."

1790 [Adam Clarke went to Trinity College, Dublin to examine the *Montfort* Codex]

1791 PRIESTELY, Joseph. *Three Tracts by Joseph Priestely, LL.D. F.R.S.* London: The Unitarian Society for Promoting Christian Knowledge and the Practice of Virtue. 136.

In the tract entitled "A Familiar Illustration of Certain Passages of Scripture" Priestely says:

> 1 John v.7 *There are three that bear record in heaven, the Father, the Word, and the Holy Ghost; and these three are one.* Sir Isaac Newton, and others, have clearly proved that this verse was no part of John's original epistle, but was inserted in later ages. It is not to be found in any ancient manuscript, and has been omitted in many printed copies and translations of the new Testament, at a time when the doctrine which it is supposed to contain was in a manner universally received. I say *supposed to contain*, because, in fact it exresses no more that that these three agree in giving the same testimony, which is the only kind of union which the *spirit*, the *water*, and *the blood*, in the verse following can have.

1791 [Travis went to Paris to examine the MSS of Stephens.]

1792 CAREY, William. *An Enquiry into the Obligations of Christians to use Means for the Conversion of the Heathen.* Leicester:

In *The Baptist Heritage: Four Centuries of Baptist Witness*, (Nashvillle: Broadman, 1987) H. Leon McBeth mentions the noteworthy fact that "William Carey was one of the Particular Baptists who shared in the evangelical renewal of the northern Midlands in the latter part of the eighteenth century." (p. 184). McBeth described this book by Carey as the "charter of the modern missionary movement."

1792 [Oct 2: Baptist Missionary Society was founded]]

H. Leon McBeth said 14 persons met in the home of Martha Wallace, and "the group voted to form "The Particular Baptist Society for the Propagation of the Gospel Amongst the Heathen." The group was popularly known by the shorter name Baptist Missionary Society or just BMS." (p. 185). The term "Particular Baptist" is noteworthy here. There is no evidence, for any objection among these Baptists to the use of the Greek Received Text for NT translations into the language of the heathen.

1793 [William Carey and his family sailed for India.]

1793   HEZEL, Wilhelm Friedrich. *Über die Aechtheit der Stelle Johannis (I John 5,7) drey sind die da zeugen im Himmel etc. Aus Gründen der höhern Kritik, nebst einer Erklärung des ganzen Abschnitt V. 4-13.* Gieszen: G.F. Heyer. [100pp.]

1794   GRIESBACH. J.J. *Bemerkungen über des Herrn Geheimen Regierungsrath Hezel Vertheidigugn der Aechtheit der Stelle I Joh. 5,7 Drez sind die da zeugen im Himmel etc. mit Anmerkngen und einem Anhange, von Hezel.* Giessen: [104pp. in the form of a letter to Hezel]

1794   [William Carey reaches Bengal.]

1794   TRAVIS, George. *Letters to Edward Gibbon, Esq., in defense of the Authenticity of the seventh verse of the first Epistle of St. John* London:

1795   MARSH, Herbert. *Letters to Mr. Archdeacon Travis, in Vindication of one of his Notes to Michaelis's Introduction...With an appendix, containing a Review of Mr. Travis's Collation of th Greek MSS. which he examined in Paris; an Extract from Mr. Pappelbaum's Treatise on the Berlin MS.; and an Essay on the Origin and Object of the Velesian Readings.* Leipzig:

In 1854, Dr. Dobbin referred to this as a "scarce volume". Dr. Dobbin says that he makes an extract from the preface of this work, but he provided neither quotation marks nor indentation. It appears that the extract extends from p. 41 to p. 44 in Dobbin's *The Codex Montfortianus; A Collation.* Accordingly, one of the statements by Dr. Marsh is:

> For though in the text of the most ancient Latin Manuscripts no traces are visible of 1 John v.7, . . .

The statement is out of date, and is clearly no longer the case.

1796   PAPPELBAUM, G.G. *Codicis Manuscripti Raviani Examen.* Berlin:

This Greek MS, *Codex Ravianus*, (also *Berolinensis* or ω 110) "has been examined by Wetstein, Griesbach, and by G.G. Pappelbaum in 1796. It contains the whole New Testament, and has attracted attention because it has the disputed words in 1

Jo. v.7,8."[226]

Many have said *Ravianus* is "obviously a forgery", that it was proved to be a 16th century copy of the Complutensian. Usually the account stops here. But such brief accounts give the impression it is an exact copy of the Complutensian. Let us raise 3 questions: First, *Ravianus* contains the entire New Testament. What would be the motive for such an immense amount of labor for this forgery? Second, it is not an exact copy, but is "with some various readings from Stephen's third edition; and the remainder (from Mark v.20. to the end of Saint John's Gospel, and Rom.i.-vi. and xiii.-16.) is a copy of the same edition, with some various readings taken partly from Stephen's margin, and partly from the Complutensian Polyglott."[227] Why is this fact omitted in modern accounts? Third, if it is a forgery, why is Metzger still citing it (by its alias "ω 110") in 1968 as a witness for the *Comma*? Fourth, we wonder if anyone questioned the forgery view. In about 1769 Gotthold Lessing questioned it:

> It's true that the remaining codicies don't have the passage, until such time as the Berlin MS, which Christian Rau (or Ravius) sold to the *Churfürsten*. But that's going too far to make Rau as the forger of it and to purport that Rau himself copied it from the Complutensian edition.[228]

1796   HEY, John. "Concerning the genuineness of 1 John V.7," *Lectures in Divinity*. vol. II, Cambridge: 280-291

Horne: "The learned author appears to have cherished a hope that future MSS. might be discovered, containing the disputed passage."

Comment: Why shouldn't he have this hope? In 1796, the *speculum* and the citation from Priscillian were not yet known. For years, it was said only one Greek MSS testifies in favor of the *Comma*. Today, NA[26] lists eight Greek MSS.

1801   [The vast increase in the number of Particular Baptists]

A.H. Newman said "By 1801 the Particular Baptist had increased to 29,000"[229] K.S. Latourette provides more detail (from Carlile) by saying "At the beginning of the nineteenth century the Particular Baptists with 417 Churches and 29,000 members,

---

226. Scrivener, *Plain Introduction*, 3rd ed., p. 196-97.
227. T.H. Horne (2nd ed., 1822) cites Pappelbaum's book and *Symbolæ Criticæ* pars i. p. clxxxi by Griesbach.
228. G.E. Lessing *Sämmtliche Schriften*. (Leipzig: G.J. Göschen'sche, 1857) part 1 of vol 11: 413-14.
229 *NSHE* IV: 465.

outnumbered the General Baptists with about 100 churches."[230]

1801   CARRY, William & THOMAS, John. *The New Testmant in Bengali*

It is impossible to imagine that Carey used anything but a printed Received Text (*textus receptus*) for his translation of the New Testament into 26 Indian languages on behalf of 300 million people. (He did not force the King James Version 1611 upon them!) Are we to believe that 300 million people were deceived from their new translations based on an "inferior" Greek text? [231] Some will ask "But what Greek text did Baptist missionaries translate from in later years, say in 1833?" See (1833: Baptists).

1801   MICHAELIS, Johann D. "Dissertation on 1 John v.7." *Introduction to the New Testament*. Cambridge: 4:412-441 [This English translation of the 4 vols. is dated 1793-1801]

QUOTE: from Michaelis
>   It is uncandid in the extreme for one Protestant to condemn another for rejecting 1 John v.7, since it was rejected by the author of our Reformation.

1801   BARRETT, John. *Evangelium Secundum Matthæum ex Codice Rescripto in Bibiotheca Collegii SSæ Trinitatis Juxta Dublin. Cui Adjungitur Apendix, Colllationem Codicis Monfortiani Complectens*. Dublin:

Dr. Dobbin said of this work "But the Appendix of Dr. Barret embraced a collation of the Epistles only. . . The very defective way in which that portion of the MS. had been collated for Walton's Polyglot, suggested strongly to the author the desirableness of submitting the four Gospels and the Acts to an entirely new examination. . ."[232]

1802   [The Freising codex was moved to Munich]

It would be wrong to create two Old Latin witnesses for the *Comma* from *q* and *r*, for these are other names for the same codex. The "Freising fragments" which contain the *Comma*, were moved in 1802 from the Freising Chapter Libary to the

---

230. K.S.Latourette *The Nineteenth Century in Europe; the Protestant and Eastern Churches* (New York: Harper and Row, 1959).
231. Carey, who is known as "the father of the modern missionary movement", also "was (and remained) a five-point Calvinist throughtout the whole of his ministry." See: Kenneth Good, *Are Baptists Reformed?* (Lorain, OH: Regular Baptist Heritage Fellowship, 1986) 58.
232. O.T. Dobbin *The Codex Montfortianus: A Collation of This Celebrated MS*...(London: Samuel Bagster, 1854) 1.

Hof-Bibliothek in Munich. "Since the time of Tischendorf it has been cited as *q*."[233] Scrivener called it *r*.

1803   MATTHAIE, Christian Friedrich, *Novum Testamentum*, Tome XI, page ix, Leipzig:

A quote by Matthaei (as provided by F. Nolan) on the mismatched genders within the comma.

> *haud plane consisteret, nisi cum violentia quadam dictionis, et per solaecismusm patentissimum.* Cum eternim τὸ μνεῦμα καὶ ὕδωρ καὶ τὸ αἷμα nomina *neutrius* generis sunt, qua ratione concordabit cum iis quod immediate praecedit; τρεῖς ςἰσιν οἱ μαρτυπἑντεσ, et quod illico sequitur, καὶ ἕτοι οἱ τρεῖς κ.τ.λ. -Sed nonne quaeso dictio naturalis hic et propria potius esset; τρία εἰσι τὰ μαρτυρἑντα ἐν τῇ γῇ, τὸ πνεῦμα, τὸ ὕδωρ, καὶ τὸ αἷμα· καὶ τὰ αἷμα·καὶ τὰ τρία εἰς τὸ ἕ εἰσιν; At illud tamen est scriptum non hoc.

1803   FULLER, Andrew. *The Great Question Answered.* London: W.Button & Sons.

1804   MATTHAIE, Christian Friedrich. *Novum Testamentum Graece ad codices Mosquenses utriusque Bibliothecae SS. Synodi et Tabularii imperialis. . .* Curiae Variscorum:Grau. 297-299.

1805   BUTLER, Charles. "A Short Historical Outline of the Disputes respecting the Authenticity of the Verse of the Three Heavenly Witnesses, or 1 John, Chap. V. ver. 7."
[Appendix II of his *Horæ Biblicæ* or vol. II of his *Collection of Essays and Tracts in Theology* Boston: 2:321-357.]

1805   GRIESBACH, J.J. *Novum Testamentum.* Leipzig:

Samuel Sharpe described this labor of Griesbach as "settling the Greek Text" and referred to it as "the corrected Greek text".[234] But the mta of today are still restless today within their never-ending endeavor to "recover" the true text, regardless of a multitude of past claims of "corrected" or "settled" texts.

1806   GRIESBACH, Johann Jacob. "Diatribe in Locum 1 Joann. V.7, 8"
[in vol. II of his *Critical Edition of the New Testament.* Hallæ:] Appendix, pp. 1-25.

---

233. H.J. White *Old Latin Biblical Texts* (Oxford: Clarondon Press, 1888)III:v.
234. Introduction to Sharpe's 1940 translation of Greisbach.

1807   CLARKE, Adam. "Observations on the Text of the Three Divine Witnesses" *The New Testament of Our Lord and Savior Jesus Christ Carefully Printed from the Most Correct copies of the Present Authorized Translation.* [at the end of his comments on First John]

> ...but the dispute has been principally confined to the *Unitarians* of all classes, and those called *Orthodox*; the former asserting that it is an *interpolation*, the latter contending that it is a *part of the original text of St. John.*

Clarke admitted that the orthodox have been defending the comma! Yet he was undecided until he was influenced greatly by Michaelis, and eventually decided against its authenticity.

1807   JOWETT, Joseph. "The Question concerning the Authenticiy of 1 John V.7. briefly examined" [In vol. 6 of the *Christian Observer*]

1808   [The American edition of Griesbach's NT.]

Rev. J.S. Buckminster "superintended the American edition of Griesbach's Greek Testament (1808);"[235] Consequently, the *Comma* dropped out of Greek New Testaments used at Harvard College.

1808   MIDDLETON, Thomas F. *The Doctrine of the Greek Article; Applied to the Criticism and the Illustration of the New Testament.* London: 633-653.

The following is taken from David D. Scott's translation from the French of L.Gaussen's *Divine Inspiration of the Bible*, pp 192-193, who introduces the passage: "We shall confine ourselves to these two remarks by Bishop Middleton:-"

> 1. Why is the word *three, the three,* in the masculine in the Greek (τρεῖς οἱ μαρτυροῦντες, καὶ οἱ τρεῖς), while the words *spirit, water,* and *blood,* to which it relates, are all neuter (for it would have been necessary to say τρία τὰ μαρτυροῦντα)? This irregularity, which is fully justified by what is called in grammar *the principle of attraction*, if the passage remains entire, becomes inexplicable when you would deprive it of the contested words.
> 2. Wherefore, above all, this word, *that one* (τὸ ἕν, the ONE), if some certain ONE have not been spoken of in the preceding words?

1808   WHITE, Josephus, S.T.P. *Novum Testamentum Græce. Lectiones Varianties, Griesbachii Judicio iis quas Textus Receptus exhibet Anteponendas, vel Æquiparandas.* Oxford: Clarondon. 319.

---

235. *NSHE* 2:290.

† ἐν τῷ οὐρανῷ, ὁ Πατὴρ, ὁ Λόγος, καὶ τὸ ἅγιον
† Πνεῦμα. καὶ οὗτοι οἱ τρεῖς ἕν εἰσι. Καὶ τρεῖς
† εἰσι οἱ μαρτυροῦντες ἐν τῇ γῇ,*

1809 PHEREZ, J. *The Critique on the Eclectic Review |of the English Version of the New Testament, published by the modern Socians| on 1 John V.7., confuted by Martyn's Examination of Emlyn's Answer; to which is added and Appendix, containing Remarks on Mr. Porson's Letter to Archbishop Travis.* London:

1810 'Η ΚΑΙΝΗ ΔΙΑΘΗΚΗ Τοῦ κυρίου καὶ Σωτῆρος ἡμῶν. London: 1026.

ἐν τῷ οὐρανῷ, ὁ Πατὴρ, ὁ Λόγος, καὶ τὸ ἅγιον Πνεῦμα. καὶ οὗτοι οἱ τρεῖς ἕν εἰσι. καὶ οὗτοι οἱ τρεῖς ἕν εἰσι 8. Καὶ τρεῖς εἰσι οἱ μαρτυροῦντες ἐν τῇ γῇ

1811 [J.S. Buckminster: appointed lecturer on Biblical Criticism at Harvard]

1811 * BUCKMINSTER, Joseph S. (article on Griesbach's Greek Testament). *The Monthly Anthology and Boston Review*.

Rev. Buckminster questioned the readings of Acts 20:28, 1 Tim 3:16, and the *Comma*, in this article. These are the same three verses which Andrews Norton, a Unitarian, found repulsive. See his "Explanations of Particular Passages of the New Testament, Adduced by Trinitarians"[236]

1811 LAURENCE, Richard. *Critical Reflections upon some imortant misrepresentations contained in the Unitarian version of the New Testament* Oxford.:

1812 [April 22; Solomon C. Malan, the noted orientalist, was born in Geneva.]

1812 [Baptist pastors planned 'The General Union of Baptist ministers and churches']

About 60 Baptist pastors met to encourage each other and renew the zeal of their churches. "Among the attenders of the meeting were Andrew Fuller, John Sutcliff, John Ryland, Jr., John Rippon, and Joseph Ivimey."[237]

---

236. A. Norton *A Statement of Reasons for Not Believing the Doctrines of Trinitarians* 2nd ed. Edited by "E.A." [Ezra Abbot] (Boston: Amer. Unitarian Association, 1856)
237. T.J. Nettles, *By His Grace and for His Glory* (Grand Rapids: Baker, 1986) 31.

1813 [Andrews Norton became librarian and Bible lecturer at Harvard College]

1813 [*Confession of Faith* of the General Union of Baptist ministers]

Nettles says "Paragraph one of this original constitution is worded in terms in which "the Calvinism of Particular Baptist churches was customarily defined."

The confession of this Baptist union maintained
> the important doctrines of "three equal persons in the Godhead; eternal and personal election; original sin; particular redemption; free justification by the imputed righteousness of Christ. . ."[238]

1814 [May: The General Missionary Convention was founded.]

Luther Rice, who used the King James Version,[239] was instrumental in this work. In Philadelphia, 33 men gathered to form a constitution for the "General Missionary Convention of the Baptist Denomination in the United States of America for Foreign Missions."

1814 LAURENCE, Richard. *Remarks Upon the Systematic Classification of Manuscripts adopted by Griesbach in his edition of the New Testament.* Oxford:

1815 FULLER, A. *The Calvinistic and Socinian Systems Examined and Compared.*

1815 NOLAN, Frederick. *Inquiry into the Integrity of the Greek Vulgate or Received Text.* Collingswood: Bible For Today,[240] 1985 reprint xvii-xviii, 276-305.

---

238. E.A. Payne, *The Baptist Union.* 26 (as quoted by Nettles, p. 32).
239. Note his quoting from the KJV ". . .could he be displeased with *the preaching* of such as: "Having PREDESTINATED us unto the adoption of children of Jesus Christ to himself, according to the good pleasure of his will." "For whom he did foreknow, he also did PREDESTINATE to be coformed to the image of his Son.". . .Similar passages are numerous, . . .the "good minister of Jesus Christ," cannot excuse himself. . .if he shuns to declare this part of the counsel of God, while he certainly ought to press the obligation of "all men every where to repent," and to "believe the gospel"; in short, to urge "repentance towards God, and faith towards our Lord Jesus Christ," as the immediate duty of all. . ."[emphasis his] *Memoirs of Rev. Luther Rice* (Nashville: Broadman Press, 2nd ed., 1937) 298.
240. Dr. D.A. Waite remarked: "His defense of 1 John 5:7 is without equal. He makes use of the LATIN MANUSCRIPTS on this verse because of an ARIAN HERETIC'S being the head of the GREEK CHURCH for a period of time. He feels that it was under this ARIAN'S direction that 1 John 5:7 was removed from the Greek texts."

A quote by R.L. Dabney concerning Nolan's work

> The acute and learned Irish divine, Nolan, in his *Inquiry into the Integrity of the Greek Vulgate*, a work which defends the received text with matchless ingenuity and profound learning, also demolished Griesbach's system.

A quote from Frederick Nolan[241] on the genders, p. 257;

> In 1 Joh. v. 7, three *masculine* adjectives, τρεῖς οἱ μαρτυροῦντες, are forced into union with three *neuter* substantives, τὸ πνεῦμα καὶ τὸ ὕδωρ καὶ τὸ αἷμα; a grosser solecism than can be ascribed to any writer, sacred or profane.

1816   [Francis Wayland's conversion]

1816   [César Henri Abraham Malan's conversion]

1817   [Baptists confirmed C.H.A. Malan's conversion]

The Baptists who "strenthened and confirmed" the conversion, were the famous Haldane brothers, Robert and James. In this year, C.H.A. Malan fearlessly began to proclaim the Gospel, but the clergy were offended, and Malan was forbidden to preach on certain topics.[242]

1817   [Harvard Divinity School was founded]

It was "maintained as a Unitarian institution to 1878, when it became the undenominational theological school of Harvard University."[243] Andrews Norton was Dexter Professor of Sacred Literature at this school from 1819 to 1830.[244]

1818   HALES, William. "Extensive Controversy about the celebrated Text, 1 John V.7." *Faith in the Holy Trinity, the Doctrine of the Gospe*. London: 2:133-226

In 1811, Dr. Hales announced that he regarded the *Comma* as spurious. This work of 1818 shows that he changed his mind, and favors it. Orme says he has over a

---

241. One may note Nolan's linquistic proficiency from his eight grammars: French (1819), Greek (1819), Italian (1819), Latin (1819), German (1821), Hebrew (1821), Spanish (1821), and Syriac (1821).
242. These themes were forbidden: (1) Union of both natures in the person of Jesus Christ; (2) hereditary sin; (3) the manner in which grace works its effects and (4) predestination *NSHE* 7:138.
243. *NSHE* 12:84.
244"Norton, Andrews" *Dict of American Biography* 13:568.

hundred pages of discussion on the *Comma*. The strength of the argument of Hales, is his detailed account of the quantity of uncollated MSS in European libraries. He is saying, in effect, that it is premature to reject the disputed verse, until these MSS are first collated.

1818   ABLER, Joanne Nepomuceno. "Annotation ad 1 Epistolam Joannis cap. V. ver. 7,8." *Institutiones Hermeneuticæ Novi Testamenti*. Pestini: 3:353-369

1819   [W.E. Channing's sermon "Unitarian Christianity"]

This sermon by William Ellery Channing (1780-1842) resulted in the "Wood 'n Ware" debate.

1820   [L. Woods's *Letters to Unitarians occasioned by the Sermon of the Reverend William E. Channing*.] Andover:

1820   [H. Ware's *Letters addressed to Trinitarians and Calvinists*.]

Henry Ware, D.D. (1764-1845) of Harvard, responded to Leonard Woods, D.D. (1774-1854) of Andover. The last two words in the title *and Calvinists* are a matter of interest in connection with the rise of Unitarianism in America. "While individuals criticized the doctrine of the Trinity, the topic was not debated in sermons and publications, and the growing liberalism directed itself mainly against the Calvinist view of human nature."[245]

1820   TITTMANN, Joh. Aug. Henr. *Novvm Testamentvm Graece ad fidem optimorvm librorvm recensvit*. Lipsiae: 425.

> (ἐν τῷ οὐρανῷ, ὁ πατὴρ, ὁ λόγος, καὶ τὸ ἅγιον πνεῦμα. καὶ οὗτοι οἱ τρεῖς ἕν εἰσι. 8. Καὶ τρεῖς εἰσι οἱ μαρτυροῦντες ἐν τῇ γῇ,)

1821   BURGESS, Thomas. *A Vindication of 1 John V.7. from the Objections of M. Griesbach, in which a new View is given of the external evidence, with Greek Authorities for the Authenticity of the Verse, not hitherto adduced in its Defence*. London:

1821   [L. Woods's *A Reply to Dr. Ware's Letters to Trinitarians and Calvinists*] 228pp.

1822   [H. Ware's *Answer to Dr. Wood's Reply in Second Series of Letters addressed to Trinitarians and Calvinists*] 163pp.

---

245. "Unitarians" *NSHE* 12:83.

1822   TURTON, Thomas (attributed to). "Review of the *Vindication* &c. in the *Quarterly Review* for March, 1822" London:

1822   BURGESS, Thomas. *Adnotationes Millii, auctæ et correctæ ex prolegomensis suis, Wetstenii, Bengelii, et Sabaterii ad 1 Joann. V.7., una cum duabus epistolis Richardi Bentleii, et Observationibus Joannis Seldeni, Christophori Matthiæ Pfaffii, Joannis Francisci Buddei, et Christiani Friderici Schmidii de eodem loco.*

1822   MARSH, Herbert. "Observations on 1 John V.7" [in part iv of his *Lectures in Divinity*. Cambridge:

1822   [L. Woods's *Remarks on Dr. Ware's Answer*] 63pp.

1823   [H. Ware's *A Postscript to the Second Seriers of Letters Addressed to Trinitarians and Calvinists, in Reply to The Remarks of Dr. Woods on those Letters.*] 48pp.

1823   BURGESS, Thomas. *A Vindication of 1 John V.7. &c.* Second edition: *to which is added a Preface in reply to the Quarterly Review, and a Postscript in answer to a recent publication entitled "Palæoromaica"* London:

1824   BURGESS, Thomas (ed.). *A Selection of Tracts and Obervations on 1 John V.7, Part the First, consisting of Bishop Barlow's Letter to Mr. Hunt; Bishop Smalbrooke's Letter to Dr. Bentley; Two anonymous Letters to Dr. Bentley, with Dr. Bentley's Answer; An Extract from Martin's Examination of Emlyn's Answer relative to that Letter; together with Notes of Hammond and Whitby on the controverted Verse; and Dr. Adam Clarke's Account of the Montfort Manuscript.* London:

1824   HORNE, Thomas Hartwell. *An Introduction to the Critical Study and Knowledge of the Holy Scriptures*, 4th edition. London:

(In his 2nd, 3rd, and 4th editions, Horne defended the *Comma*! Orme says he was influenced by Nolan, Hales, and Burgess. In later editions, "among them the eighth" he rejected it.)

1825   SCHOTT, Heinrich August: *Novum Testamentum Græce; secundum editiones probatissimas expressum Nova Versione Latina*: Lipsiae. 638.

In this edition, the *Comma* is omitted. No verse is assigned to be verse #8; thus the sequence is #6,#7, #9, but the standard numbering is retained. Schott's footnote begins:

> quae vulgo post οἱ μαρτυροῦντες adduntur, a S.V. Griesbachio propterea ad marginem relegantur, quod a) in omnibus codicibus graecis, excepto uno

Britannico, et versionibus antiquis pluribus (v.c. Coptica, Aethiopica, Syriaca utraque) desiderentur: b) quod codices latini ante saecul. 10. nulli locum nostrum habeant, eorum vero, in quibus verba compareant, permulti ad marginem haec ablegent, neque uno modo exhibeant; . . .

1825   DAVID, Ben [John Jones, LL.D.]. *Three Letters addressed to the Editor of the Quarterly Review, in which is demonstrated the Genuineness of the Three Heavenly Witnesses, 1 John V.7.* London:

1825   OXLEE, John. *Three Letters addressed to the Rev. Frederick Nolan on his erroneous Criticisms and Mis-statements in the Christian Rememberancer, relative to the Text of the Heavenly Witnesses..* York:

This publication was the result of a controversy with Nolan begining in 1822. Orme (*Memoirs*, 112) says Oxlee's style is "unmeasured severity and contempt."

1825   BURGESS, Thomas. *A Letter to the Clergy of the Diocese of St. David's on a Passage of the Second Symbolum Antiochenum of the Fourth Century, as an evidence of the authenticity of 1 John V.7.* London:

1825   TURTON, Thomas {attributed to}. *Review of the two preceding Articles in the Quarterly Review for December 1825.* London:

1825   [The British and Foreign Unitarian Association was founded][246]

1825   [The American Unitarian Association (AUA) was founded]

1827 * DIBDIN, Thomas Frognall. *An Introduction to the Knowledge of Rare and Valuable Editions of the Greek and Latin classics. Together with an Account of Polyglott Bibles, polyglott Psalters, Hebrew Bibles, Greek Bibles and Greek Testaments, the Greek fathers and the Latin fathers.* London:

1827   CRITO CANTABRIGIENSIS [Rt. Rev. Thomas TURTON, D.D.] .*A Vindication of the Literary Character of Professor Porson from the Animadversions of the Rt. Rev. Thomas Burgess, D.D. Lord Bishop of Salisbury, in various publications of 1 John V.7.* Cambridge:

1827   [anonymous] "Versuch einer Ehrenrettung der Stelle 1. Joh. 5, 7.8. gegen den Vorwurf einer Interpolation" [Attempt of a Vindication of the Passage 1 John 5:7-8 against the Reproach of an Interpolation] *Paulus Sendschreiben an die Galatier und Johannes erster Brief, übersetzt.* Neustadt a. d. Dria: 134-137.

---

246. *Encyclopedia of Religion*, ed. Mircea Eliade, 15:144.

1827   HUYSHE, Francis. *A Specimen of an intended publication, which was to have been entitled: A Vindication of them that have the rule over us, for their not having cut out the Disputed Passage 1 John V.7,8 from the Authorized Version. Being an examination of the first six pages of Professor Porson's IVth Letter to Archdeacon Travis, of the MSS. used by R. Stephens.*

1828   OXLEE, John. *Two Letters, respectfully addressed to the Lord Bishop of Salisbury, in Defence of certain Positions of the Author, relative to 1 John V.7; in which also the recent arguments of his Lordship are shown to be groundless surmises and evident mistakes.*
London:

1828 * 'British Critic'. (A review of *Vindication of Porson*). *Quarterly Theological Review and Ecclesiastical Record*. vol. IV: 1-32.

1828   [C.H.A. Malan wrote of his intent to leave Protestantism]

The Protestant clergy of Geneva, who had warned Malan to discontinue preaching, dismissed him as a preacher on September 18. E. Barde said "His severance from the state church caused him great pain, and he was willing to re-enter it whenever the free preaching of the Gospel should be permitted."[247]

1829   BURGESS, Thomas. *A Letter to the Rev. Thomas Beyon, Archdeacon of Cardigan, in Reply to a Vindication of the Literary Character of Professor Porson, by Crito Cantabrigiensis; and in further Proof of the Authenticity of 1 John V. 7.*   Salisbury:

1829   KNITTEL. {transl. by William Alleyn EVANSON, M.A.} *New Criticism on celebrated Text. A Synodical Lecture, by Francis Anthony KNITTEL, Counsellor to the Consistory, and the General Superintendent of the Grand Duchy of Brunswich Lünenbourg. Published at Brunswich in 1785.*

1829   CLEMENS ANGLICANUS [The Rt. Rev. Thomas TURTON]. *Remarks upon Mr. Evanson's Preface to his Translation of Knittel's New Criticisms on 1 John V.7.* London:

1829 * Dr. SMITH. *Smith's Rejoinder to Taylor*

Dr. Smith claims that John Bowring, Esq., searched for the MSS used by the editors of the Complutensian Polyglot. Bowring is to have "found *THE SAME* Scripture manuscripts which had been described as being in the library, by

---

247. *NSHE* 7:138.

Alvaro Gomez, who died in 1580." Bowring is claimed to announce his results as follows:

> That the manuscripts referred to are *modern* and *worthless*, there can be no longer any question.

1829   PAULUS, Heinrich Eberhard Gottlob. *Die drey Lehrbriefe von Johannis*. Heidelberg: 241-252.

Paulus[248] regards the *Comma* as spurious.

1830   [C.H.A. Malan became a missionary.]

"He traveled also through France, Belgium, Holland, some parts of Switzerland and Germany, and through the valleys of the Waldenses in Piedmont, preaching everywhere.[249] His son, Solomon, was 18 years old at this time.

1830   [Isaac Newton's treatise on 1 John 5:7 is reprinted]

Bludau says it was reprinted "in support of the Socinian system, and the views expressed have been quoted as proving Newton to be an anti-Trinitarian."

1830   SCHOLZ, J. Mart. Augustin. *Novum Testamentum Graece textum ad fidem testium criticorum recensuit, lectionum familias subiecit*. Lipsiae: 2:152-153.

The first paragraph of his footnote reads:
> testes quideam pauci sed= codices graeci, qui eplistolas catholicas habent, fere omnes videlicet: A B (hiat a 4,3 - 2 Jo 3) GH 1-33, 35-52, (53 m. hoc loco) 54 (55 solam Judae epist. cont.) 56-73, 75-82, 83*, 84, 86-89 (90 solam Jacobi eep. cont. 91 non coll. h.l.) 92-102, 104-107 (103 tota pericopa, cuius est versus noster, caret, 108- 112 h.l. coll. non sunt) 113-119 (120. 122. 130. 157. 159. h.l. mut) 121. 123-129, 131-156, 158. 160-192

---

248. Hills informs us that Paulus "was especially active in devising a naturalistic explanation for each one of the miracles of Christ. Jesus' walking on the water, Paulus explained, was an illusion of the disciples." *King James Version Defended*. 4th ed. (Des Moines, IA: Christian Research Press, 1984) 68.
249. *NSHE* 7:138. In this source, E. Barde reported "He clung to the harshest formulas of Calvinism, and yet loved souls so fervently that his benevolence often conquered the people who were at first repelled by his theology. He preached predestination without glossing even the most repulsive features, without shrinking from the consequences, but still with the simplicity of a child and the joy of a conqueror."

1830   ORME, William [alias CRITICUS]. *Memoir of the Controversy respecting the Heavenly Witnesses, 1 John V.7, including critical Notices of the Principal Writers on both sides of the Question* London:

This contains a wealth of data supplied by Orme, who regarded the *Comma* as spurious. Although this work provides the most comprehensive review of the history until 1830, certain treatises (e.g. by Hezel, Goeze) on the *Comma* are entirely neglected.[250]

1830   NOLAN, Frederick. *Supplement Into the Integrity of the Greek Vulgate, or Received Text of the New Testament; Containing the Vindication of the Principles Employed in its Defense.*

(This obscure book was listed on col. 642 of vol. 172 of *British Museum General Catalog of Printed Books*).

1831   LACHMANN, Karl. *Novum Testament Graece*. Berlin: 297, 488.

7 ὅτι τρεῖς εἰσὶν οἱ μαρτυροῦντες, 8 τὸ πνεῦμα καὶ τὸ ὕδωρ καὶ τὸ αἷμα, καὶ οἱ τρεῖς εἰς τὸ ἕν εἰσιν. 9.

Many mta claim that Lachmann's edition and the year 1831 mark a transition toward further decline of the use of the Received Text. For example, B.B. Warfield said "Many years passed away before the hardening bondage to the received text could be shaken, and it was not until 1831 that it was entirely broken."

1831   [Trinitarian Bible Society founded in London]

1831   CAREY, Willaim. [Oct 25: Letter to his sisters Ann & Mary]

"I wish to see Idolatry, Mahomedanism. . .swept from the face of the earth. . .I account Socianism and Arianism as nothing but modifications of Mahomedanism."[251]

1831   MALAN, César Henri Abraham. *Jesus Christus ist der ewige im Fleisch*

---

250. According to certain theology professors in Tübingen, the three names assosiated with the three fiercest debates in the history of Germany are M. Luther, G.W. Lessing, and D. Strauss. Goeze is said to be remembered by his debate with Lessing (who obtained and published *Wolfenbütteler Fragmente* by the Deist, H.S. Reimarus (1694-1768). Though old encyclopedias correctly say he is remembered for his debate with Lessing, there is no special entry for Goeze in *Allgemeine Deutsche Biographie* (1897) nor in *Neue Deutsche Biographie* (1964).
251. E.A. Payne "A 'Carey' Letter of 1831" *The Baptist Quarterly* IX No.1 (Jan 1938) 241.

geoffenbarte Gott.

This treatise was a reply to Chenevièr, who denied the divinity of Christ.

1832   [John Leland's re-affirmation of his views on redemption.]

In a letter to James Whitsitt, Leland affirmed his continued belief in certain articles of faith.[252] He had adopted them since 1774.

1832   [Reorganization of the Baptist Union]

Tracing the decline of belief in the doctrines of Sovereign Grace among Baptists, Nettles says with reference to the 1813 *Confession of Faith* of the Baptist Union:

"Article one, containing the distinctive doctrines of Calvinism, gave way to an extraordinary short doctrinal statement susceptible to the most extreme abuse. . ."[253]

Is it merely incidental that the point of decline of the transitional stage away from the Received Text ("A" below) occurred a year prior to the point of decline among Baptists of adherence to the doctrines of Sovereign Grace ("B" below)?

xxxxxxxxxxxxxxxxxxxxxxxxxxxxxxxxxxxxx
| 1831 "A" (Lachmann's text)

xxxxxxxxxxxxxxxxxxxxxxxxxxxxxxxxxxxxxx
| 1832 "B" (Baptist Union reorganisation)

1832   [New evidence for the *Comma*. Latin manuscript *m* (the Speculum) was discovered in this year. It is dated to the 5th century]

---

252. These articles include "2. That Christ did, before the foundation of the world, predestinate a certain number of the human family for his bride, to bring to grace and glory. 3. That Jesus died for sinners, and for his elect sheep only. 4. That those for whom he did not die, had no cause to complain, as the law under which they were placed was altogether reasonable. 5. That Christ would always call his elect to him while on earth, before they died." *The Writings of John Leland*, ed. L.E. Greene (1833, New York: Arno Press, 1969) 625. T.J. Nettles in *By His Grace and for His Glory* p. 140 says "For sixteen years he preached all over the area, and according to R.R. Sample, was the most popular preacher who ever resided in Virginia.
253. *By His Grace and For His Glory* 33.

Significance: *m* is regarded as an Old Latin MS. Thus the source of the inverted-*Comma* was not directly from the late Vulgate MSS, but from MSS which Jerome may have had, of which some would be similar to this 5th century Old Latin MS. The *Comma* in *m* is inverted.

In 1968 Metzger said the *Comma* "was taken into the text of the Old Latin Bible during the fifth century." There was no question that it was Old Latin. However, in 1977, he includes *m* with four others "that no longer are generally regarded as Old Latin".[254] But no explanation is provided.

1833 ERNESTI, J.A. *Principles of Biblical interpretation*, transl. from *Institutio interpretis* by Charles H. Terrot.

Ernesti's comment on the *Comma*:

> If the genuineness of the seventh verse depended on Greek MSS. alone, and was to be estimated by them solely, Griesbach would have gained his cause. But although the Greek MSS. take a lead in this inquiry, yet learned and skilful critics require other helps also. In my opinion, its connexion with the antecedent and subsequent verses prevents me from subscribing to their decisions, who think this verse ought to be expunged: for, in the ninth verse, a comparison is introduced between the testimony of men, and the tesimony of God himself; in which the apostle undoubtedly refers to these heavenly witnesses, of whom he had made mention a little before."[255]

1833 *The New Hamshire Confession of Faith*

Robert J. Barnett (of Grayling, Michigan) says "The New Hamspire Confession dropped many specific statements about God's sovereignty and replaced them with beautiful, short, pregnant statements which could have been interpreted one way by the Arminians and another by the Calvinists."[256]

How did this happen? Pastor Barnett explains "the historical decay of Bible preservation in Baptist circles" and provides a quote from W.L. Lumpkin's *Baptist Confessions of Faith*:

> These "Free Will" or Arminian Baptists were opposed to the strong stand on the sovereignty of God as found in the Philadelphia Confession of faith. As a

---

254. *Early Versions of the New Testament* (Oxford: Clarendon, 1977) 295. On p. 299, it is still dated to the 5th century.
255. *Institutio* as quoted by T.H. Horne *An Introduction to the Critical Study. . .*(1822) 521 n.1.
256. Barnett, *Word of God on Trial*, (Wyoming, MI: Paris Press, 1981) 7.

result, there was "a revolt against the rigid theological system of some Calvinistic Baptists. The New Hampshire thus sought to restate its Calvinism in very moderate tones."

1833 (Calcutta Baptist Missionaries) *The New Testament of Our Lord and Savior Jesus Christ, in the Bengallee Language; Translated from the Greek.* Calcutta, India: Baptist Mission Press, 22,196.

On page 22, we find Acts 8:37, and on page 196, we find the *Johannine Comma*, the only verse in the translation with brackets around it. Perhaps the missionaries had sincere doubts, but they did not cast out the verse.

1833 NORTON, Andrew. *Statement of Reasons for not believing the Doctrines of Trinitarianism concerning the Nature of God and the Person of Christ.*

When Erza Abbot obtained a copy of this book, he "wrote to the author expressing delight in the work, stating that he had made an index of it, and adding some discriminating remarks. Pleased with the letter, Norton invited the writer to visit him. The result was that Abbot went to Cambridge. . .rendering years of editorial service to Norton."[257]

A quote from section ix, "Explanation of Particular Passages fo the New Testament, Adduced by Trinitarians" revealing Norton's bitterness towards defenders of the *Comma*:

> 1 John v.7 . . .The value that has been formerly attached to this passage, though unquestionably interpolated, may be estimated from the obstinacy with which it has been contended for. . .and from the pertinacity with which the more ignorant or bigoted class of controversialists continue to quote and even defend it.

After this comment, he began discussing 1 Tim 3:16 in his next paragraph. He argued not for the reading θεος (God), nor for ὅς (he who), but rather for ὅ (which)!

---

257. *Dict of American Biography* 1:10.

1834   [Solomon C. Malan won the Boden (Sanskrit) Scholarship]

Solomon was about 22 at the time.

1834   HUYSHE, Francis. "Dr. Wiseman on 1 John V.7,8." *British Magazine*, (1835) v.702-707

1835   (The planting of a modern Baptist church in Hamburg, Germany.)

As a result of the further church-planting efforts of J.G. Oncken, Baptist churches of the modern type spread throughout Germany. By 1849, there were delegates from 37 Baptist congregations at the general conference in Hamburg. According to Professor Günther Balders of the Baptist Seminary[258] in Hamburg, the "kalvinistisch gesinnte Oncken"[259] "Calvinistic-minded Oncken" used the Authorized Version while he was in England. The Bibles he brought into Germany to distribute were editions by Martin Luther. Oncken was in favor of the doctine of verbal inspiration.[260]

1835   BURGESS, Thomas. *An Introduction to the Controversy on the disputed verse of St. John, as revived by Mr. Gibbon: to which is added Christina Theocracy; [or the doctrine of the Trinity and the Minstration of the Holy Spirit, the leading and pervading Doctrine of the New Testament in] a Second Letter to Mrs. Joanna Baillie* Salisbury:

1835   WISEMAN, Nicholas. *Two Letters on some parts of the Controversy concerning 1 John V.7.; containing also an Enquiry into the Origin of the first Latin Version of Scripture, commonly called the Italic.* Rome:
Cardinal Wiseman dealt with the question, "Why is Augustine said never to have quoted 1 John 5:7?" He argues on page 42 that

> The verse belongs essentially to the African text, and this writer used the Italian.

1835 * HUNT, William H. "Authenticity of 1 John v.7,8," *Literary and Theological Review*. New York: 2:141-148

1836   SCHOLZ, Martini Augustini. "Diatribe brevis in locum 1 Joannis V.7, 8." [In

---

258. The Theolgischer Seminar is on Renn Bahnstraße 115. I am grateful to Michael Kißkalt, a student at the seminary, who spoke with Prof. Günther on my behalf.
259. H.Luckey, *J.G. Oncken; und die Anfänge des deutschen Baptismus* 3rd ed. (Kassel: J.G. Oncken Verlag, 1958) 83.
260. Accordingly, he had tension with the Baptist preacher G.W. Lehmann (1799-1882), who held more lenient views.

vol.II. pp. 132,133. in his *Critical Edition of the New Testament*] Lipsiæ:

1836 * LÜCKE, Friedrich. *Commentar über die Briefe des Evangelisten Johnannes.* Bonn:

1836 [Baptist Board of Foreign Missions planned to form a separate organization for Bible translation: AFBS]

1837 [AFBS founded: American & Foreign Bible Society] Convention met at the First Baptist Church in Philadelphia.

Spencer H. Cone was elected as president of the AFBS.

1837 [S.C. Malan won the Pusey and Ellerton (Hebrew) Scholarship]

1837 BURGESS, Thomas. *Three Letters to the Rev. Dr. Scholz, Editor of a new Edition of the Greek Testament, Lips. 1836, on the Contents of his Note on 1 John v.7.* Southampton:

1837 * BLOOMFIELD, Samuel Thomas. Η Καινὴ Διαθήκη *The Greek Testament with English Notes, critical, philological, and exegetical.*

In 1828, in his *Recensio Synoptica*, vol. VIII, p. 776, he said it is "*probable* that the verses are genuine". In 1831, he considered the *Comma* as "verging to probability". In 1836, he was doubtful, and by 1839 he rejected the *Comma*.

1838 *The New Testament* by the AFBS.

1838 [AFBS resolution: "in the distribution in the English language, they will use the commonly received text version"]. This resolution was abandoned in 1849.

1839 * GAUSSEN, Samuel-Robert Louis. *Le Pleine inspiration des saintes Ecritures ou Théopneustia.*

Gaussen's book was translated into English in 1841, and into German in 1870. Kregel published David Scott's translation in 1971, (reprinted in 1979), and gave it the title *The Divine Inspiration of the Bible*. Gaussen, a French scholar, agrees with Middleton that the grammatical argument in defense of the *Comma* is valid. Apparently Scrivener read Gaussen in haste, for in reference to 1 John 5:7-8 he says that Gaussen "has still spirit remaining to press the masculine forms οἱ μαρτυροῦντες ver. 7 and οἱ τρεῖς vers. 8 as making in favour of the intervening clause: 'Remove it, and the grammar becomes incoherent:' a reason truly, but one not strong enough to carry his point"[261] But the statement is not from Gaussen. It is from Middelton, whom Gaussen quoted.

1840 [Jan: S.C. Malan departed from India due to failing health]

1840 SHARPE, Samuel. *New Testament, translated from the Greek of J.J. Griesbach.*

F.F. Bruce says the translator is "a Unitarian scholar."[262]

1842 BERNARD David, AARON Samuel *Revising and Amending King James' Version of the Holy Scripture.*

1842 [June 28: Letter by J.G. Oncken to a brother]

"The service.....are most numerously attended and the Spirit of God is.....own truth in the ingathering of God's elect."[263]

1842 [Discovery of the Curetonian Syriac]

It contains only portions of the Gospels, and is defective in the remainder. "It was found by Archdeacon Tatam in 1842, with 550 other MSS., in a convent of the Nitrian Desert". . .[264] This MS, denoted "sy^c", is noteworthy since Scrivener, Schaff, et al. have said it agrees closely with D (which is defective in 1 John) and the Old Latin, (which often contains 1 John, where we find the *Comma*).

1845 [Andrew Fuller's tract *Universal Atonement Refuted* was reprinted][265]

1846 [JUDSON: "Obedience to Christ's Last Command a Test of Piety"]

---

261. *Plain Introduction*, 3rd ed., p.654.
262. *The English Bible; a History of Translations* (London: Lutterworth Press, 1961) 130. Rev. Alexander Gordon said in the *DNB* 51:426 "His Greek text was that of Griesbach, and to this he always adhered, taking little interest in the progress of purely textual studies." See also (1862: SHARPE) and (1870: SHARPE).
263. "A Letter From J.G. Oncken to J.L. Angas." *The Baptist Quarterly* XII (1946-48) 42.
264. P. Schaff, *Companion to the Greek Testament* (London: MacMillan, 1883) 156.
265. The reprint was made by the Baptist Churches of Scotland. They merely gave a new title to Fuller's *Reply to Philanthropos*. The Baptists appended a supplement, from which on p. 20 they said "These churches never taught nor allowed to be taught amongst them that Jesus died for all men, for the whole human family, for Judas as well as for Peter, that many for whom he shed his precious blood shall perish."

Adoniram Judson, after more than 33 years (1813-1846) of missionary work, returned to American for less than a year and wrote this sermon, in which he asked "For what purpose did he leave the bosom of the Father, the throne of eternal glory, to come down to sojourn, and suffer and die in the fallen rebellious world?. . .-to redeem his chosen people from death and hell-. . ."[266]

1847 [J.J. Herzog accepted a call to teach at the Univ. of Halle]
"While there he became much interested in the Waldenses, two of his students being members of that sect, and he devoted himself to a historical investigation of their origin. . ."[267]

1848   PORTER, J. Scott. *Principles of Textual Criticism.* London: 494-512

Orme says "Professor Porter, however, is a Unitarian."

1848   HERZOG, J.J. *De Origine et Pristino Statu Waldensium secundum antiquissima eorum scripta cum libris Catholicorum ejusdem aevi collata.*

A.H.Newman said "This was the first serious effort to ascertain the exact historical facts regarding the origin and pristine condition of the Waldenses, by a careful comparison of Waldensian and Roman Catholic documents."[268]

1849   [May 11: AFBS abandoned its resolution made in 1838 to abide with the commonly received text] Isaac Davis made the motion for revision of the English version.

1849   CARTER, William. [lengthy paper against revision]

His paper was a long argument "against altering the common version [KJV] at all" (Armitage, *A History of the Baptists,* p. 900)

1850   [Apr 4: one of many meetings held to denounce the revision movement to correct the English version]

Many Baptists were "full of fiery denunciation of Cone, Wyckoff, and Colgate, and their sympathizer; as if they were guilty of the basest crimes for desiring" to

---

266. *Memoirs of the Life and Labors of the Rev. Adoniram Judson* (Boston: Phillips, Sampson, & Co) 519. [as quoted in *By His Grace and for His Glory* p.150.]
267. *NSHE* 5:252.
268. A.H. Newman "The Early Waldenses" *Baptist Quarterly Review* VII (1885) 301. According to Newman, J.J.Herzog argues in this thesis that Peter Waldo derived his name from a pre-existing sect.

supplant the KJV. (Armitage, p. 901). These Baptists felt their KJV "was now to be taken from them by force."

1850   [May 22: the 13th anniversary of the AFBS] A motion by Rev. Isaac Wescott was "that this Society . . .be restricted to the commonly received version, without note or comment"]

Wyckoff, Colgate and 10 others "all known revisionists" were banished. Armitage (p. 903) said "No person then present can wish to witness another such scene in a Baptist body to the close of life." Spencer H. Cone resigned as president.

1850   [May 27: meeting of 24 revisionists: defectors of the AFBS]

Thomas Armitage was one. Spencer Cone presided. Wm Colgate led in prayer. Armitage proposed this ecumenical resolution: "*Resolved* That in such as association we will welcome all persons to co-operate with us, who embrace the principles upon which we propose to organize, without regard to their denominational principles in other respects." (Armitage, *A History of the Baptists*, 907).

1850   [Jun 10: American Bible Union (ABU) was founded]

Although the ABU "had always disclaimed that it was a Baptist Society, yet a large majority of its life members and directors being Baptists. . ." (Armitage, p. 912). Cone, Wyckoff, and Colgate were respectively president, corr. secretary, and treasurer. Among the ABU revisors were Joseph Angus and J.L. Dagg, as well as even Philip Schaff. Rule #3 of the general rules for revision:

> 3. Translations or revisions of the New Testament shall be made from the received Greek text, critically edited, with known errors corrected.

1851   DIECKHOFF, August Wilhelm. *Die Waldenser im Mittelalter; Zwei Historische Untersuchung*. Göttingen:

A.H. Newman concurred with Herzog that Dieckhoff "went farther than the facts" when he concluded that most of the literature for which the Waldensian "claims of antiquity had been made. . .was the result of deliberate forgery on the part of Waldensian teachers after the beginning of the Reformation."[269]

1851   HORT, F.J.A. (letter to a friend)

---

269. Ibid. However, Dr. Newman also provides this quote from Dieckhoff: "The Waldensian sect belongs as a single member to a series of developments reaching far beyond it"

In volume I, page 211 of *Life and Letters of Fenton John Anthony Hort*, a letter by Hort reveals that he

> . . .dragged on with the villianous *Textus Receptus*. . . .Think of that vile *Textus Receptus* leaning entirely on late MSS.

The question arises: How do we explain the bias of so many conservative scholars in the late 1800's and throughout the 1900's, who are Trinitarians, against the *Johannine Comma*, the clearest proof-text for the doctrine of the Trinity? Adam Clarke described the attitude prior to 1807, that the opposition to the verse was "confined to the Unitarians of all classes." Such a bias from conservatives was generally unheard of in former centuries. Perhaps the real bias (whether expressed or not) of Trinitarians of the 20th century who protest against the *Comma*, is not so much against this Trinitarian citation, but against the settled-for-centuries nature of the Received Text. What else could the underlying bias be?

Their bias may range from slight to even the intensity expressed here by Hort. Perhaps they perceive they have no license to "restore the original text" by "correcting" the RT, until they find one spuriuos verse within it. Once they "discover" at least one error, then they assume a license to search for other errors. The *Comma* may be perceived as a barrier, that once overcome, is now a gateway that leads to liberty to begin attempts of "restoration." The *Comma* is seen as a weak spot. Hence, in chapters on the "orgins of the Textus Receptus" we see enormous efforts expended not on other verses, but upon what they perceive as the barrier to justify their attempts at "correction" and "restoration."

1851   NEANDER, August. *Der erste Brief Johannis; In berichtigter Lutherscher Uebersetzung von K.F.Th. Schneider*. Berlin: 232-233.

1852   DAVIDSON, Samuel. *Treatise on Biblical Criticism*. Edinburg: 403-426

1852   [The Bible Revision Association was founded]

The BRA co-operated with the ABU in the revision work. The BRA "was located in Louisville, KY." (Armitage, p. 918).

1852   LILLIE, John. *2 Peter, the Epistles of John and Jude.*

This work is of interest since it contains 1 John. A.S. Herbert, *Historical Catalog of Printed Editions of the English Bible 1525-1961* reports that a copy of this portion of the ABU Bible is at the ABS in New York. C.S. Malan selected to critique the first chapter of John's Epistle. The critiques extends from p. 332 to p.348 in *Vindication of the Authorized Version of the English Bible* (1856). Malan said Lillie's translation "deviates *twenty-one* times from the AUTHORIZED VERSION, in this short chapter of *ten* verses." (p. 332).

----------<The end of Horne's list>---------------------------

1853   HERZOG, J.J. *Die romanischen Waldenser, ihre vorreformatorischen Zustände und Lehren, ihre Reforation im 16. Jahrhundert und die Rückwirkungen derselben, hauptfächlich nach ihren eigenen Schriften.* Halle: Edwuard Anton. [470pp.]

In preparation for this work, Herzog "made himself master of the entire body of known Waldensian manuscripts"[270] and copied unprinted documents, and collated printed documents with the MSS.

1853   [J. Newton Brown revised the New Hamspire covenant]

This convenant "is still the accepted covenant of most Baptist churches."[271]

1853   [A paper read before the Royal Irish Academy]

The paper dealt with the Montfort Codex. A quote from p. 432:

> Forming his opinion from the sundry aspects of the Manuscript, its history, its readings, its character, its paper, Dr. Dobbin declared his conviction to be, that the Codex Montfortianus was written, from first to last within the last fifty years of the fifteenth century, and that by some half-learned scribes, -not by any one 'bold critic', as has been averred, nor by any unprincipled forger.

1854   DOBBIN, Orlando Thomas. *The Codex Montfortianus; A collation of this celebrated MS. in the library of Trinity College, Dublin, throughout the Gospels and Acts with the Greek text of Wetstein, and with certain mss. of the New Testaments.* London: C.J. Clay & Sons. [196 pp.] 40-57.

Scrivener says that in his day, Dr. Dobbin (1807-1890) was the last collator of this famous 61 ms. containing the *Comma*. Dr. Dobbin noted (p. 12):

> . . .the volume is of a small octavo size, contains in the whole 455 folios, and has only one leaf glazed--that exhibiting 1 John v.7--with white of egg, it would seem, or some other varnish, to protect this particular leaf, oftentimes referred to, and much handled, from fatal injury.

---

270. A.H.Newman, "Early Waldenses", *Baptist Quarterly Review* VII(1885) 305.
271. See "Southern Baptists and Church Covenants" *Baptist History and Heritage.* IX No. 1 (Jan 1974) 6, where R.A. Parker is quoted.

Dr. Dobbin makes on comment on p. 9 and refutes himself on p. 10. He says on page 9.

> The strongest proof of the identity of the Codex Britannicus with the Codex Montfortianus is that the text of the third edition of Erasmus, printed in 1522, differs in this interpolated passage from all other editions, except those which were immediately copied from it, and at the same time agrees word for word with the Codex Montfortianus.

He told us it agrees "word for word." Now he says on page 10:

> [Britannicus] agrees word for word with the text of the Codex Montfortianus, except in the omission of the word ἅγιον and of the article οἱ before μαρτυρουντες, which are clearly typographical errors. . .

Forster's argument that Britannicus is not the Montfort had not been published until 1867. Yet in 1854, despite Dr. Dobbin's bold claim on page 9, he does reveal his own doubt about the matter, by his careful use of the word "probably" in this clause from page 5:

> The Codex Montfortianus, called the Dublinensis, probably the same which Erasmus entitled Britannicus. . .

1855   CONANT, Thomas J. *Specimen of a Revision of the English Scriptures of the Old Testament*. New York: American Bible Union.

S.C. Malan has critiqued the revision by Conant (a Baptist revisionist) of Job 1 on pp. 165 to 232 of *A Vindication of the Authorized Version of the English Bible*.

1856   NOYES, George R. (ed.) *A Collection of Theological Essays from Various Authors* Boston: Amer. Unitarian Assoc. (See Appendix 3)

1856   [Ezra Abbot was appointed assistant librarian at Harvard]

1856   MALAN, Solomon Caesar. *A Vindication of the Authorized Version of the English Bible, from Charges brought against it by recent writers*. London: Bell & Daldy. [348 pp.] 229.

Malan "was descended from an old Waldensian family".[272] From his father Dr. C.H.A. Malan (1787-1864), Solomon "gained a conversational knowledge, not only of German, Spanish, and Italian, but also at an early age of Latin. He had also begun English, Hebrew, Arabic, and Sanskrit."[273] He studied Tibetan under Csoma Körösi, and "translated many works, chiefly religious, from the Russian, Welsh, Armenian, Arabic, Syriac, Coptic, Ethiopic, Georgian, Chinese, Japanese, and other languages;"[274] He was "acquainted with twenty-five to thirty languages."[275] Of his knowledge of ancient Egyptian, F.H.A. Scrivener said "a few Biblical scholars, as Bishop Lightfoot and especially the Rev. S.C. Malan, have made good progress in the ancient Egyptian; the rest of us must remain satisfied with a confession of ignorance, or apply our best diligence to remedy it."[276]

What was S.C. Malan's view on the *Comma*? From p. 229, we read:

> Take for instance 1 John v.7, than which, no verse in the Bible has been, and is, more contested; or St. John viii. 1-11, and like passages. We should still believe in the Most Holy Trinity, and we should still condemn adultery, if neither of those portions of Scripture had ever been written. At the same time, we should not welcome a version, or a revision, of the Bible, in which they were not found.

1856   ANGUS, Joseph. "Criticisms-Various Readings" *The Bible Hand-book; An Introduction to the Study of Sacred Scripture.* [revised by F.S. HOYT] (Philadelphia:) 65-67

1858   TRENCH, R.C. [his treatise on the "urgent need of revision"]

> ...I am persuaded that a revision ought to come. I am convinced that it will come.

1858 * TURNBULL, Joseph. *The Seven Epistles of James, Peter, John, and Jude, and the Revelation. Translated from the Original Greek, with Critical Notes, and a Dissertation on 1 John v.7,8.*

Dr. Turnbull argues in defense of the *Comma*. Tregelles reviewed it and according to Orme, he exposed a number of Turnbull's errors. One of the errors was said to

---

272. *DNB Supplement* 3: 133. For a biography, see Arthur Nolan Malan's *Solomon Caesar Malan, D.D. Memorials of his Life and Writings by his eldest surving son, Rev. A.N. Malan* (London: J. Murray, 1897) [445pp.].
273. Ibid.
274. *NSHE* 7:139.
275. Ibid.
276. *Plain Introduction* 3rd ed. p. 311.

be a confusion of *Codex Guelpherbytanus* XIV. 7 with *Codex Guelpherbytanus* D. The former is said to have the *Comma* in the margin, that latter is said to have it in the main text.

1859 REICHE. Johann Georg. *Commentarii in Novum Testamentum*. Göttingen: 326-327.

> Vs 7. Verba celeberrima, quae in textu recepto post μαρτυροῦντες sequuntur: ἐν τῷ οὐρανῷ --ἐν τῇ γῇ, de quorum authentia diu acerrime nec semper sine ira et studio, disputatum est, non esse manus Apostolicae, sed serius additamentum inter latinos ortum et post plura secula e latino in graecum versum, et quoque in graecum N.T. textum primo typis expressum a Complutensibus e Vulg. graece translatum illatum esse. . .

1860 [July: Tregelles examined the 3 Latin MSS of Ximenes]

1860 [The predominance of belief in an "inerrant" Bible]

"In the 1860's Baptists shared a predominant belief in the inerrancy of the Bible. During the period under survey [1865-1918], many men came to acknowledge the presence of a fallible human element in the Scriptures"[277]

1860 JOWETT, Benjamin, et al. *Essays and Reviews*. London:

In Jowett's essay he argued "that the only proper way to interpret it was to treat it 'like any other book'. The phrase was a refrain repeated throughout the lengthy essay. . ."[278]

---

277. Norman H. Maring, "Baptists and Changing Views of the Bible, 1865-1918 (Part I)", *Baptists; The Bible, Church Order and the Churches* (New York: Arno Press, 1980) 53.

278. N.M. de S. Cameron "Dean Burgon and the Bible: an Eminent Victorian and the Problem of Inspiration", *Themelios* 7 (Jan 1982) 16.

1860-1872 [E. Robinson was president of Rochester Theol. Seminary]

Ezekiel G. Robinson "was considered by some the foremost figure in the [Baptist] denomination in the latter half of the nineteenth century."[279] He acquired his "spirit of inquiry" from Barnas Sears.

1861   BURGON, John W. *Inspiration and Interpretation; seven Sermons preached before the University of Oxford. . .being an answer to the volume entitled 'Essays and Reviews'* Oxford and London:

A quote from page 89:

> The Bible is none other than *the voice of Him that sitteth upon the Throne!* Every Book of it--every Chapter of it--every verse of it--every word of it--every syllable of it--is the direct utterance of the Most High!

1862   SHARPE, Samuel. *The New Testament Translated from Griesbach's Text.* London: 382.

Sharpe had 8 editions of this work. This was his fifth.

> For there are three that bear witness, the spirit and the water and the blood; and these there agree in one. If we receive the witness of men. . .

1864   [C.H.A Malan died at the age of 76.] [280]

1864   *The New Testament.* American Bible Union.

The ABS Bible was such a miserable failure that "No separate copy of Part III (Galations to Revelation) has been located. . ." A.S. Herbert, *Historical Catalog of Printed Editions of the English Bible 1525-1961* (London & NY: BFBS & ABS, 1968) p. 412. Despite the fact that it was produced by Baptists "eager for an English 'immerse' version" (A.S. Herbert, p. 412), despite how T. Armitage praised it, it fell into such disfavor, that Baptists themselves abandoned it and returned to the Authorized Version.

---

279. Ibid. 56.
280. There are at least two biographies in English: *The Late Rev. Dr. Cesar Malan of Geneva* (1864), and *The Life, Labours, and Writings of Cæsar Malan* (1869) by Solomon Malan.

1865-1869   [Eberhard Nestle studied "im Seminar Blaubeuren"[281] Blaubeuren is a small town 7 miles east of Ulm. The old Benedictine cloister is located there.]

1866   TREGELLES, S.P. "On the Reading of 1 John v.7", *An Introduction to the Critical Study and Knowledge of the Holy Scriptures*. 4 vols., 11th ed. London: 4:355-384

1866   HORNE, T.H. "Appendix to Chap xxxvi", *An Introduction to the Critical Study and Knowledge of the Holy Scriptures*. 4 vols., 11th ed. London: 4:384-388.

This is the source from which this update has been made. Horne cites 55 distinct entries in his bibliography.

1866   ORME, William. *Memoirs of the Controversy Respecting the Three Heavenly Witnesses...A New edition with notes and appendix by Ezra Abbott.*

According to the *National Union Catalog*, these new editions of Orme were published in 1866, 1867, 1869, 1872, 1875, 1883; each with the notes of Erza Abbot. This is one of the most valuable sources for reading summaries from the various arguments, which have nearly always (with the exception of Charles Butler) been presented from the perspective of those objecting to the *Comma*.

1866   [H.B. Hackett was co-editor with a Unitarian]

H.B. Hackett was a Congregationalist, but became a Baptist in 1835. "In 1866 he began to edit an American edition of *Smith's Dictionary of the Bible*. Its publication took place between 1867 and 1870, and in this task he had the special co-operation of Prof. Ezra Abbot, D.D., LL.D., and some of the most able scholars of America." Cathcart, *The Baptist Encyclopedia; A Dictionary...* (1988 reprint, Paris, AR: Baptist Standard Bearer, 1881) 483.

1867   [December: letter from Henry G. Weston to Alvah Hovey]

Weston was, at the time, soon to be president of Crozer Theological Seminary. But his letter revealed "his unfamiliarity with Biblical problems which were coming to the fore."[282]

> . . .having to review in a slip-shod way Curtis on *Inspiration* before our Pastor's Conference, and that subject being one in which I am all at sea,

---

281. Erwin Nestle. "Eberhard Nestle: zu seinem 100. Geburtstag" *Kirchlich-theologische Halbmonatsschrift*, Nr. 9 (1951)
282. N.H. Maring, "Baptists and Changing Views of the Bible" *Baptists, The Bible, Church Order and the Churches*, 53.

except as a dogged belief in inspiration goes, without being able to define what "Inspiration" is, or what its metes and bounds are. . .I want you to give me what ideas you can conveniently put on two pages of note-paper. I'll fight for them to the death, for I shall heartily believe what you say.[283]

1867   [Baptists were not prepared for the onslaughts upon the Bible]

"Even men who were fairly well informed about theological currents in 1867 were hardly prepared to recognize the imminence of a revolution in Biblical thought and theology."[284]

1867   CURTIS, Thomas F. *The Human Element in the Inspiration of the Sacred Scriptures.*

"Although the prevailing spirit among Baptists was very conservative" Curtis was "one Baptist whose wide reading and inquiring mind had led him to break out of traditional paths much sooner than others."[285]

Curtis wrote on page 8 of his introduction;

> For many years I conscientiously and earnestly struggled to maintain the current theories of Infallibility and of Scripture Inspiration, until all possibility of doing so reasonably and honestly was gone.

"Unable to satisfy the doctrinal requirements any longer, he resigned [as professor of theology (1855-65)] from the University at Lewisburg."[286] He denied that "an infallible revelation" was possible, though he believed "firmly that the writers of the Scriptures were inspired."[287] But he denied inspiration of the words. "This broadside against infallibility was the first one fired by a prominent Baptist, and the only one for several years."[288]

1867   FORSTER, Charles. *A New Plea for the Authenticity of the Text of the Three Heavenly Witnesses, or Porson's Letter to Travis Eclectically Examined.* Cambridge: Deighton Bell & Co.

---

283. George R. Hovey, *Alvah Hovey; His Life and Letters* (Phila: Judson Press, 1928) 161 (as quoted by N. Maring in "Baptists and Changing Views of the Bible" 53.)
284. N.H. Maring, "Baptists and Changing Views of the Bible, 1865-1918" *Baptists, The Bible, Church Order and the Churches,* 53.
285. Ibid. 54.
286. Ibid.
287. Ibid. 55
288. Ibid.

From p. 126:

> Bishop Marsh labours hard to identify the Codex Britanicus used by Erasmus, with the Codex Montfortianus. Erasmus's own description of the Codex Britannicus completely nullifies the attempt: 'Postremo: Quod Britannicum etiam in terrae testimonio addebat, καὶ οἱ τρεῖς εἰς τὸ ἕν εἰσι, quod non addebatur hic duntaxat in editione Hispaniensi.' Now as this clause is also omitted in the Montfort Codex, it cannot possibly be the same with the Codex Britannicus. In this as yet undiscovered MS., we have a second and independent Gr. MS. witness to the seventh verse.

Porson (1790) did not anticipate this objection, and F.H.A. Scrivener acknowledged it, but did not adequately respond to it.

Forster also notes that Chark and Ussher were not only collators of the Montfort Codex "which its dogmatic censors, Marsh, Michaelis, and Porson, *never saw*" (p. 127) but Chark and Ussher were "its possessors; and who make no note whatever of its recency in their time." (p. 128).

1868   [New evidence in favor of the *Comma*. The disputed prologue of Jerome was discovered in manuscript *fu*.]

1868   CATHCART, William. *The Remarkable Preservation by Divine Providence of the Hebrew and Greek Scriptures*. American Baptist Publication.

This was an address delivered by Cathcart, author of *The Baptist Encyclopedia*, at the September meeting of the Baptist Sunday school Association of Philadelphia.

1869   MALAN, Solomon Ceasar. *A Plea for the Received Greek Text and for the Authorized Version of the New Testament, in Answer to some of the Dean of Canterbury's Criticism of Both*. London: Hatchards. [212pp.]

1869   [William Witsitt studied at Leipzig under Tischendorf]

W. Whitsitt, who later became president of the Southern Baptist Theological Seminary, had finished as a student at the U of Virginia (1866) and at the SBTS in

KY (1868). Then he "studied in 1869-'70 at the University of Leipzig"[289] and Berlin (1870-71). He studied under Luthardt, Curtius, Lipsius, "and L.F.K. Tischendorf". [290]

1870 [Samuel Sharpe was invited to be on the ERV committee.]

"When, in 1870, the project of a revised version was undertaken by the convocation of Canterbury, Sharpe was one of four scholars of his denomination invited to select a member of their body to co-operate with the New Testament Company." Sharpe was "president of the British and Foreign Unitarian Association in 1869-70. . ."[291]

1871 KRAUTH, Charles P. *The Conservative Reformation and Its Theology*. Minneapolis: Augsburg Publ. House, 1978 reprint. 98.

A quote from Krauth concerning the *Johannine comma*:
> Luther rejected it on critical grounds, and it did not appear in any of his Bibles published in his lifetime.

1871 DABNEY, Robert L. "The Doctrinal Various Readings of the New Testament Greek" *The Works of Robert L. Dabney*. 3 vols. London:Banner of Truth. 1967 reprint. 1:377-382

The following is the GRAMMATICAL DEFENSE as given by Dabney. Frederick Nolan remarked "This objection was first started by the learned Abp. Eugenius, . . . and may be seen in a letter prefixed by M. Matthæi to his Greek testament".[292] For some reason, the critics seldom notice the problem of mismatched genders[293] if the *Comma* is removed. Tregelles, in the article preceding Horne's bibliography of the *Comma*, did not object to the argument! He even refers to an article in *Classical Journal*, vol. ii. pp.869-871. Jack A. Moorman notes that the "leading Greek scholars as Metzger, Vincent, Alford, Vine, Wuest, Bruce, Plummer, do not make the barest mention of the problem."[294]

---

289. *Appleton's Cyclopedia of Amer. Biography* (NY: D. Appleton & Co., 1889) VI: 491.
290. *Dictionary of Amer. Biography* (NY: Charles Scribner's) 20: 170.
291. *DNB* 51:426.
292. *Inquiry into the Integrety of the Greek Vulgate or Received Text of the New Testament*, p. 257
293. I.A. Marshall in *The New Testament Commentary;* rejected the *Comma* as "such a weakly attested reading" whose "added words cause a break in the sense". Then he admits the mismatched genders! He comments "It is striking that although *spirit*, *water*, and *blood* are all neuter nouns in Greek, they are all introduced by a clause expressed in the masculine plural: τρεῖς εἴσιν οἱ μαρτυροῦντες.
294. *When the KJV Departs from the "Majority Text"*

The internal evidence against this excision, then, is in the following strong points; *First*, if it be made, the masculine, article, numeral, and participle, οἱ τρεῖς μαρτυροῦντες, are made to agree directly with three neuters -an insuperable and very bald grammatical difficulty. But if the disputed words are allowed to stand, they agree directly with two masculines and one neuter noun, ὁ Πατὴρ, ὁ Λόγος, καὶ τὸ ἅγιον Πνεῦμα; where, according to a well known rule of syntax, the masculines among the group control the gender over a neuter connected with them. Then the occurrence of the masculines τρεῖς μαρτυροῦντες in the eighth verse agreeing with the neuters, Πνεῦμα ὕδωρ and αἷμα may be accounted for by the power of attraction, so well known in Greek syntax, and by the fact that the Πνεῦμα, the leading noun of this second group, and next to the adjectives, has just had a species of masculineness superinduced upon it by its previous position in the masculine group.

1871 [Erza Abbot, a Unitarian, was appointed lecturer at Harvard]

Mr. Ezra Abbot's position was lecturer on the Textual Criticism of the New Testament.

1871   BURGON, John W. *The Last Twelve Verses of the Gospel according to Mark Vindicated against Recent Critical Objectors and Established*. Oxford and London: James Parker and Co. 15.

> But it is a known rule in the Law of Evidence that *the burthen of proof lies on the party who asserts the affirmative of the issue*. We have therefore to ascertain in the present instance what the supposed proof is exactly worth; remembering always that in this subject-matter a *high degree of probability* is the only kind of proof which is attainable. When, for example, it is contended that the famous words in S. John's first Epistle (1 S. John v. 7,8,) are not to be regarded as genuine, the fact that they are away from almost every known Codex is accepted as a proof that they were also away from the autograph of the Evangelist. On far less weighty evidence, in fact, we are at all times prepared to yield the hearty assent of our understanding in this department of sacred science.

In *Demystifying the Controversy over the Textus Receptus*, D.S. Chinn and R.C. Newman interpreted this paragraph as indicating that "Burgon in this passage rejects the authenticy of I John 5:7." But to arrive at this conclusion they admitted "Burgon's style of writing is perhaps somewhat unclear in this section. He is discussing what would consitute sufficient evidence to reject the authenticity of this ending of Mark. As an example of what would constitute "proof" for the ending of Mark to be counterfeit, he cites the manuscript evidence for I John 5:7, i.e. "the fact that they are away from almost every known codex is acepted as a proof that they were also away from the autograph of the Evangelist." At this point, one might wonder whether or not this "fact. . . is accepted" by Burgon himself." (p. 24). Agreed!

1872   [S.C. Malan visited the Crimea, Georgia][295]

1872   TISCHENDORF, Constantine. *Novum Testamentum Graece: Editio Octava Maior*. Lipsiea: Giesecke & Devrient. 377-341

These notes on 1 John 5:7, which A.T. Robertson recommended, must have had a widespread influence. For this reason, his notes on 1 John 5:7 here, and perhaps in any of his correspondence [296] deserve special treatment in a new edition of this work.

1873   [C.R. Gregory left America and settled in Leipzig]

He went to Leipzig for study "perhaps under incentive from Ezra Abbot"[297]

1873   [Adolf von Harnack received his doctorate from Leipzig.][298]

1874   [Eberhard Nestle received his doctorate from Tübingen.]

1874   [F.H. Kerfoot studied at the Univ. of Leipzig]

"In 1874 after a visit to Egypt and the Holy Land, Kerfoot studied at the Univ of Leipzig."[299] In 1889, Kerfoot (1847-1901) succeeded J.P. Boyce in the Chair of Systematic Theology at the Southern Baptist Theological Seminary.

1874   [The death of K. Tischendorf]

1874? HALEY, John W. *Alleged Discrepancies of the Bible*. 1977 Reprint. Grand Rapids: Baker.

> I John 5 v.7 is a spurious passage. It is found in no Greek manuscript before the fifteenth or sixteenth century, and in no early version. It is rejected by

---

295. Here "he was the guest of Bishop Gabriel and preached in Georgian at the cathedral of Kutais" *DNB Supp* 3: 134.
296. The *Inventar der Wissenschaftlichen Nachlässe* (Leipzig: Kleine Schriften der Universitätsbibliothek, 1985) by Dr. Detlef Döring, indicates that it consists of 32 Kapseln, 2 Bände, 3 Päckchen.
297. *Dictionary of American Biography* 1:11.
298. *TRE* 14:451 "Auf die Promotion 1873 folgte ein Jahr später die Habilitation in Leipzig." He was about 22 at the time.
299. *Encycl of Southern Baptists* 2:749.

Alford, Abbot, Bleek, Scrivener, Tischendorf, Tregelles, Wordsworth, and most modern critics.

1874 [Eberhard Nestle was a *Stadtvikar* in Ravensburg, and a *Stiftbibliothekar* in Tübingen. In the spring, he went to Leipzig.]

1875-1877 [Eberhard Nestle studied in England.][300]

1875 [New evidence for the *Comma*. The Old Latin manuscript *q* was discovered in this year.]

Kenyon says it was "noticed by Tischendorf, and published by Ziegler in 1876."

1876 [C.R. Gregory earned his Ph.D. at the University of Leipzig.]

1876 [B.B. Warfield studied at the University of Leipzig]

He began his study abroad soon after his graduation at Princeton. Tischendorf had passed away in 1874.

1877 HOVEY, Alva. *Manual of Systematic Theology and Chistian Ethics* (Boston:)

It was said of Hovey, "Probably no other American Baptist ever spoke with more *ex cathedra* influence than he,"[301] Maring said "many Baptists considered him a veritable oracle."[302]
On page 77 of his *Manual* he claims inspiration, not for the words of Scripture, but for the writers:

> . . .that the sacred writers were moved, and assisted by the Holy Spirit to put on record all which the Bible, apart from ERRORS IN THE TEXT, now contains. [emphasis mine]

Maring says "he rejected the theory of verbal inspiration"[303] in favor of *dynamical inspiration*. Maring refers to a quote from a student that Hovey once said in class "The verbal theory of inspiration is a gigantic swindle."[304]

1878-1879 [C.R. Gregory was pastor of the Amer. Chapel (Leipzig).]

---

300. He studied Syriac MSS in the British Musuem.
301. W.H. Allison, "Alva Hovey" *Dict. of American Biography*. 9: 270.
302. "Baptists and Changing Views of the Bible" 54.
303. Ibid. 59.
304. Ibid. 60. See E.G. Robinson's *An Autobiography, With a Supplement*...(1896)

1879   [Crawford H. Toy resigned from the SBTS in Louisville KY]

"Irwin T. Hyatt, Jr., reports that Toy did in fact join the Unitarian Church when he went to Harvard. . ."[305]

1879   LASHER, George W. "Inspiration," Part II *The Baptist Review* I,#2,260.

Lasher, editor of *The Journal And Messenger* was one of the few Baptists, who did not conform to the fashionable criticism of the Bible. His admirable stand for inspiration was that it "extends to the very language employed by the writer. . . so that one jot or one tittle of the Word cannot be removed or altered.[306]

1880   KITTO, John, *Cyclopædia of the Biblical Literature*. New York: American Book Exchange. 2:137-141

1881   *English Revised Version; New Testament*

If the renumbering of the Greek text of I John 5:6-8 indeed first occurred in 1776, we ought to be interested when the renumbering[307] first occurred in the English text. For anyone interested in tracing back to this event, they are welcome to obtain and check each of over 2000 English versions listed in *Catolog of Printed English Bibles* by A.S. Herbert. Perhaps it was the English Revised Version. Recently, in 1990, a professor Emeritus of New Testament actually spoke in defense of the 1881 renumbering:

> When the English Revised Version (1881) dropped the spurious passage concerning the three witnesses, the verse numbering was moved back to give a more balanced verse division. This numbering was also used in the ASV (1901), the NASB, and the RSV. [308]

After only a few decades, the ERV fell into relative disuse. Many Christians in this generation have never heard of it. In his valuable article "Baptists and Changing View of the Bible 1865-1918" covering over 50 pages, Norman H. Maring was completely silent about the ERV.

1881   [Solomon Malan joined Burgon in the fight against the ERV]

---

305. *Baptists and the Bible*, 239.
306. As quoted by Maring "Baptists and Changing Views of the Bible" 69.
307. I John 5:6 was divided into two verses (6a & 6b) and verse 6b was then renumbered as verse 7
308. D.Edmond Hiebert, "An Exposition of I John 5:1-12," 147 *Bibliotheca Sacra* Apr-Jun 1990 #586, 225 n25.

"In 1881 Malan joined in the onlslaught made by John Willaim Burgon [q.v. Suppl.] on the revised version of the New Testament, contributing to his articles, and himself publishing a new version of Matthew i-vi, with an appendix giving the Lord's prayer in seventy-one languages. This he followed up in 1882 by a work directed against the Greek text of Drs. Westcott and Hort..."[309]

1881   EACHES, O.P. "What Latitude of Belief is Allowed by the Doctrine of Inspiration?" *Baptist Review* III, #2, 196.

In this article, Eaches uttered this absurdity:

> We cannot and ought not to start with the theory that there can be no mistakes in God's word; . . .

1881-1889   [Higher Criticism prevailed]

"The so-called "higher criticism" did not assume great importance in the United States until the eighties. . ."[310]

1882   [Ezra P. Gould was dismissed from Newton Theol. Institution]

The Baptist professor was teaching unorthodox view of the Scriptures.

1882   [J.P. Boyce studied the Hort-Westcott theories]

James P. Boyce, the principle founder of the first Southern Baptist Seminary in Louisville, KY, "was especially interested in Text-criticism. . .When the second volume of Westcott and Hort's Greek Testament appeared, containing their elaborate system of text-criticism, he went carefully through it, though the style is difficult, and mastered with great satisfaction its scientific method and interesting results." J.A. Broadus, *Memoir of James Petigru Boyce, D.D., LL.D.* (NY: A.C. Armstrong & Sons, 1893) 270.

---

309. *DNB Supp* 3: 134.
310. "Baptists and Changing Views of the Bible" 61.

1882   HORT, F.J.A. "Notes on Select Readings" *The New Testament in the Original Greek*. New York: Harper's & Brothers. Appendix 2:103-106

> Three new and interesting testimonies on behalf of the inserted words have subsequently come to light, those of *m* in 1832, of *q* in 1875, and of the occurrence of the Pseudo-Hieronymic Prologue in *fu* in 1868.

1882   SAMSON, George Whitefield. *The Text Used for the Revised New Testament Shown to Be Unauthorized*. Cambridge, MA: Moses King. Reprint. 1988. Bible For Today. 76-78

1882   KELLER, Ludwig. "An Apostle of the Anabaptists." *Preussische Jahrbücher*. (transl. by Henry S. Burrage, D.D. for the *Baptist Quarterly Review*).

This article reveals the duration (3 centuries!) of the erroneous views towards Anabaptist.

Keller, who was of the German Reformed Church, and archivist in Münster, and later in Berlin, began his article:

> Whenever, at the present time, the name "Anabaptist" is mentioned, the majority think only of the fanatical sect, which under the leadership of John of Leyden, established the kingdom of "New Jerusalem" at Münster. The history of of the religious ideas whose caricature appears in the communism at Münster, however, in no wise connects itself with the beginning and end of that short episode. There were "Baptists" long before the Münster rebellion, and in all the centuries that have followed, in spite of the severest persecutions. . .

1883   [Tübingen appointed Eberhard Nestle to their faculty.]

1883   MORGAN, Thomas J. [May 22-23 resolution of The Baptist Bible Convention (with 436 delegates)] Saratoga:

> Resolved. . .whatever organization or organizations shall be designated as the most desirable for the prosecution of Home Bible work among American Baptists should now circulate the commonly received version, *The New Revised Version, with the corrections of the American Revisors incorporated in the text*, and the translation of "The American Bible Union," according to demand. . .

Schaff comments "The American Baptists, the most numerous denomination in the United States, next to the Methodists. . .came to the unanimous conclusion to adopt and circulate ...*the Anglo-American Revsion*"

1883   [The Baptist Congress]

The president of Bucknell University said at this congress

> ...even WERE IT CONCEDED that the Scriptures are FULL OF ERRORS, containing solar myths, legends, and fables, they still remain as witnesses to the fact that man is a religious being,...Religion stands or falls with the living God. It is not a question of manuscripts. [emphasis mine] [311]

1883   BURGON, John William. *Revision Revised*. Paradise, PA: Conservative Classics, 483.

Commenting on Griesbach's corruption of 1 Tim 3:16, Burgon says:
> At first indeed (viz. in 1777) he retained Θεός in his Text, timidly printing ὅς in small type above it...But, at the end of thirty years (viz. in 1806), waxing bolder, Griesbach substituted ὅς for Θεός...

The quote is from page 482. On the next page, Burgon remarked that Griesbach's own reasoning on 1 John 5:7 can also be applied against himself for chosing ὅς.

> My only wonder is, how an exhibition of 1 Tim. iii. 16 so feebly attested, -so almost *without* attestation, -can have come to be seriously entertained by any. "Si," -(as Griesbach remarks concerning 1 John v.7)-"si tam pauci...testes....sufficerent ad demonstrandum lectionis cujusdam γνησιότητα, licet obstent tam multa tamque gravia et testimonia et argumenta; *nullum prorsus superesset in re criticâ veri falsique criterium*, et *textus Novi Testamenti universus plane incertus esset atque dubius.*"

In other words, if Griesbach argues against 1 John 5:7, on the basis of a paucity of MSS support, why doesn't he likewise argue against ὅς in 1 Tim 3:16? In this context, Burgon did not reveal his opinion about the *Comma*. The context is 1 Tim 3:16.[312]

1883   SCRIVENER, F.H.A. *A Plain Introduction to the Criticism of the New Testament*. 3rd. ed. Cambridge: Deighton Bell & Co. 8,187,196,258

---

311. *The Baptist Congress 1883*, 70-71 (as quoted by Maring "Baptists and Changing Views of the Bible," 65.)

312. Gary Hudson, in his article "Why Dean Burgon Would Not Join the Dean Burgon Society"(1990), has attempted to prove from Burgon's quote of Griesbach that "Oh yes, Burgon would have to be included in Scrivener's list of those credible scholars of his day who rejected 1 John 5:7!" [p.11]. But Mr. Hudson quoted out of context, and by carefully avoiding any mention of 1 Tim 3:16 in his article, he misleads his readers.

n.1,314,345,355,360,408,411,425,427,432,433 and n.1,434 n.2,435 n.2,445 n.1, 496,498 n.2,511,513,648-655.

With all these pages numbers, each referring to the *Comma*, one can't help but wonder why such a scholar would give so much attention to one verse. In the section on "The Amenian Version", the inclusion of *Comma* is mentioned in the first printed Armenian Bible (A.D. Uscan). However, in the fourth edition (1894), the section on the Armenian version has been rewritten by E. Miller. Thus neither the one MS out of Zohrab's eighteen, nor Uscan's Bible, both of which contain the *Comma*, are mentioned any more.

1883   WARFIELD, B.B. *An Introduction to the Textual Criticism of the New Testament*. London: Hodder & Stoughton.

1883   SCHAFF, Philip. *A Companion to the Greek Testament and the English Version*. London: 192-193,429.

Schaff says Luther did not translate the *Comma*. "Strange to say, it is retained in the recent authoritative revision of Luther's text, though in brackets" He continues "Truth, honesty, and piety demand its expulsion from the Word of God."

1883   ARMFIELD, Henry T. *The Three Witnesses, the disputed text in St. John's Considered Old and New*. London: Bagster. [219 pages]

1884   [J.H. Thayer succeeded Ezra Abbot at Harvard Divinity School]

Thayer "resided in Cambridge, first assisting his friend, Ezra Abbot, and after his death in 1884, succeding him as Bussey professor of New Testament criticism and interpretation in the Harvard Divinity School."[313] Thayer was a member of the American committe of the ERV (1881) as well as the American Standard Version (1901). "The honary degree of S.T.D. was conferred on him by Harvard, Yale and Princeton universities. . ."[314]

1884   HUTTLE, Max, ed. *Der Codex Teplensis enthalend Die Schrift des Newen Gezeuges*. Augsburg-München: Literarischen Institute von Dr. Max Huttler. [Comba: "F. Klimesch, author of the publication of the Codex Teplensis"] (Check "Dritte Theil", 21, for appearance of the *comma*)

(There are three reasons why this MS ought to be of extreme interest. First, it contains the *Comma*. Second, it is claimed to have been <u>widely</u> used by the Waldenses. To grasp the importance of this medieval group, let us quote from three

---

313. *Nat'l Cyclopedia of Amer. Biogr.* 6:428-29.
314. Ibid.

Reformed scholars. Theodore Beza referred to these *Valdenses* as *veteris Christianæ purior Ecclesiæ semen*, i.e., "the very seed of the Christian Church.[315] A.A. Hodge said that "The Waldenses, of whom were the 'slaughtered saints whose bones lie scattered on the Alpine mountains cold,'. . .were all Calvinists."[316] Jonathan Edwards said in a sermon "there was a certain people called the Waldenses that lived separate from all the rest of the world, that kept themselves pure" Later he said "One of the popish writers speaking of the Waldenses, says the heresy of the Waldenses is the oldest heresy in the world."[317] Third, the Tepl contains Received Text readings, as shown in appendix four. D.A. Carson speaks of the Received Text as "the standard one at the time of the Elzevirs."[318] The RTa, however, claim that the RT was in use during the time of the Elzevirs, and centuries *before* the Elzevirs.[319] After the 1885 debate in Germany over its origin, interest was soon lost in the Tepl, and the debate and even the codex was forgotten.[320] But let it be known that the facts indicate that the *Comma* was transmitted through the Received Text by the Waldenses in their Latin, French,[321] and even Old German translations, centuries before Erasmus. But this stage is often bypassed in modern accounts, which merely state that the *Comma* came from the late MSS of the Vulgate, and finally entered the printed Greek editions.)

During his post-graduate studies, John T. Christian, D.D.,spent five different periods at European Universities,[322] He may have even been aware of the Tepl, since it contained the Laodicean epistle:

The Waldenses translated the Bible into the Romance and Teutonic languages

---

315. Samuel Morland, *The History of the Evangelical Churches of the Valleys of Piedmont*, (1658, Gallatin, TN: Church History Research and Archives, 1982), p. a6. Moreland's marginal reference reads "Icones Theod. Bezæ, de Vald. GENEVÆ apud Joan. Laonium An. Dom. 1580. Excus."
316. *Johnson's New Universal Cyclopedia;* (NY: A.J. Johnson & Sons, 1875) 1:733.
317. *Works of Edwards*, 419.
318. *The King James Version Debate*, p. 36
319. In *Revision Revised*, p. 392, Dean Burgon, who is a MTA, said in reply to Ellicot:"For my own part, being fully convinced, like yourself, that essentially the Received Text is full 1500 years old, -(yes, and a vast deal older,) . . .
320. J. Andorf did write a dissertation on the Tepl in 1964. See (1964: ANDORF) in this paper.
321. At the Third Lateran Council of 1179, Walter Map saw French translations of the Psalter "and other books of the Bible. Investigations undertaken on the order of Innocent III in 1199 revealed nothing in these works contrary to orthodoxy, although the translations were associated with the Waldenses" Raymond C. St-Jacques "Bible,French", *Dictionary of the*

early in the thirteenth century, the Baptists retained these versions two hundred years after Luther's version. The oldest German Bible is of Baptist origin. In these versions alone the Epistle of Paul to the Laodiceans appears.[323]

1885   FOX, Norman. "The Inspiration of the Apostles in Speaking and Writing," *The Baptist Quarterly Review* VII, #28, 469-82.

On p. 469 of this aritical, Mr. Fox, formerly a student of E.G. Robinson, believed that inspiration should be:

> . . .declared of an apostle's oral deliverances not that they *were* the word of God, but that they *contained* the word of God.

When asked "How then will we ever decide which parts of the Bible are the word of God and which are not?" he replied:

> The answer is EASY. . .We decide by examining. . .whether it accords with the teachings of the Old Testament prophets and with the still older revelation of God found in the HUMAN CONSCIENCE and COMMON SENSE.[emphasis mine]

The views of Norman Fox stirred up much debate. Heman Lincoln said that if Fox is right, then "The ultimate authority is no longer the Bible but the human reason."[324]

1885   KELLER, Ludwig. *Die Reformation und die älteren Reform parteien.*

(Quote from Comba's *History of the Waldenses from Italy*) "...Keller, an original writer, .. and versed in the history of the sects of the middle-ages, declared the Tepl manuscript to be Waldensian."

1885   HAUPT, Herman. *Die Deutsche Bibelübersetzungen der mittelalterlichen Waldenser in dem Codex Teplensis and der ersten gedruckten deutschen Bibel nachgewiesen*. Würzburg: Druck und Verlag der Stahel'schen Universitäts-Buch-und Kunsthandlung.

Middle Ages, (New York: Charles Scribner's Sons, 1983) 2:218.
322. *National Cyclopedia of American Biography*. (NY: J.T. White, 1929), 20:449.
323. J.T. Christian, *A History of the Baptists*, 2 vols. (Texarkansas: Bogard Press, 1922), 1:91.
324. *Baptist Quarterly Review*, 1886, VIII, No. 1, p. 65 (as quoted by N. Maring "Baptists and Changing Views of the Bible", 71.)

(Haupt, an Old Catholic, argues for a Waldensian orgin of this German codex)

1885   JOSTES, Franz. *Die Waldenser und die vorlutherische deutsche Bibelübersetzungen.*

(A Reply to Haupt's work)

1885   SCHAFF, Philip. "The Waldensian Bible" *The Independent,* October 8,
A quote regarding the Tepl Codex:

> This is a MS of the German New Testament dating probably from the close of the fourteenth century, and is identical with the printed German texts before Luther.

At least in one respect, they differ. The pre-Lutheran bibles have the *Comma* inverted, with the earthy witnesses first. The Tepl has the heavenly witnesses first.

1885   ABBOT, Ezra. [His notes on Scrivener's *Plain Introduction.*]

These notes were edited by J.H. Thayer.[325]

1886   *Proceedings of the Fifth Annual Session of the Baptist Congress*

In general, what was the prevailing view of inspiration among Baptists at this time. One professor said (on page 24 of this report):

> ...orthodox opinion on the subject of inspiration is undergoing a change.

1886   SCHEPPS, Georg. *Priscillian, ein Neuaufgefundener Lat. Schriftsteller des 4. Jahrhunderts.* Würzburg: 13-14

This is from the lecture delivered by Dr. Schepps on May 18th, 1886 at the Philological-Historical Society in Würzburg:

> Die Zeit gestattet nicht, heute auf diese Fragen näher einzugehen, doch will ich noch kurz berühren, dass in den Bibelcitaten Priscillians oft die frappanteste Ähnlichkiet mit dem berühmten "Speculum Augustini" hervortritt, daß u. a. wie in letzterem auch das Comma Johanneum citiert wird...

1886   MARTIN, Jean Pierre Paulin. *Introduction à la critique textuelle du Nouveau Testament; Paritie Pratique.* 5 vol. Paris: Maisonneuve, (1884-1866), vol. 5.

---

325. See "Thayer" *National Cyclopedia of American Biography* 6:429.

1886   DELITZSCH, F. *Fortgesetzte Studien zur Entstehungsgeschichte der Complutensischen Polyglottenbibel.* Leipzig: 51-52.

In these two pages, Delitzch commented on the 3 Latin MSS which Tregelles reported were owned by Cardinal Ximenes. All contained the *Comma*, but comparisons led to the conclusion that the Complutensian editors did not use these 3 MSS.

1886   BERGER, Samuel. "deutsche Bibelübersetzungen" *Revue Historique,* Jan-Apr 30:184-190. Microfiche.

A quote:
> Who else then, in Germany, if not a Vaudois, could have had the idea to translate the Bible from provencal, when the Latin text was in everybody's hands?

1886   [H.C.Hoskier visited Dean Burgon at Chicester.]

1886   [C.R. Gregory married the daughter of J.H. Thayer]

"In 1886 he was married at Cambridge, Mass., to Lucy Watson Thayer, daughter of Joseph Henry Thayer [*q.v.*]; They had one son and three daughters."[326] Two years earlier (1884) B.W. Bacon said that Ezra Abbot "also coöperated with his pupil, Prof. Caspar René Gregory, in bringing out the *Prolegomena* to Tischendorf's last critical edition. . ."[327] C.R. Gregory was not only a pupil of a famous Unitarian (E.Abbot) but married the daughter of the Unitarian, J.H. Thayer.

---

326. "Gregory, Caspar René" *Dictionary of Amer. Biogr.* 7:601.
327. *Dict. of Amer. Biog.*

1886   BERGER, Samuel. "Haupt: Die Bibelübersetzung der Waldenser" *Revue Historique*, Sep-Dec 32:164-169. Microfiche.

> ...in 1231 a synod gathered at Treve, states that all the heretics of the town, many of whom seem to have been Vadois had the German Bible in their hands.

1886   HAUPT, Herman. *Die waldensische Ursprung des Codes Teplensis und der vorlutherischen deutschen Bibeldrucke gegen die Angriffe von Dr. Iostes.*

1886   JOSTES, Franz. *Die Tepler Bibelübersetzung; Eine Zweite Kritic.*

(Jostes challenges Haupt again, and argues for a Catholic origin)

1886   KELLER, Karl Ludwig. *Die Waldenser und die deutschen Bibelübersetzungen*. Leipzig:

Dr. Keller "studied classical philology at the universities of Leipzig and Marburg" (*Mennonite Ency*, vol. iii, p.162)

1886   BILTZ, Karl. "Die neuesten Schriften...", *Archiv für das Studium der neuereu Sprachen und Litteraturen*. vol. 76, n.1 and 2.

Regarding the Tepl MS, the "learned philologist Biltz" (1830-1901), says:

> I have more than one reason for believing it to be a certain fact, that the first German translation originated outside the orthodox centre, and in the midst of dissidence.

SIGNIFICANCE: The Tepl Codex contains RT readings in German. Anyone outside the orthodox "centre" was labeled "heretic". It is this sense of the term Verduin has in mind when he said "It is quite certain that as Luther worked at his translation of Scripture he leaned heavily upon "heretical" translations already in existence; it has been argued that he simply copied over whole pages from the "Picard Bible." a procedure for which his enemies in the Catholic Church rebuked him.[328] ")

1886   MARTIN, Jean Pierre Paulin. *Introduction à la critique textuelle du Nouveau Testament. Partie Practique.* t.v. Paris:

1886   MILLER, Edward. *A Guide to the Textual Criticism of the New Testament.*

---

328. Leonard Verduin, *Anatomy of a Hybrid*, (Grand Rapids: Eerdmans, 1976),192. The Waldenses were called Picards as well as Beghards.

Collingswood: Bible For Today. 1979 reprint. 9.

> Erasmus was, however, attacked by Stunica, and also by Edward Lee ...because he had omitted the testimony of the heavenly Witnesses in I John v. 7, as well as on other grounds. Erasmus replied that he could not find the passage in his Greek manuscripts... But at length he promised that if any Greek manuscripts were produced containing the words, he would in future insert them.

Actually, Erasmus never made such a promise. See (1980: de JONGE).

1887   HARRIS, J. Rendel. *The Origin of the Leicester Codex of the New Testament*. London: C.J. Clay & Sons. 48.

> For Roy had ceased to be a Franciscan by 1524, and the Montfort Codex makes its appearance in history between the second and third editions of Erasmus; *i.e.* between 1519 and 1522; nor can the Codex Britannicus, as Erasmus called it, be very many years earlier, if earlier at all, than this period. I believe, therefore, that for the main part of the codex, including the forgery in 1 John v.7, Roy is responsible.

Notice the word "nor" in his sentence. The "neither...nor" construction is used to deny two components. A rewording with equivalent meaning is "Neither the Montfort, nor the Britannicus can be earlier than the period 1519-1522. Britannicus might be earlier than this period, if earlier at all, but not earlier by very many years."

However one reads the sentence, three conclusions can be drawn. (1) Harris believe the Monfort is dated between 1519-1522. (2) He is unsure of the date of Britannicus (3) He is referring to Britannicus as a MS separate from the Montfort.

The conclusion, however, cannot be made that Harris, is positively certain that they are two separate MSS. For the paragragh above, and from a sentence from page 5 of his introduction "This MS., the Codex Monfortianus of Mill, the Codex Britannicus of Erasmus, has been..." we may say that Harris was confused about it, or that he inadvertently contradicted himself.

1888 [A. von Harnack became a professor at the Univ. of Berlin.][329]

1888 ABBOTT, Ezra. "1 John v.7 and Luther's German Bible" *The Authorship of the Fourth Gospel and Other Critical Essays*. Boston: George H. Ellis. 458-463.

A quote from p. 463:
> We may observe, finally that the other early Reformers and friends of Luther generally rejected the passage; so Zwingli, Bullinger, Æcolampadius, Bugenhagen... So also ... Melanchthon, Cruciger (or Creutziger), Justus Jonas, Förster, Aurogallus.

According to *National Cyclopedia of Amer. Biogr.* 6:429, J.H. Thayer edited this work.

1889 [S.C. Malan completed part one of his *Notes on the Proverbs*][330]

1892 WESTCOTT, B.F. *The Epistles of St. John*. 3rd ed. with introduction by F.F. Bruce. Berkshire: Abington Press.

1893 BERGER, Samuel. *Histoire de la Vulgate pendant les premiers siècles du Moyen-Age*. Paris: (New York: Burt Franklin, 1958 reprint)
10, 27, 64, 73, 83, 103, 104, 107, 111, 121, 128, 143, 163.

A quote from p.9 where Berger is referring to a Leon (in Spain) palimpsest of the 7th century:

> Dans la première Epître de saint Jean, et spécialement dans le fameux <<passage des trois témoins>>, nous retrouvons, non sans plaisir, un texte antérieur à saint Jérôme, ...

A brief sketch of this Protestant author is given in *NCE* 2:323, from which we read:

> His lifework was the study of the Latin vulgate and the versions of the Bible in the Romance languages.

---

329. "Because of his liberal theological views, especially with respect to the validity of the historical Christian creeds, his appointment to the post at Berlin was opposed by the supreme council of the Evangelical Church of Prussia, but the opposition was overruled by Chancellor Otto von Bismark. . .Throughout his life. . .Harnack was denied ecclesiastical posts. *NBrit* 5:712.

330. The full title of Malan's work is *Original Notes on the Book of Proverbs According to the Authorized Version*. It consists of vol. I (1889, 489pp.), vol. II (1892, 726pp.), and vol. III (1893, 603pp.).

1894   GREGORY, Caspar René. *Novum Testamentum Graece ad Antiquissmos Textes Denua Recensuit Apparatum Critcum Apposuit.* Vol. 3: *Prolegomena* (to Tischendorf's 8th ed.) 207,211.

> . . .produiit anno 1552 editio tertia, quae prima illum locum 1 Io 5,7 exhibuit, Erasmo repugnante, ex codice Montfortiano nunc Dubliensi (Evv 61 Act 34 Paul 40 Apoc 92) teste minime bono.

1894   SCRIVENER, F.H.A. *A Plain Introduction to New Testament Textual Criticism.* 2 vols. 4th ed. Collingswood: Bible For Today. 1:86,199-200, 2:10,180, 185-186, 250, 265, and esp. 401-407

A quote from page 405:
> ...it is surely safer and more candid to admit that Cyprian read ver. 7 in his copies, that to resort to the explanation of Facundus [vi], that the holy Bishop was merly putting on ver. 8 a spiritual meaning;

1895   [S. Berger discovered *p*, new evidence for the *Comma*.]

> Quia tres sunt: qui testimonium dant in terra. S$\bar{p}$a. aqua. et sanguis. Et hii tris: unum sunt qui testimonium dant in ce lo. Pater. uerbum. s$\bar{p}$s. Et hii tres: umum sunt.

Metzger refers to *p* as one of three examples of Old Latin MSS which had a "remarkable feature" of longevity into the 12th or 13th centuries. He lists 9 sources[331] that date the MS to the 13th century.

1895   BERGER, Samuel. *Un Ancien Texte Latin des Acts des Apôtres.*

This works deals with the Perpignan MS (also known as *p*), an Old Latin MS. Buchanan says its orthography proves "that *p* was copied from a MS not later than the sixth century."[332]

1895-1901   [J.H. Ropes taught New Testament Criticism at Harvard]
He was assistant professor 1898-1903 and "Bussey Professor, 1903-10, succeeding in this chair Prof. Joseph Henry Thayer."[333]

1896   SCHELLHORN, Rudolf. *Über das Verhältnis der Freiberger und der Tepler Bibelhandschrift zu einander und zum ersten vorlutherischen Bibeldrucke.* Freiberg:

---

331. See *Early Versions of the New Testament*, 303.
332. E.S. Buchanan "An Old-Latin Text of the Catholic Epistles" *Journal of Theological Studies*, xii (1911) 497.
333. *Dict of Amer. Biog* 16:151.

Gerlachsche Buchdruckerei

The book is divided into two parts. Part one consists of 23 pages. Part two has 40 pages.

1897   [A.N. Malan's biography of his father C.S. Malan]

1897   [declaration by Sacred Congregation of the Inquisition in Rome]

This declaration, made on January 13, forbade the denial and the doubt of the authenticity of the *Comma*. On January 15, Pope Leo XIII confirmed the declaration.

1897   VAUGHAN (Cardinal) *The Guardian* of June 9, 1897

This was a letter to Wilfrid Ward, concerning the above named declaration

1898   VAUGHAN (Cardinal) *Revue Biblique* 15, p.149

In 1905, C.R. Gregory commented on this article concerning the *Comma*.

1898   WORDSWORTH, John and WHITE, H.J. (The Gospels of) *Novum Testamentum. . .latine secundum editionem S. Hieronzmi ad codicum manuscriptorum fidem.* Oxford:

This work is the completion of the Gospels of the new definitive edition of "the Vulgate". With respect to the MSS of the Vulgate, Kenyon says "but White estimated the total as at least 8000. For the Gospels Wordsworth and White used 29 MSS., for Acts 17, for the Epistles 21."[334] This project for a new edition of the Vulgate began by dismissing about 99.6 percent of MSS for the Gospels, the majority of which have never been cataloged! It is important to note three stages, toward the goal of the 20th century expulsion of the *Comma* from a major Vulgate edition. For stage one, the "printed test is based upon. . .codex Amiatinus"[335] (which omits the *Comma*). For stage two, see (1905: WORDSWORTH, & WHITE)

1898   NESTLE, Eberhard. *Novum Testamentum Graece cum apparatu critico ex editionibus et libris manu scriptis collecto.*

His son, Erwin, explained the appearance of this first (of 26 editions) Nestle edition of the Greek NT:

Schon lange hatte er bedauert, daß die Ergebnisse der großen Ausgaben besonders von Tischendorf (ed. octava 1869-1874) und den Engländer Westcott und Hort (1881), dem gewöhnlichen Studenten und Pfarr zu wenig zur Verfügung stehen. Deshalb erschein 1898. . . seine *Novum Testamentum*. . .Er bot ja nicht sein Eigenes, sondern wollte nur die Ergebnisse der Arbeit anderer handlich und billig darbieten.[336]

In short, Eberhard had regretted for a long time, that the large editions as Tischendorf's and Wescott-Hort's were hardly available to regular students and ministers. Thus, his 1898 edition appeared. He offered not only his own, but wanted

---

334. Kenyon *The Text of the Greek Bible* (1949) 145.
335. Metzger *Early Versions* 350.
336. Nestle, Erwin, *Kirchlich-theologische Halbmonatsschrift* Nr. 9, "Eberhard Nestle: zu seinem 100. Geburtstag" (1951)

to offer handy and inexpensive works of another.

SIGNIFICANCE; The admission is that the Greek text containing the *Johannine Comma*, the Received Text, STILL had not been overthrown in 1898!

1899   MILLER, Edward. *A Textual Commentary upon the Holy Gospels; Largely from the Use of Materials and Mainly on the Text Left by the Late John William Burgon, B.D. Dean of Chichester*, Part I, St. Matthew, Division I, I-XIV. London: George Bell.

If the title had been *The First Attempt to Print a Majority Greek Text*. it might have been remembered as *The Unfinished Attempt of 1899*. After contrasting proposals to correct the TR by Miller and Burgon, with those of Hodges & Farstad, the following conclusion was made: "that the majority text advocates of two generations have no unanimity of opinion ." [337]

Moreover, the proposals by Burgon and Miller extended only to Matthew 14. The MTA have serious problems: If their view is correct, why have no printed editions of 𝔐 been available to the public from 1514-1982? [338] Why was the attempt of 1899 to "restore" the true NT text of 𝔐 in printed form, quenched after Matthew 14, and delayed for another century? 1899 seemed like a excellent year to "restore" to text. Was the decree of our Lord frustrated in 1899? Why won't the MTA openly say that they believe the TR has lied (for over 400 years) to all Christians world-wide via the printed text "in something over a thousand places, most of them being very minor differences."[339] Why did the author say that papyri "lie" but that the TR only "differs"? Non-Anglicans are seeking to adopt a high Anglican principle which failed Burgon. Dr. E.F. Hills explained how it failed Burgon. ;lm+5
"For from Reformation times down to his own day the printed Greek New Testament text which had been favored by the bishops of the Anglican Church was the Textus Receptus, and the Textus Receptus had not been prepared by bishops but by Erasmus, who was an independent scholar."[340]

1902   GREGORY, Caspar René. *Textkritik des Neuen Testament*. Leipzig: J.C. Hinrich. II: 824-845.

---

337. T.P. Letis, "Introduction", *The Majority Text; Essays and Reviews in the Continuing Debate*.(Grand Rapids: Institute for Biblical Textual Studies, 1987) 4-5.
338. In desparation, some MTA have claimed the Complutensian for their side. See (1990: HUA).
339. Pickering. *The Identity of the New Testament Text*. (Nashville, TN: Thomas Nelson, 1977) 177. Though buried in the end-notes, this is perhaps the most often quoted passage in the book!
340. *King James Version Defended* 4th ed. p. 192. This statement by Dr. Hills is entirely appropriate in considering the current efforts of the MTA.

At the time of this writing (1991), we may say that in 11 years, this work by Gregory will be 100 years out of date. Note the current dependence on Gregory's outdated list:

Kenyon (1912) on Latin MSS:
"No complete catalog of them exists, and the precise total is unknown;"
Kenyon (1949) on Latin MSS:
"Gregory in 1909 (appendix to his *Textkritik*) enumerated 2472, but White estimated the total as least 8000."[341]

Metzger (1977) on the Syriac MSS:
". . .Gregory was able to enumerate more than 300 Peshitta manuscripts of the New Testament. Actually the number is much larger, for Gregory did not include all the manuscripts that are in the libraries in the East. And since Gregory's time other manuscripts have come to light."[342]
Vööbus (1988) on the Syriac MSS:
"C.R. Gregory's list (*Textkritik des NT*,II [1902], 508ff., 1298ff.) includes 182 Gospel MSS and more than 150 MSS of the Apostolos; and the total number is actually much larger. . ."[343]

SIGNIFICANCE: The boast is made decade after decade that "today" we have "more manuscripts." But today (A.D. 1991) the Syriac (350+? MSS), Latin Vulgate (8000+? MSS) documents are still largely unexamined. How many Latin and Syriac MSS contain the *Comma*? No one knows. We do not even know the precise totals of these MSS. Why do we have only estimates? Why do Kenyon (1949) Metzger (1977) and Vööbus (1988) still refer to Gregory's outdated listing? Why isn't Gregory's list updated? Because the Latin and Syriac MSS are not studied!

But why is there still no complete catalog?

Metzger (1977) on Syriac MSS:
"In view of the abundance of manuscripts of the Peshitta, some of them of great antiquity, it is to be regretted that during the twentieth century so little effort has been directed to solving the many problems that clamour for their attention."[344]
The first problem is that they are not even cataloged.

1902   BLUDAU, August. *Die Beiden Ersten Erasmus-Ausgaben Des Neuen Testaments und Ihre Gegner*. Freiberg im Breisgau: Herdersche Verlagshandlung.

1902   BLUDAU, August. "Der Beginn der Kontroverse über die Echtheit des comma

---

341. *Text of the Greek Bible* 145.
342. *Early Versions* 49.
343. *ISBE* 4: 975.
344. *Early Versions* 63.

Johanneum im 16. Jahrhundert" *Der Katholic.* Jahrgung 82, 2 Hälfte, 3 Folge, t. xxvi. 25-51, 151-179.

1902   BAUMSTARK, Anton. "Ein syrisches Citat des 'Comma Johanneum,'" *Oriens Christianus* 2; 438-441.

Dr. Baumstark studied classical and Oriental philology.[345] He was an honorary professor at Bonn, and a Professor of Arabic at Utrecht. Raymond Brown says that Baumstark considered it a "possibility that Jaqub knew a Latin or Greek" manuscript that contained the Comma. Jaqub (d. 708) is said to be the author of two copies (133,159) of a Syric commentary "On the Holy Mysteries" which refer to the *Comma*.

1903   BLUDAU, August. "Das Comma Ioanneum (I Io 5,7) im 16. Jahrhundert". *Biblische Zeitschrift.* I: 280-302, 378-407.

1903   BLUDAU, August. "Das Comma Johanneum in den orientalischen Übersetzungen und Bibeldrucken". *Oriens Christianus.* t. iii, 126-147.

1903   NESTLE, Eberhard. *Salz und Licht; Vorträge und Abhandlungen in zwangloser Folger.* No. 8. "Vom Textus Receptus des Griechischen Neuen Testaments". Barmen: Wupperthaler Traktat-Gesellschaft. 9, 14-15, 26-27, 37, 38-40, 50.

1904   BLUDAU, August. "Das Comma Johanneumin den Schriften der Antitrinitarier und Sozinianer des 16. und 17. Jahrhunderts". *Biblische Zeitschrift.* II: 275-300.

1904   BLUDAU, August. "Richard Simon und das Comma Johanneum". *Der Katholic.* Jahrgung 84, 3 Folge, t. xxix, 29-42, 114-122.

1904   NESTLE, Eberhard. *Novum Testamentum Graece.* 3rd ed.

Erwin remarked that it was *eine besondere Freude* (a special joy) to his father, Eberhard, when the BFBS (British & Foreign Bible Society) untertook his third edition. The BFBS accordingly distributed 170,000 Nestle editions as of 1914, and 500,000 as of 1950.

SIGNIFANCE: Although other mta Greeks texts were in print, it was not until 1904, by Nestle's admission, that a Greek text lacking the *Comma* was widely distributed and accepted by students of the Greek NT.

Now the Nestle text became the foundation for English translations (NWT, RSV, etc), but since they "involved liberal translators, we Fundamentalists tended not to use them. . ." Chinn & Newman *Demystifying the Controversy over the TR*, 2.

---

345. Otto Spieß, "Baumstark" *New Deutsche Biographie.* (Berlin: Duncker & Humblot, 1952) 1:669.

1905   WORDSWORTH & WHITE. (The Acts of their new Vulgate edition)

This is stage two. For this section the editors used (according to Kenyon) only 17 MSS from at least 8000 MSS extant, by White's esitmation. They dismissed about 99.7 per cent of the evidence for Acts. For stage three, see (1954: SPARKS & ADAMS).

1905   CLARKE, William Newton. *An Outline of Christian Theology*. 14th ed.

In J.E. Tull's *Shapers of Baptist Thought*, W.N. Clarke (1841-1912) is regarded as the Baptist representative of liberalism. Clarke's *An Outline of Christian Theology* went through 20 editions between 1894 and 1914 and "became the most widely used textbook among liberal Baptists."[346]

On p. 40 Clarke rejected 2 Tim 3:16 and instead said:
> Primarily men are inspired, not writings. . .

This widely known "Baptist" scholar even went so far to say:
> . . .our present Sriptures differ (we know not just how widely) from the original Scriptures. For us, therefore, there are no verbally inspired Scriptures. . .

---

346. *Baptists and the Bible*, 331.

1905   KÜNSTLE, Karl. *Das Comma Johanneum auf seine Herkunft untersucht.* Freiburg im B.:, Herder. [64pp.]

Künstle suggested that Priscillian himself inserted the *Comma* into John's Epistle.

1905   GREGORY, Caspar René. *Theologische Literature Zeitung.* No. 16. August 5, col.445.

The article refered to in this journal, edited by Adolf Von Harnack and Emil Schürer, is a review of Künstle's work.

1905   JÜLICHER, Adolf, and KÜNSTLE, Karl. "Das Comma Ioanneum". *Göttingische Gelehrte Anzeigen.* 167: 930-935.

1906   KURRELMEYER, William. *Die erste Deutsche Bibel.* 10 vols. Tübingen:

This is a modern printing of the 1466 German translation by Johann Mentel, which contains several RT readings including the *Comma.* The article on the MSS extends from p. XIX to p. XXX.

1907   MANGENOT, Eugène. *Le Comma Johanneum.*

1908   HÖPFL, Hildebrand. *Kardinal Wilhelm Sirlets Annotationen zum Neuen Testament; Eine Verteidigung der Vulgata gegen Valla und Erasmus* (Freiburg im Breisgau: Herdersche Verlagshandlung, 1908) 65-67.

1908   NESTLE, Eberhardt. "Bible Versions, German". *The New Schaff-Herzog Encyclopedia of Religious Knowledge.*

> The verse of the "three witnesses" (I John v.7) was first introduced into a Frankfort edition of 1575, into a Wittenberg impression in 1596)

In 1828, Karl Rickli wrote "that it did not appear in Luther's version till 1593 (not 1574 as erroneously stated by Panzer and others.)"[347] Just before the index of Orme's 1866 edition of *Memoirs of the Controversy* begins, an update is given on this matter, viz., the research of Dr. Klose has shown that the *comma* was "interpolated in Luther's version" in a Frankfurt edition as early as 1582.

1908   DUMMELOW, J.R. *The One Volume Bible Commentary.* NY: MacMillan Publ. Co. 1057.

---

347. *The First Epistle of John, explained and applied in Sermons delivered before the Evangelical Reformed Church at Lucern.*

It is quite certain that these words did not belong to the original text. They are found in no Greek manuscript earlier than the 14th cent., and are generally quoted by none of the Fathers before the middle of the 5th cent.

1908   SANDYS, John Edwin. *A History of Classical Scholarship*. 3 vols. Cambridge: Cambridge University Press. 2:425-431.

The first work that made him [R. Porson] widely known was his *Letters to Travis* (1788-79), in which he proved the spuriousness of the text on the 'three that bear witness in heaven' thus supporting an opinion which had long been held by critics from Erasmus to Bently...

1909   [Alfred Gudemann's reproach of American classical scholars]

This German scholar said "Not a single contribution marking genuine progress, no work on a extensive scale, opening up a new perspective or breaking entirely new ground, nothing, in fact, of the slightest scientific value can be placed to their credit."[348]

1909   BABUT. *Priscillien et le Priscillianisme*. (Bibliothèque de l'École des hautes études, Sciences historiques et philolgiques, 169) Paris: Appendix, iv. 3, p. 267ff.

Babut argues against Künstle's theory made in 1905. A.E.Brooke summarizes Babut's argument. Referring to Priscillian, he says

"(1) His opponents never accuse him of having falsified the text of a Canonical Book. (2) To quote his own interpretation in his *Apology* would have been an inconceivable act of audacity. (3). Such a falsification could hardly have been accepted by all Catholic theologians, and as Künstle has shown, the reading was universally accepted in the ninth century. (4). The verse is found in several orthodox works of the fifth century."[349]

1909   KNOPF, D. "Comma Johanneum" *Die Religion in Geschichte und Gegenwart*. 1st ed. Tübingen: 1867.

The 2nd and 3rd editions of this reference work (known as "RGG") appeared respectively in 1927 and 1957. The length of these articles on the *Comma* is progressively enlarged.

1909   von SODEN, Hans Freiherr. *Das Lateinische Neue Testament in Afrika zur Zeit Cyprians nach Bibelhandschriften und Väteryeugnissen*. Leipzig: J.C. Hinrichs'sche. [663 pp.] 280.

---

348. "Classical Review" June, 1909, p. 116.
349. Brooke, *Critical and Exegetical Commentary on the Johannine Epistles* (Edinburgh: T & T. Clark, 1912) 160.

page 161

In the forward, on pp. iv, Hans von Soden says "With gratitude, I would like to mention. . .the editor of the "Texts and Investigations" the *Wirkl.* privy senior government councillor Professor Dr. Harnack, my highly honored instructor, whose advice and interest was never lacking upon my research.

> 1 J 5,8 (Citate c 15 p 87,35, c 19 pp 92,7): *quia tres testimonium perhibent spirtus et aqua et sanquis, et isti tres in* (das *in* add Cod Reg. p 87, nicht p 92; in den Ausgaben fehlt es und beiden Stellen) *unum sunt.*

1910 [Presbyterian General Assembly adopts 5 fundamentals][350]

1910 DRUM, Walter. "John". *The Catholic Encyclopedia.* 15 vols. New York: Robert Appleton Co. 8:436.

> ...(I John, v. 7-8). Throughout the past three hundred years, effort has been made to expunge from our Clementine Vulgate edition of canonical Scripture the words that are bracketed.

> However, the Catholic theologian...cannot pass over the disciplinary decision of the Holy Office (13 January, 1897), whereby it is decreed that the authenticity of the *Comma Johanninum* may not with safety (*tuto*) be denied or called into doubt. This disciplinary decision was approved by Leo XIII two days later.

(Note the contrast, by observing the artice in the *New Catholic Encyl* of 1967!)

1910 KROPATSCHECK, D. Friedrich. "Die Trinität; ein Bericht über den gegenwärtigen Stand der Frage" *Biblische Zeit= und Streitfragen* VI Serie 7. Heft. 14.

The audacity of the author is revealed in this statement:

> It's very beneficial for every Christian, if he breaks himself away from intimate Bible verses as 1 John 5:7, as soon as they are taken from him by the Bible critic.[351]

1911 WINDISCH, Hans. *Die Katholischen Briefe.* Tübingen:

---

350. The "five points of fundamentalism" adopted were "1) the verbal inerrancy of Scripture, 2) the Virgin Birth of Jesus, 3) Jesus' substituion of himself as victim for the sins of humanity, 4) the physical Resurrection and bodily return of Jesus, and 5) the authenticity of the miracles." M.Fahey, "What Makes a Fundamentalist?" *Ecumenism* 91 (Sept 1988) 7.

351. He also said "Erst Schweizer Drucke und spätere Wittenberger Ausgaben bringen sie (zuerst die Wittenberger Ausgabe von 1596; nach machen Schwankungen seit der Quartausgabe von 1620 als regelmäßigen Zusatz").

J.C.B. Mohr. 129

1912   NESTLE, Eberhard. *Begleitwort zu den (für die Privileg. Württ. Bibelanstalt in Stuttgart) bearbeiteten Ausgaben des griechischen, lateinischen und deutschen Neuen Testaments.*

Only one sample page of each of the three editions mentioned, is included in this small booklet. The selected passage is the same for all three, viz. the passage beginning with 1 John 5!

1912   BROOKE, Alan England. "Separate Note: The Text of I Jn v.7" *A Critical and Exegetical Commentary on the Johannine Epistles.* New York: Charles Scribner's Sons. 154-165.

1914   [A.T. Robertson admits his dependence on German scholarship]

"But I wish to record my conviction that my own work, [on Greek grammar] such as it is, would have been impossible but for the painstaking and scientific investigation of the Germans at every turn."[352]

1915   HARNACK, Adolf von. "Zur Textkritik und Christologie der Schriften des Johannes: Zugleich ein Beitrag Würdigung der ältesten lateinischen Überlieferung und der Vulgata" *Sitzungsberichte der Preussischen Akademie der Wissenschaften* (Berlin), XXXVII, 534.

1915   BLUDAU, August. "Das Comma Johanneum bei den Griechen". *Biblische Zeitschrift.* xiii: 26-50, 130-162, 222-243.

1918   [The term "Fundamental", as designating anti-Liberalism.]

According to *The Oxford English Dictionary*, 2nd ed. (1989) p. 267, the term derived from a "religious movement, which orig. became active among Protestant bodies in the United States after the war of 1914-1918, based on strict adherence to certain tenets (e.g. the literal inerrancy of Scripture) held to be fundamental to the Christian faith."

1918-1921 BLUDAU, August. "Der Prologue des Pseudo-Hieronymus zu den katholischen Briefen," *Biblische Zeitschrift.* 15; 15-34, 125-138.

1919   BLUDAU, August. "Das Comma Iohanneum in dem Glaubensbekenntnis von Karthago vom Jahre 484". *Theologie und Glaube.* 11: 9-15

1919   BLUDAU, August. "Der hl. Augustinus und I Joh v.7.8. *Theologie und Glaube.* 11:

---

352. *A Grammar of the Greek New Testament in the Light of Historical Research*, 3rd ed. (Cambridge: Univ Press, 1919) ix.

379-386.

1920   BLUDAU, August. "Das 'Comma Johanneum' bei Tertullian und Cyprian," *Theologische Quartalschrift*. 101; 1-28.

1920   [The term 'Fundamentalism' is used among Baptists]

> 'Fundamentalism'. . .appears to have been used first in connexion with the (American) Northern Baptist Convention of 1920 to describe the more conservative delegates. . .[353]

1922   BLUDAU, August. "The Comma Johanneum in the writings of English critics of the eighteenth century". *The Irish Theological Quarterly*. t. xvii. 66-67.

353.*Times* (25 Aug 1955) as quoted in *Oxford English Dictionary*, 2nd ed. (1989) 267.

1924   TURNER, Cuthbert Hamilton. *Early Printed Editions of the Greek Testament.* Oxford: Clarendon Press. 23.

Many who lived in the 1970's through 1990's did not question Metzger when he said (in 1964) that Erasmus "indicates in a lengthy footnote his suspicion that the manuscript had been prepared expressly in order to confute him." But in 1980 H.J. de Jonge had said that such a suspicion "cannot be shown from Erasmus' works." See (1980: de JONGE) in this paper. But this suspicion-myth is recent. It was not accepted in the 1920's. C.H.Turner, who read extensively in Latin from Mill and Erasmus said on p. 23:

> If indeed [Erasmus] had known that the English manuscript was in the strictest sense contemporary, and was probably written in Oxford about 1520, he might have entertained the suspicion that the manuscript was written for the purpose of providing the evidence.

Accordingly, Turner agrees with de Jonge, that Erasmus did NOT suspect a recent fabrication "prepared expressly in order to confute him." (These are Metzger's words in *Text of the NT*, p. 101, which is the same page where he recommended C.H.Turner's booklet! p. 101 note 3) Did Metzger read the Turner's booklet? Did he correctly read the lengthy footnote of Erasmus? We wonder.

1927   von SODEN, Hans. "Comma Johanneum", *Die Religion in Geschichte und Gegenwart; Handwörterburch für Theologie und Religionswissenschaft.* 2nd edition. Tübingen: J.C.B. Mohr (Paul Siebed).1712-1713.

1927   "Declaration Supremae Scarae Congregationis Sancti Officii Circa Decretum de Authentia Textus I Io. 5,7". *Biblica.* 8: 494.

1927   [pre-1927: The Vetus Latina Institute was founded.]

Vetus Latina means "Old Latin." This institute, also known as the "Beuron Institute", is located in the Obere Donau in a Cloisture in the city of Beuron located near the Donau River. Its address is D-7792 Beuron, W. Germany. Because of the ambiquity of the sigla (e.g., r^1 r^2 r^3 and q are four sigla for the same MS!) the VLI has assigned numbers to the MSS, hence the term "Beuron numbers."

The Old Latin evidence for the *Comma* is critical, and "Most editors of a Greek New Testament take the evidence of the early versions seriously and this is especially true of the Old Latin."354 The UBS and NA editions depend heavily on the VLI for the latest Old Latin evidence. For these reasons, it is worth inquiring into the origin of the VLI. To begin "a parish priest named Joseph Denk (1849-1927), drew up plans and began to collect patristic quotations of the Old Latin Scriptures. Before his death" his quotations were passed down "to the monastery at Beuron under the care of P. Alban Dold (1882-1960)."355 Bonifatius Fischer, a monk, was instrumental in its leadership until Ursmar Engelmann, replaced him in 1973. According to the 22nd Report of the Institute (of 1989), the board of directors includes three men: H. Herder, H.J. Frede, and Jerome Nitz, O.S.B., who is the chief abbot of the Beuron. The board of trustees consists of 25 members. At the top of the list of this board are three Papists: (1) "Se. Eminenz" Carlo M. Martini, Archbishop of Mailand; (2) "Se. Exzellenz" Karl Lehmann, bishop of Mainz; (3) "Se. Exzellenz" Walter Kasper, bishop of Rottenburg- Stuttgart. The names of 3 princes follow. Then the list becomes alphabetical: Kurt Aland is second, and Bruce M. Metzger is listed as 13th. 356

Concerning the possibility of a visit to the Beuron Institute, the inquirer will be told it is closed to the public, because it is a *Kloster*!

1928   STUMMER, Friedrich. *Einführung in die lateinische Bibel; ein Handbuch für Vorlesungen und Selbstunterricht*. Paderborn: 152-153.

1928   [Baptists celebrated the 400th aniversary of Hübmaier]357

1928   RIVIERE, J. "Sur 'l'authenticité' du verset des trois témoins," *Revue Apologétique*. 46; 303-309.

1928   RIGGENBACH, Eduard. *Das Comma Johanneum; ein nachgelassenes Werk*. Gütersloh: [43pp.]

1928   ROBERTSON, A.T. *An Introduction to the Textual Criticism of the New Testament*. 2nd ed. Garden City and New York: Doubleday, Doray, & Co. 17-19, 27.

Years after the death of Hort, the attacks upon the *Comma* persisted, since the consensus was that everyone ought to wear Hortian eyeglasses to determine the identity of the NT text. But what is so amusing, is that although the Hortians regarded the debate on the *Comma* as settled, they did not let the issue rest. They continued to write page after page against it! The *Comma* continued to endure, despite all the hammer blows it took.

---

354. J.K. Elliot "Old Latin Manuscripts in Printed Editions of the Greek New Testament" *A Survey of Manuscripts Used in Editions of the Greek New Testament*. (Leiden, New York, Copenhagen, Coln: E.J. Brill, 1987)
355. B.M.Metzger *Early Versions of the New Testament* (1977) 320.
356. *Vetus Latina; 1989 33rd Arbeitsbericht der Stiftung 22nd Bericht des Instituts*
357. The Baptist "celebrated the 400th anniversary of his martyrdom with a special observance in Vienna in 1928." *ME* 2:826.

A.T. Robertson, the world famous Greek scholar, regarded the *Johannine Comma* as spurious. Thus, some have suggested that we Baptists ought to follow the example of our 19th century modern heritage.

1933   ROBERTSON, A.T. *Word Pictures in the New Testament*. Reprint 1960 Grand Rapids: Baker. 240-241.

In this quote, Dr. Robertson reveals more of his bitterness against the *Comma*, after saying that Erasmus "rashly offered to insert it if . . ." Here he describes a theory on its transmission:
> Some Latin scribe caught up Cyprian's exegesis and wrote it on the margin of his text, and so it got into the Vulgate and finally into the Textus Receptus by the stupidity of Erasmus.

1933   BÜCHSEL, Friedrich. "Excurs 11: Das Comma Johanneum 5, 7.8", *Theologischer Handkommentar zum Neuen Testament XVII Die Johannesbriefe* Leipzig: D. Werner Scholl. 82-83.

Büchsel was one of the few scholars of the 20th century to differ from the view that Cyprian made an allegorical reference to the Trinity. Instead, Büschel regarded the Cyprian reading as an actual citation of the verse. R. Brown (1982) would have us believe that no recognized authority since the 19th century would hold such a view. However, the following recognized authorities have had their views published in the respective years, that the Cyprian reading was an actual citation of the *Johannine Comma*: Büchsel (1933), Pieper (1950), Hills (1956), and Thiele (1959).

1934   FICKERMAN, Norbert. "St. Augustinus gegen das Comma Johanneum?" *Biblische Zeitschrift*. 21: 350-358.

From Raymond Brown's article we read that Fickerman "has recently raised the possibility that in fact he did know the Comma but rejected it (and for that reason never quoted it). Fickermann points to a hitherto unpublished eleventh-century text which says that Jerome considered the Comma to be a genuine part of I John. . ."[358]

1934   LEMONNYER, A. "Comma Johanique". *Dictionnaire de la Bible. Supplement*. vol. 2: 67-74.

1935   LAGRANGE, P.M.-J. *Critique Textuelle II; La Critique Rationnelle*. Paris: Librairie Lecoffre. 38, 298, 299, 547, 570.

---

358. "Appendix IV: Johannine Comma" vol 30 of *The Anchor Bible; The Epistles of John*, 785.

A quote concerning the Coptic versions (Sahidic and Boharic), p.570:
> The two versions have omitted with all the other witnesses *le comma iohanneum* (I Jo. v.7).

1935   PANIN, Ivan, ed. *The New Testament From the Greek Text as Established by Bible Numerics*. 2nd ed. Toronto: Book Society of Canada.

A quote from his modified text of 1 John 5:7:
> 7)Because the witnesssing ones are three: the Spirit, and the water, and the blood: and the three agree in one.

In his preface, Panin says "The standard used for comparison was: for the Greek, the Revision by Westcott & Hort; and for the English, the American Revised Version." Hence, the *Comma* is omitted.

1937   POPE, Huge, O.P. *The Catholic Student's "Aids" to the Bible*. 5:331-336.

(In 1952 Rev. Pope, who was professor of N.T. exegesis in the Collegiio Angelico in Rome, referred to this earlier book of his as containing "arguments in favor of the authenticity of the passage- arguments much more forcible than is generally known")

1940   POPE, Hugh. *A Brief History of the English Versions of the N.T. first published at Rheims in 1582. Continued down to the Present Day*. London:

Dr. M. Robinson said, "in 1940 the Roman Catholic scholar (and Mariolater!) Hugh Pope confidently affirmed that in matters of text he was a committed Burgonite."[359]
Dr. Robinson did not cite a page number or title. If Huge Pope was a Burgonite, then it proves that even a committed Burgonite may be an advocate of the *Comma*!

1942   JENKINS, C. "A Newly Discovered Reference to the 'Heavenly Witnesses' (1 John 5:7-8)" In a Manuscript of Bede. *Journal of Theological Studies*. 43 (1942), 42-45. [microfilm 6981, reel 6]

> The purpose of this note is . . . to call attention to a remarkable treatment of the passage unnoticed, so far as we are at present aware, in any of the printed editions of Bede's works. It is to be found in a codex given to Balliol College, Oxford, c. 1477 by a former alumnus, the magnificent and generous prelate William Grey, Bishop of Ely... MS. Ball. 177 is assigned to the end of saec. xii, and this date must be accepted, if with a little hesitation.

Jenkins, made an especially valuable comment here:

---

359. Maurice Robinson, *Whose Unholy Hands on What? A Review Article*, (1990) 12.

Since the days of Porson the most important contribution on the Latin side has been the discovery of the tractates of Priscillian in the Würzburg MS. Mp. th. q. 3 (saec. v-vi) which throw the evidence back to the fourth century and quote the passage (Prisc. *Tract*. i.4, Schepps, Vindobonae, 1889) as:

> Sicut Ioannes ait: Tria sunt quae testimonium dicunt in terra aqua caro et sanguis et haec tria in unum sunt: et tria sunt quae testimonium dicunt in caelo pater verbum et spiritus et haec tria unum sunt in Christo Iesu.

1942   FISCHER, Bonifatius. "Der Bibeltext in den pseudo-augustinischen Solutiones diversarium quaestionum ab haereticis objectarum," *Biblica* 23; 139-164.

1943   del ALAMO, Mateo. "El 'comma Joaneo'", *Estudios bibicos*. seg. ep., ii, 75-105.

1946   DODD, C.H. *The Johannine Epistles*. London: Hodder and Stoughton, Ltd. 127.

1946   *The Revised Standard Version: (New Testament)*

In reference to E.J. Goodspeed, "Along with eight others he laboured for 15 years on the Revised Standard Version of the Bible, published in 1946." [360]

A quote from the Catholic scholar, Rev. Hugh Pope:

> I John 5:7f is simply omitted, as in the Revised Version, without a note

1947   AYUSO, Marazuela Teofilo. "Nuevo estudio sobre el Comma Ioanneum". *Biblica*. 28: 83-112.

1948   AYUSO, Marazuela Teofilo. "Nuevo estudio sobre el Comma Ioanneum". *Biblica*. 52-76.

1949   KENYON, F.G. *The Text of the Greek Bible*. 2nd ed. London:

The first ed. appeared in 1937.
> The most important, historically, of these is Stephanus' of 1550, because it became the Received Text which was reprinted, with very slight alteration, in all Greek New Testaments (with negligible exception) down to the nineteeth century, and still is the standrd text in general use.

1949   IRONSIDE, Henry Allan. *Epistles of John. Jude*. 2nd ed., Neptune, NJ: Loizeaux Brothers. 196-197. (1931, 1st ed.)

> I do not think that I need to take very much time pointing out the fact that we do not actually have six witnesses in the chapter; that is three in heaven and three on earth . . .This is not found in any critical translation of the New Testament. My statement may trouble some of you who have never looked into this question, and you may say "What, is there some part of Scripture that cannot be depended upon?"

1950   BACH, H. *Bidrag til den Danske Bibels Historie* Kopenhagen:

Was the translation underlying the *vorlutherische* Bibles from a Waldensian origin? K. Strand said Walther and Kurrelmeyer "virtually shattered the hypothesis."[361] But even Strand is wavering on the question, for he says

> H. Bach declared that "this hypothesis is now given up";[36] but some scholars writing even more recently have raised anew the thought of Waldensian origin or

---

[360]*Britannica; Micropedia* (Chicago *et al*. :Ency Britannica, 1985) 5:364.
[361]. *German Bibles Before Luther* (Grand Rapids: Eerdmans, 1966) 38.

influence.[362]

In footnote 36, he says H. Bach "may have failed to note, however, that a few scholars of a decade or two earlier had not fully given up the viewpoint."

1950   PIEPER, Franz Otto. *Christian Dogmatics*. St. Louis: Concordia Publishing House. 1:241

QUOTE: from Pieper on Cyprian's words *et iterum scriptum est*:
> Griesbach counters that Cyprian is here not quoting from Scripture,...Cyprian states distinctly that he is quoting Bible passages

1951   PREISKER, Herbert, ed. *Die Katholischen Briefe*. 3rd ed. by Windisch, Tübingen: Verlag J.C.B. Mohr (Paual Siebeck) 132-133

1952   POPE, Hugh, O.P. *English Versions of the Bible*. St. Louis: B. Herder Book Co. 547.

1953   SCHNACKENBURG, Rudolf. "Die Textüberlieferung- Das Comma Johanneum". *Herders Theologischer Kommentar zum Neuen Testament*. Band XIII: Faszikel 3. *Die Johannesbriefe*. Frieburg in Breisgau: Herder & Co. GmbH. 36-39.

1953   MARAZUELA, Teofilo Ayuso. *La Vetus Latina Hispana*. Madrid: Consejo Superior de Investigaciones Cientificas. 1: 396, 406.

> Estudiando el *Comma Ioanneum* (10), pudimos llegar a la evidencia no sólo de que el famoso versículo es una interpolación de la *Vetus Latina*, sino que esta interferencia es sólo un caso más de las varias interpolaciones que existen en ese capítulo de *1 Ioh*.

1954   SPARKS, Hedley F. & ADAMS, A.W. *Nouum Testamentum Domini Nostri Iesu Christi Latine*. London: Clarendon. 3:230,373-374.

This is stage 3 and the long-awaited completion of the new printed Vulgage edition which was begun about 1877 by John Wordsword, and later assisted by H.J. White. According to Kenyon, only 29 MSS were used for the epistles! As mentioned, *Codex Amiatinus* was used as their printed base. Thus we may say, they dismissed about 99.63 per cent of the quantity of at least 8000 Latin MSS, many never cataloged or glanced at, in order to tell us what Jerome actually wrote.

---

362. Ibid.

SIGNIFICANCE: Apart from printed collations from *Amiantinus* (Tischendorf, Tregelles[363], etc.) the Vulgate tradition, until now, has always been regarded to contain the *Comma*. Ersamus said it was in his Vulgate. Porson and Scrivener granted that it was perhaps in 49 out of every 50 Vulgate MSS. It is present in the Sixtine Vulgate (1590), the Clementine Vulgate (1592), Walton's Vulgate (1657), Sabatier's Vulgate (1751), and others prior to 1590. But this Vulgate edition, known as "the Oxford edition" of 1954, marks a major turning point in the 20th century. It entirely changes answers to questions such as "Is the *Comma* in the Vulgate?"

1956   HILLS, Edward F. "The Johannine Comma (1 John 5:7)". *The King James Version Defended! A Christian View of the New Testament Manuscripts*. Des Moines: Christian Research Press.

In 1953 Günther Zuntz said "The Textus Receptus died an undeservedly slow death". Three years later, Dr. Hills, the Yale-Harvard graduate, published the most scholarly defense of the Received Text, of any that appeared in the 20th century. In his defense of the *Comma*, four sections are discussed:

a. How the Johannine Comma entered the Textus Receptus
b. The Early Existence of the Johannine Comma
c. Is the Johannine Comma an interpolation?
d. Reason for the possible omission of the Johannine Comma

In part "c" he re-introduced the forgotten grammatical argument, which had already been used by several scholars before him: Archbishop Eugenius (c.1662), T.F. Middleton (1808), F.Nolan (1815), L. Gaussen (1839), and R.L. Dabney (1871).

1957   GREEVEN, Heinrich.[364] "Comma Johanneum". *Die Religion in Geschichte und Gegenwart: Handwörterbuch für Theologie und Religionswissenschaft*. 3rd ed. Tübingen: J.C.B. Mohr. I:1854

1957   CLARK, Kenneth L. "The Transmission of the New Testament". *The Interpreter's Bible*. vols. :622.

> Erasmus introduced the passage into his third edition of 1522. Five years later it was exscinded again from the fourth edition. But the third edition had already been used by Tyndale, whose English translation is still embedded in the King James Version, and this spurious passage was to remain for centuries.

---

363. Tregelles entitled the Latin portion of his work of 1857-1879 *The Latin Version of Jerome*.

364. In order to celebrate Greeven's 80th birthday, a festschrift (ed. by W. Schrage) was written in 1986, viz., *Studium zum Text und Ethik des Neues Testaments*

Question: Of the 5 editions of Erasmus, which contain the *Comma*? The variety of replies is amusing, and it testifies to either confusion, or pure bias, if not both. Does this edition ... contain the *Comma*?

```
--------edition:  |1516|1519|1522|1527|1535|----|1555|
(1860) W. Orme:   | no | no | yes| yes| yes|
(1827) T.Dibdin:  | no | yes|  ? |  ? |  ? |
(1953) Ancestry:  | no | no | yes| no | no |
(1957) K. Clark:  | no | no | yes| no |  ? |
(1964) B Metzger  | no | no | yes| yes| /// |----|yes|
(1982) R. Brown:  | no | no | yes| yes| yes|
--------correct:  | no | no | yes| yes| yes|
```

The 15th printing of *The Ancestry of Our English Bible* makes a serious error. The claim is that Erasmus "omitted the passage in his later editions"[365] K.L. Clark is not to be confused with K. Willis Clark.

1958   EULE, Wilhelm. *Zwei Jahrtausende Bibelbuch*. Berlin:

In 1966 K. Strand said "Eule. . .referred to the said version [underlying the pre-Lutheran German editions] as an "antiquated translation probably stemming from the Waldenses."[37]

Footnote 37 refers to page 60.

1958   THIELE, Walter. *Wortschatzuntersuchungen zu den lateinischen Texten der Johannesbriefe*. Freiburg: Verlag Herder.

This was his doctoral dissertation. The Latin MSS are divided into the Afrikanische texts (text types K & C), Europäische texts (text types S,T,& V), and the remainder without text description (text types LUC, & AU).

1959   [Institute für Neutestementliche Textforschung was founded]

The world's largest collection of N.T. MSS are located here. The institute is located on Georgskommende 7 in Münster, W. Germany.
What is the origin of the INTF? This is a matter of great interest since, beginning in 1912 with Nestle[12], many Americans place great confidence in the German-produced crititial apparatus (textual notes) of the UBS and NA editions, which are base on INTF data. They who argue against the *Comma*, or other RT verses, ultimately depend on the INTF.

The concept for the INTF began when Kurt Aland consulted a Papist, viz., Bishop Herman

---

365. *Ancestry of Our English Bible*. Rev. ed. by William A. Irwin and Allen P. Wikgren (New York: Harper & Bros., 1953)

Kunst. In 1989, Meinold Krauss interviewed him. One of the questions, with the Bishop's reply in part, follows:

> Krauss: Have you demonstrated the ability not only to encourage *ökumenisch-wissenschaftliche Arbeit* [ecumenical-academic study], but also to organize all ecumenical groups and circles by the establishment of the internationally recognized Institute for New Testament Text Research in Münster?
>
> Kunst: There, I must go further back in time. . . .As other people cultivate roses, I've had friends who do such upon the investigation of the text of the New Testament. Then Professor Kurt Aland came to me. He's a pupil of Hans Lietzmann. He understood somewhat of the situation; *mit ihm habe ich mich zusammengeschlossen* [I formed a close alliance with him]. From this encounter, the Institute for New Testament Research then emerged in Münster.[366]

1959   THIELE, Walter. "Beobachtungen zum Comma Iohanneum (I Joh 5.7 f)" *Zeitschrift für die neutestamentliche Wissenshaft und die Kunde des Urchristentums.* 50: 61-73.

Commenting on Thiele's article, Raymond Brown disagrees with Thiele, who "argues that since some Latin additions may have been translated from lost Greek originals, we cannot deny the possibility of a Greek original for the Comma."

1960   *The New American Standard Bible* [NT portion]

We have noted previously (1898: NESTLE) that Eberhard *bedauert* [bemoaned] the disuse of the mta Greek text, and sought to rescue it. Similarly, the Lockman Foundation (La Habra, CA) felt a "disturbing awareness that the American Standard Version of 1901 was fast disappearing from the scene." They "felt an urgency to rescue" the ASV, an mta translation, "from an inevitable demise," ("Preface to the New American Standard Bible A.D. 1963", p. vi.)

Versions after 1881 followed the H-W Greek text. "However, since the major English translations before 1960 involved liberal translators, we Fundamentalists tended not to use them so that there was no immediate need to spark an in-house controversy. But with the advent of the New American Standard Version NT (NASV) in 1960. . .reputed to be largely the product of fundamental and evangelical translators, the situation changed." *Demystifying the Controversy over the TR*, 2.

--1960---------

Thus, in spite of the availability of the Nestle editions and other mta Greek texts, many

---

366. *Herman Kunst im Gespräch mit Meinhold Krauss*, (Stuttgart: J.F.Steinkopf Verlag, 1989) 73-74.

Fundamentalists continued to use the KJV for their English text up through 1960, as evidenced by the relative disuse of the ASV, RSV, etc. The year 1960 is a major turning point, the first time in history, when a generation of youths in Fundamentalist churches, observed their parents and church leaders, abandon the Authorized Version, without hearing or reading of any massive protests.

In contrast, numerous protests were made against the ERV, ASV, and RSV. Nevertheless, because the NT (of the NASB) follows the 23rd ed. of the Nestle text, Fundamentalists now embraced a version deprived of many pillars of Fundamental doctrines. Major verses for the deity of Christ were now removed. Act 20:28, 1 Tim 3:16, now accomodate those with Unitarian sympathies. 1 John 5:7-8 is now absent.

QUOTE from the marginal note on 1 John 5:8, (v.8 in the NASB):
> A few late mss. read *in heaven, the Father, the Word, and the Holy Spirit, and these three are one. And there are three that bear witness on earth. The Spirit*

The note is misleading. An improvement would be "a few late *Greek* mss., as many as eight Old Latin MSS, and thousands of Vulgate MSS. read..."

1963   CONSIDINE, J.S., and Van DODEWAARD, J.A.E. "Johannine Comma". *Encyclopedic Dictionary of the Bible*. New York, Toronto, London: McGraw-Hill Book Co., Inc. 1175. (This work is a translation and an expansion of Dr. van den Born's *Bijbels Woordenboek* (1957).

QUOTE:
> The first to call the authenticity of the words into question was R. Simon...

Actually, an Arian questioned it before him. See (1669: Sand)

1963   SCHÖNMETZER, Adolfus. "De commate Iohanneo" *Enchiridion Symbolorum*, 32nd ed.

> *Qu:* Utrum tuto negari aut saltem in dubium revocari possit, esse authenitcum textum s. Iohannis in Epistola I, cap. 5 vs.7, qui sec se habet: "Quoniam tres sunt, qui testimonium dant in caelo: Pater, Verbum et Spiritus Sanctus: et hi tress unum sunt"?
> *S. Officium ad hoc dubium 13. Ian. 1897 Responsum dederat:* Negative.
> *Declaratione 2. Iun. 1927 S. Officium illud Resp. retractavit:* Decretum hoc latum est, ut coerceretur audacia privatorum doctorum ius sibi tribuentium, authentiam commatis Ioannei aut penitus reiiciendi aut ultime iudicio suo saltem in dubium vocandi...

1963   HALL, Basil. "The West from the Reformation to the Present Day", *Cambridge History of the Bible*. Cambridge: Cambridge University Press. 60-61.

1964   ANDORF, Josef. *Der Codex Teplensis enthaltend "Di schrift dez newen gezeugz".*

This dissertation of 101 pages, was presented to the Theological Faculty of the

Albert-Ludwig University, Freiburg im Breisgau. Father Josef Andorf contended against the *zählebige* (hard-to-kill) Waldensian hypothesis, which claims that the MS from Tepl should be of Waldensian origin. But Hermann J. Frede of the Vetus Latina Institute, says "Andorf's opposition to the 'Waldensian hypothesis' in his textual critical investigations is not convincing. He also doesn't answer the question how the relationship of the middle-European texts of the late Middle Ages is to be explained with the Southern-French texts, which S. Berger and F. Blass had already demonstrated."[367]

1964   METZGER, Bruce M. *The Text of the New Testament*. 1st ed. New York and Oxford: Oxford University Press. 136.

> The anachronistic views of Burgon have been resuscitated recently by Edward F. Hills in his booklet...in which the author outdoes Burgon in defending the Textus Receptus, arguing even for the genuineness of the *Comma Johanneum* of 1 John v. 7-8.
>
> The passage does not appear in manuscripts of the Latin Vulgate before about A.D. 800.

(The *Comma* appears in a palimpsest, MS. 15 of the Cathedral Library of Leon, Spain. Scrivener dates it to the 7th century in *Plain Introd* 4th ed., 2:72.) Berger, said of this manuscript:

> In the first Epistle of St. John, and particularly in the famous passage of the three witnesses, we find not without pleasure, a text prior to St. Jerome[368]

1964   GREENLEE, J. Harold. *Introduction to New Testament Criticism*. Grand Rapids: Eerdmans. 70-71
QUOTE:

> When Stunica...protested...Erasmus rashly promised to include it in a later edition if it could be found... Erasmus dutifully fulfilled his promise in his edition of 1522. He again omitted it in his later editions.

---

367. H.J. Frede, "Ein Sonderzweig der Vulgata-Überlieferung" *Vetus Latina; Die Reste der Altlateinischen Bibel; Epistulae ad Philippenses et ad Colossenses*, (Freiburg: Verlag Herder, 1971) 288.
368. *Histoire de la Vulgate pendant les premiers siecles du Moyen-Age*, 9.

Greenlee says the "promise" resulted from the objection of Stunica, but Raymond E. Brown, says it was from the objection of Lee, not Stunica. Brown, who is aware of de Jonge's exposure of the myth of the "promise", says "Erasmus replied to Lee that he would have inserted the Comma. . .if he had found a Greek MS. that had it."

1964 DEMOTROPOULOS, Panagotes Ch. Ἡ ηνησιότης τοῦ χωρίου I 'Ιωάν. 5.7 Β -8α περὶ τῶν ἐν τῷ οὐρανῷ μαπρύρων. *Actes du XIIe Congres international d'Etudes byzantines*, Ochride, 10-16 septembre 1961, tom. ii (Belgrade, 1964), 429-38.

1965 THIELE, Walter. *Die Lateinischen Text des 1. Petrusbriefes*. Freiburg: Verlag Herder. 106, 115.

"Facing that, the dogmatic content of the interpolation 1:20 is noteworthy; however it is not unusual in the Catholic Epistles. The Old Latin text offers interpolations of a similar nature; first of all, to mention the *Comma Johanneum* and the interpolation in 1 John 5:20. For the *Comma Johanneum*, the antiquity of the interpolation is assured in the Latin Bible through Cyprian;

1966 REICKE, BO. "Erasmus und die neutestamentliche Textgeschichte". *Theologische Zeitschrift*. 22: 254-265.

1966 ALAND, BLACK, METZGER, WIKGREN. *Greek New Testament*. United Bible Society.

1966   THIELE, Walter. *Vetus Latina: Die Reste der altlateinischen Bibel nach Petrus Sabatier neu gesammelt und herausgegeben von der Erzabtei Beuron*. (Lieferung 1 Jo 3:17-3 Jo 3). Freiburg: Verlag Herder. 360-366. [see app # 18]

1967   BULTMANN, Rudolf. *Die drei Johannesbriefe*. 2nd ed. Göttingen: Vandenhoeck & Ruprecht.

1967   LADD, George Eldon. *The New Testament and Criticism*. Grand Rapids: Eerdmans. 60.

A quote from page 55 on Ladd's guide: [369]

> The author is deliberately following professor Metzger's excellent book as a guide.

1967   DRAINA, C. "Johannine Comma". *New Catholic Encyclopedia*. 15 vols. Washington D.C. : Catholic University of America. 7:1004.

> No scholar any longer accepts its authenticity. But even though the Comma is not a Biblical passage, it is a firm witness to the the fact that the faith of the 5th-century Christian was fully Trinitarian.

1968   BRIGHTON, Louis, "The Comma Johanneum". *Christian News*. (Now called *Lutheran News*) (reprinted in the July 22, 1974 issue, p.1663).

1968   *Biblia sau Sfînta Scriptură*. [Rumanian Bible]

> 7. (căci trei sint cari mărtrisesc în cer: Tatăl, Cuvîntul si duhul Sfînt, si acesti trei una sint.)

1968   BROWN, FITZMEYER, & MURPHY. "Note on the Johannine Comma". *The Jerome Biblical Commentary*. Englewood Cliffs: Prentice-Hall, Inc. 411.

> By a decree of 2 June 1927, the Holy Office clarified an earlier decree that had passed in favor of the authenticity of the passage, explaining that the purpose had not been to inhibit the critical study of the text but to safeguard the teaching authority of the Church...

1968   METZGER, Bruce M. *The Text of the New Testament*. 2nd ed. New York and Oxford: Oxford University Press. 62,101-102,136.

---

369. (Greenlee, Fee, Carson, Ladd, Custer, and a multitude of others regard Metzger as their guide and closely follow him in textual matters. Ladd admits it!)

Erasmus stood by his promise and inserted the passage in his third edition (1522), but he indicates in a lengthy footnote his suspicion that the manuscript had been prepared expressely in order to confute him.

Erasmus initially defended his omission of the verse. According to de Jonge, Metzger misinterpreted the footnote (1980: de JONGE). Metzger not only left the impression that Erasmus retained an alledged "suspicion" of a conspiracy involving a fabricated copy, but he remained silent about a defense Erasamus adopted. D.A.Carson went further and said Erasmus "still judged the *Comma* to be non-original."

1969   BAINTON, Roland. *Erasmus of Christendom*. New York: Charles Scribner's Sons.

Bainton, Professor at Yale, indicates that Erasmus eventually defended his restoration of the verse. Why did he restore it, and keep it in all his successive editions?

> Was his motive simply to quell the storm? His own defense was that the verse was in the Vulgate and must therefore have been in the Greek text used by Jerome.

Bainton's documentation was the 1527 edition, p. 697. D.A. Carson provided no documentation.

Dr. Dobbin remarked in his book *The Codex Montfortianus; A Collation. . .*(p. 56) "Erasmus argues cogently all the while against the genuineness of that very verse, and professes his contempt for the manuscript whose text he follows in admitting it. . .but we confess we are struck with wonder that the logic of so clear an understanding, should be stultified by the weakness of so infirm a will as yielded to in insertion after the consideration he had so well advanced against it." Dr. Dobbin continued "His entire testimony leans one way, while his verdict proceeds in a diametrically opposite direction.

If Bainton interpretated his source correctly, then scholars have excessively leaned upon the testimony of Erasmus' 3rd edition, rather than upon that of his 4th edition. If this is the case, there ought to be no reason for anyone to be "struck with wonder" any longer at the judgement of Erasmus.

1969   [Revival of interest in J.A. Bengal]

A revival of interest in the scholarship and piety of J.A. Bengel, one of most noted defenders of the *Comma*, resulted in the founding at the end of this year, of the Albrecht-Bengel-Haus, which is a *Theologiestudium* located on Ludwig-Krapf-Straße 5 in Tübingen, Germany.

1969   FISCHER, B., SPARKS, H.F., GRIBOMONT, J., THIELE, W. *Bibia sacra iuxta Vulgatam versionem*, Württembergische Bibelanstalt.

The Oxford edition begun by Wordsworth, which took 77 years to complete (1877-1954), was already superceded 15 years later! This new edition is known as the Stuttgart Vulgate, 1st ed. Once again, in a 20th century printed Vulgate, the *Comma* did not appear. Is is any wonder that Metzger could not suppress his delight? He exclaimed:

> In agreement with the Oxford edition and the *Vetus Latina* the new edition rejects the *comma Johanneum* of the Clementine Vulgate.[370]

Perhaps it is as if they imply that now the RTa do not have a "leg to stand on" to support the verse. Perhaps they feel that they have taken away all our props, and hope that we have forgotten history!

Of the thousands of verses to comment on in his one-page coverage of this new edition, Metzger chose two. One was 1 Thess 2:7 were he only commented on the substitution *lenes*. It is noteworthy that the other verse he focused on, was the *Comma*. The Stuttgart Vulgate is an ecumenical Vulgate, for it was edited "under supervision of both Roman Catholic and Protestant scholars."[371]

1970 BRUCE, F.F. "Note on the 'Three Heavenly Witnesses' " *The Epistles of John*. Grand Rapids: Eerdmans. 129-130.

> The classic formulations of Nicaea (325), Constantinople (381) and Chalcedon (451) were the work of theologians who knew nothing of the 'three heavenly witnesses'.

However, "it was invoked at Carthage in 484" according to the Catholic scholar, Raymond Brown.

1971 PARKER, T.H.L. *Calvin's New Testament Commentaries*. Grand Rapids: Eerdmans Publ. Company. 96, 113.

QUOTE: from p. 113
> The third edition [of Erasmus's Greek NT] ...is notorious for being the first printed edition, apart from the Complutensian, to contain the so-called Johannine comma, i.e., the insertion of I John 5.7, supplied in a thoroughtly reprehensible honoring of his word to print it if it could be found in any one Greek manuscript. Nowhere is sixteen-century irresponsibility in things textual exposed so drammatically as in Erasmus' action and in the subsequent almost general acceptance of this sentence.

1972 THIELE, Walter. "Probleme der Versio Latina in den Katholischen Briefen." *Die Alten Übersetzungen des neuen Testamenst, des Kirchenväterzitate und Lektionare*. ed. Kurt Aland. Berlin & New York: Walter de Gruyter. 93-119.

---

370. *Early Versions of the New Testament* 351.
371. Ibid.

1973   HILLS, Edward F. *The King James Version Defended*. 2nd ed.
QUOTE:
> ...it was not trickery which was responsible for the inclusion of the *Johannine Comma* in the Textus Receptus, but the usage of the Latin speaking Church.

1973   BULTMANN, Rudolf. *The Johannine Epistles*. trans. O'Hara, McGaughy, and Funk. Philadelphia: Fortress Press.

1973   *The New Testament, New International Version, An Ecumenical Bible Study Edition*. New York: Paulist Press [published in 1986].

QUOTE from the footnote on 1 John 5:7-8:
> 7,8 Late manuscripts of the Vulgate *testify in heaven: the Father, the Word and the Holy Spirit, and these three are one. 8 And there are three that testify on earth: the* (not found in any Greek manuscript before the sixteenth century)

REFUTATION of footnote's claim: Metzger says it appears in the Greek ms. 629, "a fourteen or fifteenth century manuscript in the Vatican"[372]

1974   REYNOLDS, L.D., and WILSON, N.G. *Scribes and Scholars*. 2nd ed. Oxford: Clarendon Press. 144.

1975   VOS, J.G. "Bible, English Versions", *The Zondervan Pictorial Encyclopedia of the Bible*. 578.

> Even after 350 years and numerous revisions and new trs., the KJV is still by far the most popular and widely circulated Eng. Bible. It has been precious to millions, who have loved it for its simple, dignified, beautiful presentation of the Word of God. It seems unlikely that the KJV will be supplanted by another VS [version] in the near future.

(This shows the pervading irony. The modern academic world says the RT is inferior, yet they don't seem to be reaching the layman, who is still perceived as clinging to his old favorite, an RT-based version)

1975   WIERWILLE, Victor Paul. *Jesus Christ is Not God*. New Knoxville, OH: American Christian Press. 18.

D.S. Chinn and R.C. Newman in their report *Demystifying the Controversy over the Textus Receptus and the King James Version of the Bible* (Hatfield, PA: Biblical Research Institute, n.d.) have said "Even among people who use the KJV alone, it seems amazing what widely different doctrines can be derived. We Fundamentalists believe in the Trinity.

---

372. *A Textual Commentary on the Greek New Testament*, 715.

Yet. . .members of The Way International believe the KJV teaches Arianism." (p. 13). Although V. P. Wierwille, the founder of The Way International, includes the statement "All biblical quotations are from the King James Authorized Version" in this book, Wierwille's statements show he does not trust the KJV. Commenting on 1 John 5: 7-8, he neglects all Old Latin and patristic evidence and says:

> These verses contain words that do not appear in any of the early manuscripts. The words added begin in verse 7 with "in heaven" and go to "in earth" in verse 8. These words are not found in any of the Greek manuscripts before the sixteenth century.

1975   METZGER, Bruce M. *A Textual Commentary on the Greek New Testament*. London and New York: United Bible Societies, Corrected from the 1971 edition. 715-717.

> The passage is absent from every known Greek manuscript except four . . .

(The four he lists are 61 and 629, where the *Comma* appears in the main text, and 88 and 635 where it appears in the margin. Metzger says four. However, the UBS3 lists twice as many: 8 MSS. Considering the view of Dr. Dobbin that 61 is a forgery, it is very odd, why Metzger still cites it, if it indeed is a forgery).

Gordon H. Clark, in his valuable *Logical Criticisms of Textual Criticism,* (Jefferson, MD: The Trinity Foundation, 1986) has exposed several fallacies contained in Metzger's commentary. On p. 38, Clark rejects the *Comma*, but his comments seem derived from one of the oft-repeated modern accounts of the "origin of the *textus receptus*".

1976   [July 26-31: The J.J. Griesbach Bicentenary Colloquium]

The colloquium was held in Münster. While works of Griesbach continue to receive praise today; works of Hezel, a defender of the *Comma*, continue to be forgotten. But we have noted Hezel's linquistic skills from a mere selection of his works under (1786: HEZEL). In addition, Hezel may have been more prominent than Griesbach in their time. In 1776 Hezel was appointed (by the Prince of Saxony) as court councillor, in 1778 appointed (by the Prince of Schwarzburg) as Count Palatinate. In 1793 he became *Definitor* at the Consistory in Geißen. He was not only a university professor, but even a Privy Councillor.[373]

1977   RICHARDS, William Larry. *The Classification of the Greek Manuscripts of the Johannine Epistles*. Missoula: Scholars Press. 253.

Richards examined only 81 MSS out of approximately 600 which contain the General Epistles.

---

373. *ADB* 12:382-83.

1977   ALAND, Kurt. "New Editions of the Greek New Testament." *United Bible Societies Bulletin*. 108/109 3rd/4th quarter.

QUOTE: concerning the 26th ed of the Nestle-Aland Greek N.T.
> It is significant that various Press publications already speak of the new text as the "standard text". This is predicting the future somewhat, but as near as can be told it will be the case soon enough because the "standard text" will in a short time be the only one circulated by the Bible Societies. Most significantly, this will be done in cooperation with the appropriate agencies of the Roman Catholic Church.

(Consequently, both Catholic and Protestants are now omitting the *Johannine Comma*!)

1978   MARSHALL, I. Howard, *The New International Commentary on the New Testament*. (Grand Rapids: Eerdmans). 236-37.

> The facts concerning the so-called "comma Johaneum" (i.e., the Johannine [interpolated] clause, from Greek κόμμα, clause, have been frequently and fully discussed.

> It is wholly improbable that such a weakly attested reading is an original part of the text of 1 John and the added words cause a break in the sense.

1978   van BRUGGEN, Jakob. *The Future of the Bible*. Nashville and New York: Thomas Nelson, Inc. 124.

> Another mistake in the KJV occurs at 1 John 5:7: ...This text is not found in newer translations

Later, in the same page he says:

> These words of the text are missing in the Greek textual tradition. They do have an old and respectable history in the Latin Church, but...as long as a translator of the New Testament wants to base his work on the Greek traditional text, these words do not belong in his translation.

(Van Bruggen is one of the few who admits the old & respectable Latin tradition of the *Comma*. The question is now: Should we have Greek as the exclusive basis for our translations, and ignore the other MSS of the "ancient versions"? None of the positions (mta, MTA, RTa, pRT) <u>both</u> openly announce and practice this discrimination against non-Greek manuscript evidence. In practice, however, only the MTA ignore all Latin evidences.

1979   HILLS, Edward F. "The Johannine Comma (1 John 5:7)". *The King James Version Defended! A Space-Age Defense of the Historic Christian Faith*. 3rd ed. Des Moines: Christian Research Press. 209-213.

QUOTE: quote concerning Calvin and Beza, respectively;

And he [Calvin] receives 1 John 5:7 as genuine

And concerning 1 John 5:7 Beza says "It seems to me that this ought by all means to be retained"

1979 CARSON, Donald A. "Thesis 8". *The King James Version Debate*. Grand Rapids: Baker Book House. 34-35, 59-61.

QUOTE from page 61
(7) The *Comma Johanneum* did not become established in the Old Latin until the fifth century. (8) It does *not* appear in Jerome's Vulgate, despite what Gill says...The *Comma Johanneum* does not appear in the Vulgate until the beginning of the ninth century or thereabout.

A check for copying or unquestioning acceptance of Metzger:
Let M= Metzger, C= Carson

M:The Origin and Dominance of the Textus Receptus (p. 95)
C:Origins of the Textus Receptus (p.33)

M:the *Comma* probably originated as a piece of allegorical exegesis of the three witnesses
C:it--------probably arose from--------------allegorical exegesis of the three witnesses

M:written as a marginal gloss ...the Old Latin Bible during the fifth century.
C:became an established gloss in the Old Latin Bible of the fifth century (p. 35)

M:The passage does not appear in manuscripts of the Latin Vulgate before about A.D. 800
C:It appears in no copy of the Latin Vulgate before about A.D. 800 (p. 35)

M:he indicated in a lengthy footnote his suspicion that. . .
C:he protested in a lengthy footnote that he did so under duress

Carson describes the verse as one which post-dates Jerome. But Samuel Berger, a scholar "whose lifework was the study of the Vulgate", spoke of this verse as *un texte anterieur a saint Jerome* [a text prior to Jerome]. See under (1893: BERGER)

1979   BROWN, Andrew J. *A Review of D.A. Carson's **The King James Version Debate** (1979)*. London: Trinitarian Bible Society. Article No. 69. page 8.

A quote from Brown's treatise:
> (However, the author's [D.A. Carson's] criticisms of [John] Gill's commentary on 1 John 5.7 are entirely correct, as this verse of the TR has practically no support from the Greek manuscripts.)

Note: This may have been the first step toward A.J. Brown's eventual transition. Presumably, he was a RTa at one time, and changed to the pRT position. He is now a MTA, as documented by D.A. Waite (CS-1561 #1 & #2)[374] on Jan 2, 1988. Andrew Brown's dismissal from the TBS was announced by the *Quarterly Record* in April 1990.

1979   GREEN, Jay Patrick (ed.). *Pocket Interlinear New Testament*

> Athough we admit that Erasmus added to this text a handful of readings from the Latin Vulgate, two or three without manuscript authority
> (e.g. Acts 9:5,6) and one from the Complutensian Bible (e.g. 1 John 5;7), we have not deleted these from the Greek text as supplied by the Trinitarian Bible Society -though we do not accept them as true Scripture

---

374. Cassettes are available from Dr. Waite at 900 Park Ave. Collingswood, NJ 08108.

This demonstrates the problem with attempting to adopt a pRT position, by rejecting ONLY the *Comma*, viz., that a rejection of a "handful of readings" must be also be rejected, in order to be consistent.

Many say the *Comma* came from "the Vulgate." Few say it came from *Britannicus*. Now, Mr. Green presents a third view: it came from the Complutensian! But Scrivener said Erasmus "had seen the Complutensian Polyglott in 1522, shortly after the publication of his third edition. . ."[375] In addition, the Complutensian is lacking in the final clause. See (1522: ERASMUS).

The 1988 edition of the *Pocket Interlinear* has a new preface, with no comment on 1 John 5:7.

1979   *The New King James Version*, New Testament. Thomas Nelson

QUOTE from the footnote on 1 John 5:7:
> NU, 𝔐 omit the rest of v.7 and through *on earth* of v.8, a passage found in only 4 or 5 very late *Greek* mss.

The NKJV note is misleading the unsuspecting reader. The verse is not found in "only" a few Greek mss., but is found in thousands of Vulgate mss, and several italic mss.

In reference to the planning stages of the New King James Version, the Executive Director of the NKJV now admits that "Early, it was planned to use the majority text as the translation base for the NKJV New Testament"[376] This implies that such verses as Acts 8:37, and 1 John 5:7 etc. were just about to be omitted for the first time in over 375 years under the name of the "Great Tradition", the King James Version! The basis was to be the majority text, in which:

> those TR readings with weak support, such as 1 John 5:7,8 are corrected.[377]

Contrary to the fashionable "let the reader decide" mood of the 20th century, their original intent was to "correct" such verses by eliminating them from the main text! However, the committee decided not to follow the very Greek text they regard as best. They knowingly left in verses they do not regard as Scripture.

1979   McGEE, J. Vernon. *I John*. Pasadena, CA: Thru the Bible. 149.

---

375. *Plain Introduction* 3rd. ed., p. 433.
376. Arthur L. Farstad, *The New King James Version in the Great Tradition* (Nashville: Thomas Nelson, 1989), 116.
377. *The New King James Version in the Great Trad.* 111.

In a very scholarly presentation, Dr. A.T. Robertson states that this verse is not in the better manuscripts. I heard Dr. Robertson lecture when I was a student in seminary, and he probably knew more Greek than anybody who has ever lived in our generation.

Dr. Robertson, a ardent follower of the views of Tischendorf, Hort & Westcott's, felt codex Sinaiticus and Vaticanus were the "better manuscripts."

1979 KING, Howard. "Book Notice: The New King James Bible..." *The Gospel Clarion*. Metamora, MI: Thornville Baptist Church. July-August. 35-36.

> There is only one textual note, and that is with regard to I John 5:7, 8 which cannot be defended by appeal to the Greek manuscript tradition at all. It is admittedly a Vulgate reading, and has no claim to be Scripture. This will bother some, but it is wrong to publish merely human words as the Word of God, just as much as it is to delete from Scripture anything which is truly from God

1980 STROUSE, Thomas M. *A Critique of D.A. Carson's "The King James Version Debate"*, Watertown, WI: Maranatha Baptist Bible College. 16.

1980 de JONGE, Henk Jan. "Erasmus and the Comma Johanneum", *Ephemerides Theologicae Lovanienses*. LVI: 381-389.

This aricle is particularly valuable since from his words of another work (1983: de JONGE), he is not even an advocate of the received text! But rather he appears undecided at the "extremely complicated question", although he is correct about how we ought to regard the Vulgate if the modern view (critical text) is correct.

QUOTE: a summary of the article in the author's words
> (1) The current view that Erasmus promised to insert the *Comma Johanneum* if it could be shown to him in a single Greek manuscript, has no foundation in Erasmus' work. Consequently it is highly improbable that he included the disputed passage because he considered himself bound by any such promise.
>
> (2) It cannot be shown from Erasmus' works that he suspected the Codex Britannicus (min. 61) of being written with a view to force him to include the *Comma Johanneum*.

QUOTE: from de Jonge concerning the tradition of the alleged promise

> Not only do Simon and Mills make no reference to Erasmus' promise, J. Clericus does not mention it either in his *Ars Critica* (1696, often reprinted) or his commentary on 1 John 5:7 (1714, 2d). Nor do we find it in J.J. Wetstein (1751/2), J. le Long, C.F. Boerner, A.G. Masch (1788-90), J.D. Michaelis (1788), G.W. Meyer (1802/9). J. Townley (the author of *Biblical Anecdotes*: 1821) or in T.F. Dibdin (1827). The earliest reference to Erasmus' promise of which I am aware is that of

T.H. Horne in 1818. It remains unclear from which source Horne derived his information. He was too scrupulous a critic to raise any suspicion that he was the inventor of the whole story.

1981 CUSTER, STEWART. *The Truth About the King James Version Controversy*. Greenville, SC: Bob Jones University Press.

QUOTE concerning the nature of verses lacking support of Greek MSS:
> The most notorious verse of this nature is 1 John 5:7. Out of the more than 5000 Greeks manuscripts there are only two (61 and 629) that have the text...

From among about 500 Greek MSS which contain the 5th chapter of 1st John. Four MSS have the *Comma* in the text, and five others have it in the margin. The ratio would be 9/500 which contain the *Comma*. Dr. Custer's wording gives the impression of a 2/5000+ ratio, as if 5000+ contained this 5th chapter!

> Only when the Roman Catholic hierarchy ordered him to follow the Latin Vulgate reading and include it did he make a rash promise that...

But Erasmus said he followed *Britannicus*, a Greek MS. Besides, the question is not whether the "promise" was rash, but rather whether there was *any* promise at all. If only Dr. Custer had read de Jonge's article, already published in 1980! But he repeated this error even in his public debate in 1983 at the Marquette Manor Baptist Church.

1982 "John, Epistles of", *International Standard Bible Encyclopedia*. Grand Rapids: Eedmans. 1095.

1982   METZGER, Bruce M., ed. *The Reader's Digest Bible*. Pleasantville, NY: Reader's Digest Association.

This "Bible" is professed to be a condensed version of the 1971 Revised Standard Version. In order to condense the fifth chapter of 1 John, Metzger has omitted from v.2 "love God and", from v.3 "And his commandments are not burdonsome. For", v. 5. (the entire verse), v. 18 (the entire verse). The *Comma* was omitted in the 1946 RSV, the 1971 RSV, and certainly in this condensed RSV. It is important to note that this "butchered Bible"[378] appeared only three years after D.A. Carson had just shown his excessive dependence upon his champion, Metzger, in *The King James Version Debate*.

1982   [Dallas, TX: "Councils on Baptist Theology"]

C.H. Spurgeon said "we believe that Calvinism has in it a conservative force which helps to hold men to the vital truth"[379] These councils in Dallas, in which Sovereign Grace Baptists (alternatively Calvinistic or Particular Baptists) gathered, prove that the "conservative force" of Calvinism is not always functional, for D.A. Carson was a guest speaker, among several other Sovereign Grace Baptists, in this council!

1982   PFEIFFER, Charles F., and HARRISON, Everett F. eds., *Wycliff Bible Commentary*. 32nd printing. Chicago: Moody Press. 1477.

> The text of this verse should read, *because there are three that bear record*. The remainder of the verse is spurious. Not a single manuscript contains the trinitarian edition before the fourteenth century, and the verse is never quoted in the controversies over the Trinity in the first 450 years of the church era.

1982   KÜMMEL, Werner Georg. "Einleitungswissenschaft II", *Theologische Realenzyklopädie*. Berlin, New York: Bd IX: 470.

Kümmel is referring to Richard Simon, who perceived because of the examination of numerous MSS and editions of the Church Fathers, that the author's information in the inscription/headings of the Gospels did not derive from the Evangelists,

---

378. In the May 1982 issue of *Plains Baptist Challenger*, a review by E.L. Bynum of this new version appeared. It was entitled "WE REJECT THE READER'S DIGEST BUTCHERED BIBLE". Within the article, E.L. Bynum refers to "Metzger and his Bible butchers." With all respect for the learning of Bruce Metzger, Ph.D., D.D., L.H.D., D. Theol., the choice of Pastor Bynum's words is shown to be remarkably appropiate. The German word "Metzger" is a masculine noun and actually means "butcher". About 40 percent of the text has been removed.
379. *Sword and Trowel*, 1887, p.195.

that in many manuscripts, Mk 16:9ff; Joh 7:53ff and the Trinitarian insertion in 1 John 5:7f (*Comma Johanneum*) is missing, that before Jerome it has given (cf. TRE 6:172ff) a Latin translation deviating from the Vulgate

1982   HODGES Z. and FARSTAD A.L. *The Greek New Testament According to the Majority Text*. (Nashville: Thomas Nelson) 713

[7] ὅτι τρεῖς εἰσὶν οἱ μαρτυροῦντες .. .., ..., ..., ... [8] ... .
.. .., τὸ πνεῦμα, καὶ τὸ ὕδωρ, καὶ τὸ αἷμα· καὶ οἱ τρεῖς εἰς ἕν τὸ εἰσιν.

(The elipses were added by the present writer to allow the reader to note the omissions at a glance).

1982   BROWN, Raymond E. "Appendix IV: The Johannine Comma" *The Epistles of John*. (*The Anchor Bible*; vol. 30). Doubleday & Company. 775-787.

The Catholic scholar, Father Brown, S.S., enquired from Metzger information on the Greek MSS which contain the *comma*. Brown lists these eight:

   61: the Codex Monfortianus (Britannicus [as alleged]), (xvi).
   629: the Codex Ottobonianus at the Vatican, (xiv or xv).
   918: an Escorial (Spain) MS. (xvi).
   2318: a Burcharest (Rumania) MS. (xviii).
   88vl: a variant reading (xvi) from Codex Regius (xii,Naples).
   221vl: a variant reading added to a MS. (x, Bodleian Library at Oxford)
   429vl: a variant reading added to a MS. (xvi,at Wolfenbüttel).
   636vl: a variant reading added to a MS. (xv, Naples.)

1983   WAITE, D.A./QUOROLLO vs. S.CUSTER/PRICE. *Debate on W/H Text vs. Textus Receptus*. (October 11) Marquette Manor Baptist Church, Shumborg, IL. Cassette #1175. Collingswood, NJ: Bible For Today.

See appendix 7 for a review of Dr. Custer's comments.

1983   ALAND, BLACK, MARTINI, METZGER, & WIKGREN, eds., *The Greek New Testament*. 3rd. edition (corrected). United Bible Societies. Stuttgart: Biblia-Druck GmbH, 824.

According to this edition, the UBS3, the *Comma* occurs in the following Greek manuscripts:

221^{mg} 2318 (629 ...ἀπὸ τοῦ οὐρανοῦ...τρεῖς εἰς τὸ ἕν...ἀπὸ τῆς γῆς; 61 629 *omit the following* καὶ οἱ τρεῖς...εἰσιν; 61 88^{mg} 429^{mg} 629 636^{mg} 918 *with other minor variants*) (it^m) vg^{cl}

The UBS3 also says it occurs in the following Latin manuscripts:

(it^{c,dem,div} *omit: in Christo Iesu*) it^{m,p} (it^q *omit: et hi tres unum sunt in Christo Iesu*) vg^{mss} Varimadum Priscillian Cassian Ps-Vigilius mss$^{acc.}$ to Victor-Vita Ps-Athanasius Fulgentius Ansbert

Since various editions which contain the *Comma* were neglected by the UBS (excluding the Vulgate editions, which were not given distinctive symbols), the following additional symbols are now being supplied (and redefined for the Vulgate):

a) SYR^{Tr-mg} SYR^{Hu} SYR^{Gu} SYR^{Sch}
b) GEO^{Mosc}
c) ARM^{Usc} arm^{Zohr}
d) lat^{Bede}
e) VG^s VG^{cl} VGst VG^{ww}
f) vg^{Leon} vg$^{over\ 7000\ others}$
g) ger^{Tepl}
h) slav^x slav^y

Capital letters indicate editions. Small letters indicate manuscripts. The symbol "vg^{mss}" indicates "some vulgate manuscripts" and thus is inadequate to indicate Porson's estimate that 49 out of 50 contain the *Comma*. Hence, vg$^{over\ 7000\ others}$ is now being suggested.

These symbols respectively apply to the following:

a) Syriac editions: Tregellius (in margin), Hutter, Gutbier, Schaaf.
b) The first Georgian edition. Published in Moscow, 1743.
c) The first Armenian edition. Published in 1666 by A.D. Uscan; The one manuscript of the 18 used by Zohrob which contained it.
d) The one manuscript by Bede which contained the *Comma*.
e) Vulgate: Sixtine, Clementine, Stuttgart (1975), Wordsworth-White,
f) The Leon mss of the vulgate dated to the 7th century by Scrivener.
g) The Codex Teplensis dated c.1400
h) The "few recent" Slavonic MSS mentioned by Scrivener which contain the *Comma*.

In the summary of implied complete accounts of evidence for the *Comma* in three ancient language versions, Greek, Latin, and Syriac, "sugg" will be used here to signify an improvement toward a more complete account, and "UBS3c" signifies The *"Third Edition (Corrected)"* of UBS. The critical apparatus for the UBS is listed in UBS3 (1975) and UBS3c (1983). NS = Nestle ed. NA= Nestle-Aland ed.

Greek witnesses:
(1927) NS^{12}: 61 ---- ----- ----- 629 635^{mg} ----- --- ----
(1932) NS^{15}: 61 ---- ----- ----- 629 635^{mg} ----- --- ----
(1936) NS^{16}: 61 ---- ----- ----- 629 635^{mg} ----- --- ----
(1952) NA^{21}: 61 88^{mg} ----- ----- 629 ----- ----- --- ----
(1957) NA^{23}: 61 88^{mg} ----- ----- 629 ----- ----- --- ----

(1960) NA²⁴: 61 88^mg ----- ----- 629 ----- ----- --- ----
(1963) NA²⁵: 61 88^mg ----- ----- 629 ----- ----- --- ----
(1966) UBS1: 61 88^mg 221^mg 429^mg 629 635^mg 636^mg 918 2318
(1968) MZHB: 61 88^mg ----- ----- 629 ----- ----- --- ---- ω 110
(1975) UBS3: 61 88^mg 221^mg 429^mg 629 ----- 636^mg 918 2318
(1975) MZCM: 61 88^mg ----- ----- 629 635^mg ----- --- ----
(1979) NA²⁶: 61 88^mg 221^mg 429^mg 629 ----- 636^mg 918 2318
(1983) UBS3c 61 88^mg 221^mg 429^mg 629 ----- 636^mg 918 2318
(1987) ANTF9 61 88^mg 221^mg 429^mg 629 ----- 636^mg 918 2318 2473

Latin witnesses: (1988 NA²⁶ = 10th printing of NA²⁶)
1927 NS¹²: --- ----- ----- --- it^m --- --- it^r ----- vg^cav.tol vg^s.cl
1932 NS¹⁵: --- ----- ----- --- it^m --- --- it^r ----- vg^cav.tol vg^s.cl
1936 NS¹⁶: --- ----- ----- --- it^m --- --- it^r ----- vg^cav.tol vg^s.cl
1952 NA²¹: --- ----- ----- --- it^m --- --- it^r ----- vg^cav.tol vg^s.cl
1957 NA²³: --- ----- ----- --- it^m --- --- it^r ----- vg^cav.tol vg^s.cl
1960 NA²⁴: --- ----- ----- --- it^m --- --- it^r ----- vg^cav.tol vg^s.cl
1963 NA²⁵: --- ----- ----- --- it^m --- --- it^r ----- vg^cav.tol vg^s.cl
1966 UBS1: --- ----- ----- --- it^m --- --- --- ----- -------- vg^cl
1975 UBS3: it^c it^dem it^div --- it^m it^p it^q --- ----- vg^mss
1983 UBS3c it^c it^dem it^div --- it^m it^p it^q --- ----- vg^mss
1988 NA²⁶: --- ----- ----- it^l it^m --- --- it^r ----- vg^mss vg^cl

1991 sugg: it^c it^dem it^div it^l it^m it^p it^q(=it^r) lat^Bede vg^over 7000?
1991 sugg   6..   2   ...div..   4..   5...   54..64   ......lat^Bede vg^over 7000?
dated: 11+ 12+   12   7   5   13   5+

Syriac witnesses:
UBS3: -------- ----- ----- ------ (none)
UBS3c -------- ----- ----- ------ (none)
sugg: SYR^Tr-mg SYR^Hu SYR^Gu SYR^Sch

UBS3c 61 88^mg 221^mg 429^mg 629 ----- 636^mg 918 2318 it^c it^dem it^div --- it^m it^p it^q ---
------; ------no syriac editions---, --no arm ed/ms-; -no geo; vg^mss: -----no vulgate examples are listed-----; -no ger-; --no slav--

sugg: 61 88^mg 221^mg 429^mg 629 635^mg 636^mg 918 2318 2473 it^c it^dem it^div it^l it^m it^p it^r lat^Bede; SYR^Tr-mg SYR^Hu SYR^Gu SYR^Sch; ARM^Usc arm^Zohr; GEO^Mosc; vg^mss: VG^Six VG^Cl vg^Leon vg^over 9000 others; ger^Tepl ger¹⁴ Hi ger⁴ Lo ; slav^x slav^y

1983   de JONGE, Henk Jan, ed. "Apologia Respondens ad ea qvae Iacobvs Lopis Stvnica Taxaverat In Prima Dvntaxat Novi Testamenti Aeditione". *Erasmi Opera Omnia*. IX-2. Amsterdam and Oxford: North Holland Publishing Company. 252-258.

QUOTE: from de Jonge from p. 19-20 of his introduction (from this volume just cited above) revealing his view that the received text (in effect) is "late and inferior"

The problem is that, in evaluating and criticizing the old translation used in the Latin church, he chose his criterion in Greek manuscripts of the Byzantine church. Within the textual tradition of the New Testament these Greek manuscripts represented not only another branch than the Vulgate, but also, as is now gererally acknowledged, a relatively late and inferior stage of transmission. From a modern point of view and if allowance is made for the limitations to which the Vulgate was necessarily subject as a translation, one must admit that the Vulgate contained a more reliable text of the New Testament than Erasmus' Greek manuscripts, let alone his new Latin translation.

1984 WAITE, D.A. *Dr. Stewart Custer Answered on the T.R. and K.J.V.* Collingswood, NJ: Bible For Today. 92-93.
QUOTE:

Hold the Line on 1 John 5:7 Until All of Burgon's Methodology is Followed for the Entire New Testament.

Now, look, I am not going to touch 1 John 5:7 until the entire process of Dean Burgon is worked out, and I don't think that will be in my lifetime, because ...nobody cares to do it.

Appendix #10 verifies that Dr. Waite is correct.
Note: Burgon's methodology included the following: a completed index to quotations of the Church Fathers, a familiarity with the contents of the "ancient versions" (which includes a mastery of the languages of Gothic, Aethiopic, Armenian, and Georgian and Slavonian versions), and an extensive time-consuming collation of all the uncollated MSS (which includes an estimated 8000 Latin MSS.)

1984   LETIS, Theodore P.   preface, *The King James Version Defended*, 4th ed., by Edward F. Hills. Des Moines: Christian Research Press.

QUOTE: from p. viii
> Finally, it must be stated that Hills did not hold to an uncritical, perfectionist view of the TR as some have assumed...nor did he advocate with absolute certainty the genuineness of the *Johannine Comma*...

1985   GREENLEE, J. Harold. *Scribes, Scrolls, and Scripture*. Grand Rapids: Eerdmans. 44-45.

> Erasmus strongly suspected that he had been tricked, but he nevertheless fulfilled his promise and inserted the "heavenly witnesses" in his third edition of 1522 with a footnote indicating his doubts about the manuscript that had been shown to him.

(A translation[380] of a portion of the footnote by Erasmus, as provided by William Orme, follows: "although I suspect that this manuscript hath been corrected and accommodated to some of our [Latin] copies.")

1985   POSSET, Franz. "John Bugenhagen and the Comma Johanneum", *Concordia Theological Quarterly*. 49 #4: 245-251.

This is the most informative of recent[381] articles which reveals the historic Lutheran position regarding the comma.

1985   SWAGGART, Jimmy. *Questions and Answers*. Baton Rouge, LA: Jimmy Swaggart Ministries. 199.

> Many people conclude that the Father, the Son, and the Holy Spirit are all one and the same. Actually they are not. These people take 1 John 5:7 to mean one in number, when that is not what is meant at all.

R.C. Sproul quoted this in his essay in Mike Horton's *Agony of Deceit*, but he declined to comment on the verse.

1986   SCREECH, M.A. Introduction. *Erasmus' Annotations on the New Testament; The Gospels*. London: Gerald Duckworth & Co. xix.

---

380. Orme, *Memoirs of the Controversy*, 6
381. The present author became aware of this article from the QUICKSEARCH computer facility in the main library at the U of AZ. It was obtained via interlibrary loan on December 15, 1989 from Ft. Wayne, IN. See above (Luther, 1527) for the quote from this article.

A quote concerning Erasmus:
> His *Annotations* show him constantly learning from a wide range of evidence. He had far less to go on than modern editors, but his methods were similar; statements to the contrary in general histories of New Testament scholarship can safely be discounted. It does set one dreaming, though, to realise that, through Paul Bombasiais, he actually had indirect access to readings of the *Codex Vaticanus*...

1986   HOLECZEK, Heinz, ed. *Novum Instrumentum*. (a facsimilie of Erasmus's work of 1516.) Basil: Frommann-Holzboog. 617-618.

A quote from Erasmus' comment on I John 5:7-8 in this Latin edition:

> There are three which give witness in heaven: In the Greek codices, I find only this about the triple testimony, ὅτι τρεῖς εἰσιν ὅι μαρτυροιῶτες, ὁ πνεῦμα καὶ τὸ ὕδωρ, τὸ αἷμα. Likewise [?] since there are three which testify, the spirit, and the water, and the blood. And these three are one.[382]

1986   [Revival of interest in J.M. Goeze]

This revival of the famous Lutheran pastor from Hamburg, who is an important defender of the *Comma*, resulted in the publication of *Vestigia Biblia; Jahrbuch des Deutschen Bibel-Archives Hamburg; Johann Melchior Goeze 1717-1786*, (Hamburg: Friedrich Wittig Verlag)

1986   ALAND, Barbara. *Das Neue Testament in Syrischer Überlieferung; I. Die Grossen Katholischen Briefe*. Berlin & New York: Walter de Gruyter. 252.

Of the Syriac MSS, there are over 350 Peshitta MSS, and 125 Harclean MSS. This edition used only 9 Peshitta MSS[383] (2.5%) and only 3 Harclean MSS[384] (2.4%)! As expected, the *Comma* is not included in this new Syriac edition. Is it a fair statement to say "The *Comma* does not occur in the Syriac!" on the basis of 2.5% (12 out of over 425) of the MSS?

1987   BORGER, Rykle. "Das Comma Johanneum in der Peschitta". *Novum Testamentum*. XXXIX, 3: 280-284

---

382. Tres sunt q. testimonium dant in cælo.) In græco codice tantum hoc reperio de testimonio triplici, ὅτι τρεῖς εἰσιν ὅι μαρτυροιῶτες, ὁ πνεῦμα καὶ τὸ ὕδωρ, τὸ αἷμα. i. quonia tres sunt q. testificant, spiritus, & aqua, & sanguis. Et hi tres unu sunt.)
383. These nine are B.L.Add. 17.121, Sinai 53/5, Vat.syr. 266, B.L.Add.14.470, B.L. Add.14.448, B.L.Add.14.473, B.L.Add.17.120, B.L.Add.14.472, and B.L. Add.18.812.
384. These three are Oxf.NC 333, B.L.Add.14.474, and Cambr.UL Add.1700.

Die Weglassung des Comma Johanneum ist nach Hutter ein *insigne erratum nec silentio praetereundum nec ulla ratione excusandum*. Für diese kühne Behauptung beruft er sich auf Hieronymus - aber der Prologus *septem epistolarum canonicarum* (Wordsworth und White III, S. 230 f.) stammt bekanntlich nicht von Hieronymus.

A translation of this paragraph is provided in this paper under (1600: HUTTER).

Why did Borger write this article? After reading the article, one gets the impression that he is writing in a defensive nature; to defend the omission of the *Comma* in Barbara Aland's edition. But he discusses only previous editions, but does not deal with Syriac MSS.

1987   LETIS, Theodore P., ed. *The Majority Text: Essays and Reviews in the Continuing Debate*. Grand Rapids: Institute for Biblical Textual Studies. 17.

QUOTE: from the Lutheran editor, on the issue of the TR non-majority readings

> ...further editions of the TR appearing after Erasmus *could* have excised the *Johannine comma* and other Latin or non-majority readings, but all sixteen and seventeenth century TR editors chose not to.

> Conservative Lutherans...would do well to reevaluate this issue in light of the judgments and arguments of the greatest of Lutheran NT critics, Johann Albert Bengel (1687-1752), who not only argued in favor of the *Pericope de Adultera* and the last twelve verses of Mark sixteen- but even for the *Johannine comma*!

1987   ALAND, Kurt. ed. *Text und Textwert der Griechischen Handschriften des Neuen Testaments. I. Die Katholischen Briefe*. Berlin, New York: Walter de Gruyter. 163-166.

This is volume nine of *Arbeiten zur Neutestamentlichen Textforschung*, or *ANTF 9*. It presents the results of the collation of the general epistles (Jam, 1Pet 2Pet 1Jo 2Jo 3Jo Jud). The collation of 1 John 5:7-8 involved 498 [=499-1] Greek MSS. It seems that MS. 496, which is listed as a witness hostile to the *Comma*, has been overlooked. It is neither listed in the *Verzeichnis* of *ANTF 9*, nor in that of NA[26]. Of 498 MSS, 97% of the hostile witnesses are dated 10th or later. There are only 6 Greek MSS dated from the 6th century or earlier, which testify against the inclusion of the *Comma*. In the display of the reading from MS. 61, there is no mention of the omission of εἰς τὸ ἕν εἰσιν.

1987   ALAND, Kurt and Barbara Aland. *The Text of the New Testament*. [From *Der Text Des Neues Testament*. (1981); transl. Errol F. Rhodes] Grand Rapids: William B. Eerdmans. 245,306

> Many other passages could be mentioned, such as the famous "Comma Johanneum" of 1 John 5:7-8. But for anyone who has read this far, a glance at the data in the critical apparatus of Nestle-Aland (which is exhaustive for this passage) should make any further comment unnecessary to demonstrate the secondary nature of this addition and the impossibility of its being at all related to the original form of the

text of 1 John.

1988   BIETENHOLZ, Peter G., ed. *The Collected Works of Erasmus.* vol. 8. Toronto, Buffalo, London: University of Toronto Press.

1988   MOORMAN, Jack A. "The Most Famous Minority Verse -I John 5:7". *When the KJV Departs from the "Majority Text" ; A New Twist in the Continuing Attack on the Authorized Version.* 2nd ed. Collingswood: The Bible For Today. 115-123.

Note: Jack Moorman's collection and summary of evidence for this verse is a welcome relief from eyes wearied from reading hackneyed accounts of Erasmus and his "promise". He presents his case admirably and in only nine pages. Credit is due to him for gleaning data on MSS evidence from various works, especially from Scrivener's 3rd edition of *A Plain Introduction to Textual Criticism of the New Testament.* From Scrivener alone, he draws our attention to the interesting Eastern editions which contain the *Comma.*

1. 1569 Tremellius' 2nd Syriac Peshitta (placed in margin)
2. 1664 G. Gutbier's Syriac edition (Hamburg)
3. 1666 Bishop Uscan's Armenian Bible (the 1st printed Armenian Bible)
4. 1789 John Zohrob's Armenian Bible (1/18 of the Armenian mss had it)
5. 1743 The first printed Georgian Bible
6. Scrivener's mention of a "few recent Slavonic MSS"

1989   WALLACE, Daniel B., "Some Second Thoughts on the Majority Text" *Bibliotheca Sacra,* Jul-Sep, 270-290

> Second, why do majority text advocates count only *Greek* manuscripts? Is is because inclusion of the Latin Vulgate, with more that 8,000 extant copies...would demolish their theory?

(Porson granted the possibility that 97.5% to 98% of the Latin MSS may contain the verse. See above (1790: PORSON). Metzger reports there are "more than 10,000" Latin MSS. [385] If Metzger's estimate[386] is fair, and if each of these 10,000 Latin MSS contained a reading of the fifth chapter of John's epistle, and if Porson guessed correctly, then between 9750 to 9800 Latin MSS contain the comma. Although Tregelles said "The disputed clause is *wanting* in more than fifty of the OLDEST Latin manuscripts, containing the ENTIRE New

---

385. Bruce Metzger, *The Early Versions of the New Testament* (Oxford: Oxford Clarondon Press, 1977), 293.
386. Presumably, Metzger knew that H.J. White's estimate of "at least 8000" is out-dated. It seems Metzger merely tagged on 2000. Dr. W. Thiele, of the VLI, does not agree with the figure. When asked for an estimate he merely says "Niemand weiß."

Testament." [387] the claim (expressed by Tregelles himself) remains undisputed that "most of the manuscripts of the Vulgate Latin contain the disputed clause..."

1989 SAWYER, John Wesley (ed.) [reprint of Tyndale's 1526 NT]

1989 DANIELL, David. (ed.) [reprint of Tydales's 1534 NT]

1989 PICKERING, Wilbur N. [July 7: Interview with Gary Hudson]

> Now one of the criticisms that Waite levels against us is that we have not yet collated all the manuscripts. That's entirely true. I grant that. We have not. But he tries to argue that Burgon would not have us revise the text until such an hour that all the manuscripts were collated...But, the problem is that Burgon himself did not do that. In fact, he left behind his own edition of the Gospel of Matthew long before...[388]

Why did Burgon prematurely begin to "correct" Matthew? Hills explained why Burgon "looked askance at the Textus Receptus and declined to defend it..."[389] It was due to his high Anglicanism. Thus, unless the MTA share the theology of high Anglicanism, they cannot justify why they also look askance at the TR, by pointing back in history to a heritage of non-Anglican MTA as their exemplary patterns to follow. Apparently none existed. It is any wonder why the MTA of today suppress the issue of theology?

1990 HUDSON, Gary R. [May 12] "Why Dean Burgon Would Not Join the Dean Burgon Society"

In this paper, Evangelist Gary Hudson announced on pages 11-12 "I plan to give I John 5:7 a complete treatment answering most of the arguments set forth in its favor by Hills and others... Hills' argument about the "gender argument" of this passage necessitating its place in the text is absolutely unfounded." [emphasis his]

Mr. Hudson also attempted to prove from Burgon's quote of Griesbach, that this indicated Burgon's own view on 1 John 5:7.

1990 MAYNARD, M. [May] *A Select Annotated Bibliography on the Johannine Comma*.

The paper was submitted for fulfillment of the requirement in "Classical Philology 510." It was completed the same month in which Mr. Hudson wrote the above paper.

---

387. T.H. Horne, *Introduction to the Critical Study*, new ed., (London: Longmans, Green, & Co., 1866), 362. His source is Bishop Marsh's Lectures, part vi. p.18
388. As quoted by Gary Hudson in "Why Dean Burgon Would Not Join the Dean Burgon Society" p. 10
389. *The King James Version Defended*, 4th ed. p. 192.

1990   ROBINSON, Maurice & W.G. PIERPONT [August] [MJT on diskette]

The Robinson-Pierpont MJT (R/P) supplements the two editions of the Hodges-Farstad MJT (H/F). Within a period of 8 years, there are now 3 Majority texts: $H/F^1, H/F^2$, and R/P. W. Pickering says the R/P text "differs somewhat from the Hodges-Farstad edition."

Dr. Robinson wrote in the same year (1990) "In a properly balanced methodology (followed by Burgon himself), one should maintain that it is in the in the *aggregate consentient testimony* of *all* texual witnesses--good as well as bad--that one finds preserved providentially the data necessary whereby to establish the near-autograph NT text."[390] Did Burgon follow this methodology? Robinson did not. Dr. Pickering admitted in July 1989 that "Burgon himself did not do that." Hence, Burgon was inconsistent. His suggested 150 "corrections" of Matthew implies impatience. Thus, to justify the Majority texts of the late 20th century, the argument amounts to this: "If Burgon was inconsistent and did not follow his own methodology of waiting for all the collated evidence to be before him, they we also may be as inconsist and as impatient to correct the TR as he was."

1990   PIERPONT, William G. *Some Improvements to the King James Version from the Majority Greek Manuscripts*.

1990   MOORMAN, Jack A. *Early Manuscripts and the Authorized Version*. Collingswood, NJ: Bible For Today. 147.

1990   HUA, Andrew S.P. "Rediscovering the Complutensian Text"
A quote concerning the "Mc" (Complutensian text):

> As expected, Mc contains the *Comma Johanneum* of 1 John 5:7-8. It is interesting to note that Greg. 629 which according to Metzger (p.101) is one of the only 3 extant manuscripts which contain the *Comma*, is in fact a 14th Century manuscript which is part of the Vatican collection and could possibly have been available to Ximenes.

Hua claims the Complutensian is similar to the current Majority Text. There is a similarity. But there are differences to be noted.
(1)Mt 6:13, (2)Jo 3:25, (3)Ac 10:21, (4)Ac 15:34, (5)Ac 24:6, (6)Ac 24:7, (7)Ac 24:8, (8)1Jo2:14, (9)1Jo5:7-8

verse	1	2	3	4	5	6	7	8	9
MJT:	-in	sg.	out	out	out	out	out	-in	out
CPG:	out	pl.	-in	-in	-in	-in	-in	out	-in

The differences are shown in detail in appendix 5.

---

390. "Whose Unholy Hands on What? A Review Article", p. 10.

1990   METZGER, Bruce M., et al. *The New Revised Standard Version.*

To no one's surprise, the *Comma* is omitted.

1990   ROBINSON, Maurice A. "Whose Unholy Hands on What?"

This review[391] portrays an MTA perspective far different than A.J. Brown's. Dr. Robinson warns against passionate invective. However, he himself proceeds to use "highly intemperate and abusive" language such as the "modern insistence of fundamentalist extremists on a particular Greek texttype" and "these extremists" and "the extremist TR/KJV defenders." Presumably, A.J. Brown would be more of a gentleman and not resort to this emotional expression of bitterness.

1990   [Apr] Quarterly Record of the TBS announces changes.

1990   [May 1] Andrew J. Brown's open letter.

Mr. A.J. Brown, is now regarded as an MTA.

> In fact, my support for the Society's historic position on the Authorized Version and its underlying Greek and Hebrew texts is well known to members of the Society. . .On the other hand it has been necessary to point out from time to time that no translation or printed edition of the Greek and Hebrew texts is perfect. . .

1990   [May 21] open letter from Trinitarian Bible Society.

In reference to A.J. Brown, the TBS Committee "there had been evidence over the years of his leanings away from the Received Text, and his support for the Authorized Version."

1990   [Dec 13] Conversation with Dr. Walter Thiele at 4:30PM

After his lecture that day, we went into the library of the Theologicum of Universität Tübingen. I had brought along the article "Beobachtungen. . .", which he wrote over 30 years ago (1959) and I pointed to the part in which he instisted that Cyprian quoted directly from a manuscript which contained the Comma. I asked if he still held this view. He nodded his head firmly as he said:
   Ja. Doch ! Aber, ich bin allein.

---

391. The article is a welcome exposure of how J.P. Green, Sr. placed his own grubby hands upon selected works of J.W. Burgon and distorted them beyond recognition.

APPENDICES

Appendix one:

pro = advocate; *contra* = opposer

TERTULLIAN (c.160-c.220)
    CYPRIAN (200-258) *pro*
        SABELLIUS (?-260)
            PRISCILLIAN (?-385) *pro*
                JOVINIAN (?-c.405)
                    EUSTOCHIUM (c370-418)
                      JEROME (c345-420)
                        AUGUSTINE (354-430)

FULGENTIUS (468-527) *pro*
  CASSIODIUS (480-583) *pro*
    ISIDORE of Seville (?-636) *pro*
      JAQUB of Edessa (?-708) *pro?*

AQUINAS (c1225-1274) *pro*

John WYCLIFFE (c1329-1384) *pro*

F. XIMENES (1437-1517) ?
    U. ZWINGLI (1481-1531) *contra*
      D. ERASMUS (1465-1536) *pro!*
        Edward LEE (1482-1544) *pro!*
          M. LUTHER (1483-1546) *contra*
        J.A. WIDMANSTADT (?-1557)
        Johannes BUGENHAGEN (1485-1558) *contra*
          Lopez de ZUÑIGA (c1465-1564) *pro*
            John CALVIN (1509-1564) *pro*
        Juan Gines de SEPULVEDA (1490-1573)
              Georg WITZEL (1501-1573)
                Wilhelm SIRLETS (1514-1585)
                  Georgio BLANDRATA (?-c.1590)   [Unitarian]
Theodore BEZA (1519-1605) *pro*
  Elias HUTTER (1553-1605) *pro!*
    Johann CRELLIUS (1590-1633)   [Socinian]
      Johann Gerhard (1582-1637) *pro!*

John COTTON (1584-1652) *pro*
John SELDON (1584-1654) *contra?*
Henry HAMMOND, D.D. (1605-1660) *pro*
Aegidius GUTBIER (1617-1667) *pro* [Syriac scholar]
Christopher SAND (1644-1680) *contra*
John OWEN (1616-1683) *pro*
Francis TURRETIN (1623-1687) *pro*
Johann LEUDSEN (?-1699)
J. SPENER (1635-1705) *pro*
John MILL (1645-1707) *pro!*
George BULL, D.D. (1634-1710) *pro*
Thomas SMITH (1638-1710) *pro*
Richard SIMON (1638-1712) *contra*
Peter ALLIX, D.D. (1641-1717) *pro*
David MARTIN (1639-1721) *pro!*
F.E. KETTNER (1671-1722) *pro!*
Francis GASTRELL, D.D. (1662-1725) *pro*
Martin Sylvester GRABE (1674-1727) *pro*
Sir Isaac NEWTON (1642-1727) *contra*
Karl SCHAAF (1647-1729) *pro!* [Syriac scholar]
Edmund CALAMY, D.D. (1671-1732) *pro*
William WAKE, D.D. (1657-1737) *pro*
Mathrin Veyssière de LaCROZE (1661-1739) *contra*
Daniel WATERLAND, D.D. (1683-1740) *pro*
Thomas EMYLYN (1663-1741) *contra*
William BERRIMAN, D.D. (1688-1750) *pro*
Johann A. BENGEL (1687-1752) *pro!*
J.J. WETTSTEIN (1693-1754) *contra*
Augustine CALMET (1672-1757) *pro*
Nikolaus ZINZENDORF (1700-1761)
George BENSON, D.D. (1669-1762) *contra*
Giuseppe BIANCHINI (1704-1764)
Thomas SECKER (1693-1768) *pro*
John GILL, D.D. (1697-1771) *pro*
James SLOSS (1698-1772) *pro*
William BOWYER (1699-1777) *contra*
Johann A. ERNESTI (1707-1781) *pro*
Gotthold E. LESSING (1729-1781)
Johann Melchior GOEZE (1717-1786) *pro!*
Johann D. MICHAELIS (1717-1791) *contra*
F.A. KNITTEL (1721-1792) *pro!*
Edward GIBBON (1737-1794) *contra*
George TRAVIS (1741-1797) *pro!*
Thomas KNOWLES, D.D. (1723-1802) *pro?*
SOSIPATER (c.1721-1803) *pro*
Gottlob Christian STORR (1746-1805)

Samuel HORSLEY (1733-1806) *pro*
Richard PORSON (1759-1808) *contra*
Johann Jakob GRIESBACH (1745-1812) *contra*
John HEY, D.D. (1734-1815) *pro*
John BARRETT, D.D. (1753-1821) *contra*
Thomas F. MIDDLETON, D.D. (1769-1822) *pro!*
Cappel LOFFT (1751-1824) *contra*
Wilhelm Friedrich HEZEL (1754-1824) *pro!!*
William HALES, D.D. (1741-1831) *pro!*
Charles BUTLER (1750-1832) *pro!*
Adam CLARKE (1762-1832) *contra*
Thomas BURGESS, D.D. (1756-1837) *pro!*
Richard LAURENCE (1760-1838) *pro?*
Thomas FALCONER (1772-1839)
Herbert MARSH, D.D. (1757-1839) *contra*
Henry John TODD (1763-1845) *pro-TR*
J.M.A. SCHOLZ (1794-1852) *contra*
Angelo MAI (1782-1854) *pro*
Rev. John OXLEE (1779-1854) *contra*
Friedrich LÜCKE (1791-1855) *contra*

Johann Georg REICHE (1794-18??)
Louis GAUSSEN, D.D. (1790-1863) *pro!*
C.H.A. MALAN (1787-1864)
Frederick NOLAN, LL.D. (1784-1864) *pro!*
Thomas TURTON, D.D. (1780-1864) *contra*
Nicholas WISEMAN, D.D. (1802-1865) *pro!*
Charles FORSTER (?-1871) *pro!*
L.F.K. TISCHENDORF (1815-1874) *contra*
Samuel P. TREGELLES (1813-1875) *contra*
Samuel SHARPE (1799-1881) *contra*
Thomas R. BIRKS (1810-1883) *pro-TR*
John William BURGON (1813-1888)
Jean Pierre Paulin MARTIN (1840-1890)
Orlando Thomas DOBBIN, LL.D. (1807-1890) *contra*
F.H.A. SCRIVENER (1813-1891) *contra*
F.J.A. HORT (1828-1892) *contra*
Solomon Caesar MALAN, D.D. (1812-1894) *pro*
George W. SAMSON (1819-1896) *pro!*
Henry T. ARMFIELD (1836-1898) *pro!*
Samuel BERGER (1843-1900) *pro?*
B.F. WESTCOTT (1825-1901) *contra*
Edward MILLER (1825-1901) *contra*
Alvah HOVEY (1820-1903)
Herman HAUPT, Ph.D. (1817-1905)

C.H. WALLER (1840-1910)
J. WORDSWORTH (1843-1911)

Dr. Eberhard NESTLE (1851-1913) *contra*
H.F. von SODEN (1852-1914) *contra*
Dr. Ludwig KELLER (1849-1915)
Ernest Ch. BABUT (1875-1916) *pro-Prisc*
Caspar René GREGORY, D.D. (1846-1917) *contra*
Albert HAUCK, Th.D. (1845-1918)
B.B. WARFIELD, D.D. (1851-1921) *contra*
Eugene MANGENOT (1856-1922)
Edward RIGGENBACH (1861-1927)
Dr. Adolf von HARNACK (1851-1930) *contra*
August BLUDAU (1862-1930) *contra*
Francis PIEPER (1852-1931) *pro!*
Karl KÜNSTLE (1859-1932)
A.H. NEWMAN, D.D. (1852-1933)
A.T. ROBERTSON, D.D. (1836-1934) *contra*
Henry Julian WHITE (1859-1934)
Hildebrand HÖPFL (1872-1934) *pro?*
Albert Curtis CLARK (1859-1937)
Herman C. HOSKIER (1864-1938)
Adolf JÜLICHER (1857-1938)

George Ricker BERRY (1865-1945) *pro-TR*
Hugh POPE (1869-1946) *pro!*
Kirsopp LAKE (1872-1946)
Mateo del Álamo (1878-1947)
Anton BAUMSTARK (1872-1948) *pro?*
Frederick G. KENYON (1863-1952) *contra*
Teófilo Ayuso MARAZUELA (?-1962) *contra*
Benjamin G. WILKINSON (1872-1968) *pro-TR*
Erwin NESTLE (1883-1972) *contra*
Ernest Cadman COLWELL (1901-1974)
Margaret DEANESLY (c1885-1977) [Historian]
Edward F. HILLS (1912-1981) *pro!*
Jean DUPLACY (1916-1983)
David Otis FULLER (1903-1988) *pro*
Harry A. STURZ (?-1989)

Leonard VERDUIN (1897-....) [Historian]
Kenneth Willis CLARK (1898-....)
Allen Paul WIKGREN (1906-....)
Heinrich Greeven (1906-....) *contra*
Herman KUNST, D.D.(1907-....) *contra*
Bruce M. METZGER, D.D. (1914-....) *contra*
Rudolf SCHNACKENBURG (1914-....) *contra*
Dr. Kurt ALAND (1915-....) *contra*
Jay P. GREEN, Sr. (1918-....) *contra*
Dr. Walter THIELE (1923-....) *pro H-W; pro-Cyprian*

D.A. WAITE, Th.D. (1927-....) *pro*
Carlo M. MARTINI (1927-....) *contra?*
Elton J. Epp (1930-....) *contra*
W.N. PICKERING, Ph.D. (1934-....) *contra*
Dr. Jakob Van BRUGGEN (1936-....) *contra*
Dr. Barbara ALAND (1937-....) *contra*
Maurice A. ROBINSON, Ph.D. (1947-....) *contra*
Theodore P. LETIS (1951-....) *pro*

Appendix Two: Pertinent quotations

An irrefutable theory to explain the preservation of the Johannine Comma will be of interest, though one has not been widely accepted yet. One theory is that in those rare instances where the Greek MS evidence is weak, the Italic has perserved it. There may be some 10,000 Latin MSS of the New Testament. Although Dr. Thiele in 1958 dealt with Latin text types K,C,S,T,V, LUC, and AU., he has said to me in 1990, that the subject of the Latin text is still largely unknown. I had also written to the ABS inquiring whether a listing similar to that available for Greek MSS is extant. In a letter dated April 7, 1989, Dr. Errol F. Rhodes, the Senior Historical Researcher for the American Bible Society (and the translator of *Der Text des Neuen Testaments* by Kurt Aland and Barbara Aland) replied, "For Biblical manuscripts in Latin, there is no single listing".

Recent discoveries: In 1975 at St. Catherine's monastery, 836 Greek MSS were discovered.[392] Questions to be asked: How many contain the fifth chapter of first John? Of them, how many have the *Comma*? Pieper remarked "...the hope voiced by Bengel that old documents might still be discovered that would throw further light on our text might not be so foolish in view of recent discoveries.[393]

1690   ALLIX, Peter. *Some Remarks upon the Ecclesiastical History of the Ancient Churches of Piedmont*. Gallatin, TN: Church History Research and Archives. 1989. Reprint. 39.

QUOTE: on the term "Italy", which Nolan refers to.

> By Italy, I do not understand here the several countries which, at this day, bear that name, but only the seven provinces to which that name was given, by way of distinction, and which constituted a particular government under the care of the lieutenant on the western Præterian Prefect. These provinces were Liguria, Æmilia, Flaminia, Venetia, the Alps, both Cottian and Greek, and Rhætia, or the country of the Grisons.

QUOTE: on the diocese of Waldenses in Italy in the seventh century and the Liturgy they used.

> ...this Liturgy has the Psalms, and divers other texts of Scripture of the ancient version called the Italic.

QUOTE: from chapter xxvii, p. 315 entitled "That the Churches of the Valleys of Piedmont

---

392. James Bently, *Secrets of Mount Sinai: The Story of the Codex Sinaiticus*, London: 206.
393. For example, in 1984 the oldest intact Christian community (Kourion) was discovered in Cyprus by Dr. David Soren (Ph.D. from Harvard) of the University of Arizona. Will Greek MSS of the NT be discovered there?

have constantly persevered in the same faith, until the time of the Reformation". Allix reports that Seisselius was his source for the following quote concerning the articles of their faith.

> "They say that the Popes of Rome, and other Priests, have depraved the Scriptures by their doctrines and glosses"

1815   NOLAN, Frederic. *An Enquiry into the Integrity of the Greek Vulgate or Received Text.*

QUOTE: concerning the "old Italick translation"

> ...the author perceived...that it derived its name from that diocese, which has been termed the Italick, as contradistinguished from the Roman. This is a supposition, which receives a sufficient confirmation from the fact,-that the principle copies of that version have been preserved in that diocese...The circumstance is at present mentioned, as the authour thence formed a hope, that some remains of the primitive Italick version might be found in the early translations made by the Waldenses, who were the lineal descendents of the Italick Church and who have asserted their independence against the usurpations of the Church of Rome and have ever enjoyed the free use of the Scriptures. In the search to which these considerations have led the author, his fondest expectations have been fully realized. It has furnished him with abundant proof on that point to which his Inquiry was chiefly directed; as it has supplied him with the unequivical testimony of a truly apostalical branch of the primitive church, that of the celebrated text of the heavenly witnesses, was adopted in the version which prevailed in the Latin Church previously to the introduction of the modern Vulgate.

1886   MILLER, Edward. *Guide to Textual Criticism of the New Testament.* Collingswood, NJ: Bible For Today. 85

> The best of the Old Latin Versions--were made two hundred years before those two manuscripts, and --especially the former--supports the Traditional Text.

1922   DEANESLY, Margaret. *The Lollard Bible and Other Medieval Biblical Versions.* Cambridge: Cambridge University Press. 1960. p.65.

QUOTE from this book on the Bible of the Lollards [394]

> The earliest existent Waldensian texts, Provençal, Catalan and Italian, were founded on a Latin Bible, the use of which prevailed widely in the Visigothic kingdom of Narbonne, up to the thirteenth century...
>
> In any case, the strongest argument for the antiquity of origin of the original of the Tepl manuscript, is S. Berger's verdict on its Latin source.

1922   CHRISTIAN, John T. *History of the Baptists*. 2 vols. Texarkana: Bogard Press. 1:91.

> The Waldenses translated the Bible into the Romance and Teutonic languages early in the thirteenth century, the Baptists retained these versions two hundred years after Luther's version. The oldest German Bible is of Baptist origin.

1922?   KENYON, Frederick. *Our Bible and Ancient Manuscripts*.
QUOTE from page 78:

> What is certain is that the version exists in two different forms, probably representing two indepenenst translations, known, from the regions in which they were circulated, as the African and the European: and that a revised form of the latter was current in Italy towards the end of the fourth century and was known as the Italic.
>
> But the Old Latin was made long before any of our manuscripts were written, and takes us back almost to within a generation of the time at which the sacred books were themselves composed. The Old Latin Version is consequently one of the most valuable and interesting evidences which we possess for the condition of the New Testament Text in the earliest times. It has already been said (p.78) that it was originally made in the second century perhaps not very far from A.D. 150, and probably, though not certainly, in Africa. Another version, apparently independently appeared in Europe.
>
> Codex Brixianus (f), sixth century, with an Italian Text.

1930   WILKINSON, Benjamin G. *Our Authorized Bible Vindicated*. Washington D.C. :1982 reprint. 37

> It is recognized that the Itala was translated from the Received Text. (Syrian, Hort calls it); that the Vulgate is the Itala with the readings of the Received Text

---

394. C.H. Spurgeon wrote: "It is also certain that many of the Lollards, perhaps the majority of them, strongly opposed infant baptism." "Review of J.M. Cramp's Baptist History", London: *Sword and Trowel*. August 1868.

removed.

1932? WILKINSON, Benjamin G. *Answers to Objections to Our Authorized Bible*. Payson, AZ: Leaves of Autumn. (First published in 1989)

QUOTE concerning Kenyon's words "The Italian Text being evidently due to a revision of those with the help of Greek copies of a Syrian type."

> Now note Dr. Kenyon's remarkable statement to the effect that the Italian text was the revision with the help of Greek copies of a Syrian type. Since Dr. Kenyon's had adopted Hort's word "Syrian" to mean the Textus Receptus, here we have positive evidence that the Itala or the Italic type of Latin manuscript was of the Textus Receptus type. It is this Itala which Dr. Nolan proves was the Bible of the Waldenses.

1940 KENYON, Frederic G. *Our Bible and Ancient Manuscripts*, 4th ed.
New York: Harpers and Brothers. 174.

> Jerome's revision, which was based on MSS of a "Neutral" (or as it seems preferable to call it Alexandrian) character, removed many of the Syrian interpolations, but still left the Vulgate a mixed text.

1956 HILLS, Edward F. *The Kings James Version Defended*. Des Moines: Christian Research Press. (p.62,190 of 4th ed.).

> For centuries it had been commonly believed that the currently received New Testament text, primarily the Greek text and secondarily the Latin text, was the True New Testament Text which had been preserved by God's special providence.

> ...we conclude...that these few Latin Vulgate readings which were incorporated into the Textus Receptus were genuine readings which had been preserved in the usage of the Latin-speaking church.

1977 METZGER, Bruce M. *The Early Versions of the New Testament; Their Origin, Transmission and Limitations*. Oxford: Clarendon Press. 285-86.

> Our information concerning the Old Latin translation of the New Testament is very defective, but it is certain that it was not one uniform work; the books were translated a number of times and no single translator did all twenty-seven books.

> The question has been raised whether the birthplace of the Latin New Testament might not have been at Rome after all.

1986 KUTILEK, Doug. (The Kutilek-Johnson correspondence debate):

A quote from Kutilek's letter to Dr. Ken Johnson, June 6, 1986:

No authority I know of declares the Waldensian Bible was the Old Latin; uniformly they say it was the Vulgate translated into the vernacular.

1989   VERDUIN, Leonard. *Mr. L. Verduin interviewed by M. Maynard* Apache Junction, AZ.

A quote from the interview of December 29, 1989:
> M: Where can I find information on what the Waldensians used as far as their translations?
> V: Ludwig Keller has quite a bit on the Tepler Codex which he contends comes out of the Waldensian camp. I think he's right. You know he got a lot of people on his neck[395] right away, because they didn't like to hear this...But the Tepler Codex, to my way of thinking, is quite certainly of "heretical" origin, whether the Waldensians [or Bohemian brethren] did it. From my way of thinking, it doesn't matter whether you say Waldensian or Lollard or half a dozen other names. They all agreed with each other on this point...They were all influenced by the Tepl Codex which came out of the camp of the underworld, the *Nebenkirche*.

1990   MOORMAN, Jack A. *Early Manuscripts and the Authorized Version*. Collingswood, NJ: Bible for Today. 29.
> Research into the text and history of the Waldensian Bible has shown that it is a lineal descendant of the Old Latin Itala. In other words, the Itala has come down to us in the Waldensian form, and firmly supports the Traditional Texts.

1990   VERDUIN, Leonard. *Where We Went Wrong*. (unpublished at this time)

QUOTE: from chapter 5, p. 62 concerning the Waldensians knowing the Gospels by heart "...so that they could repeat them without a halt and with scarely a word here or there.
> This remark about "a word here or there" may be taken to imply that they of the Nebenkirke translated from a Latin text other than the one approved by "Christendom". The question of the Latin text favored by the Nebenkirke is one that deserves to be researched further than has been done.

---

395. This is verified by the statement "Keller was violently attacked" *Mennonite Encyclopedia*, 3:162. This German Reformed scholar "published his epoch-making works, vindicating Anabaptism." He was also attacked for being an "ardent exponent that there was a direct connection between the Waldenses and the Anabaptists."

Appendix three:

F.A.G. [sic] Tholuck's essay "The Doctrine of Inspiration" was included in *A Collection of Theological Essays from Various Authors with an introduction by George R. Noyes, D.D.* (Boston: Amer. Unitarian Assoc., 1856). On page 92, Tholuck says:

> What does it avail you, says the Roman Catholic, to have an infallible *document*, unless you have also an infallible *translation?* And what could an infallible translation avail you, without an infallible *interpretation?* Nay, verily, your learned men themselves, who abide by the original text, -whence derive they certainty concerning its correctness? Does not the number of various reading in the New Testament alone, accouding to modern calculation, exceed fifty thousand? On e can andy must yield to our pious friend, Professor Gaussen, and confess that, essentially, the great majority of thes readings are immaterial. But this is by no means the case with them all. That it is not indifferent, for example, whether the passage concerning the Trinity in 1 John v.7,8 be genuine or not, Professor Gaussen so decidedly acknowledges, that he believes the defence of the received reading must at all risks be undertaken, notwithstanding the passage is found in no Greek Codex except the *Codex Britannicus** of the sixteeth century; in the *Codex Ravianus,* which is a copy partly from the *Complutensian Polyglot* and partly from the third edition of Erasmus; and in the Vulgate only since the tenth century. If *one* credible testimony in reference to this subject were not of equal weight with many, a host of others might easily be added; but this instance must now suffice.

From John Biddle's *The Faith of One God Who is only the Father; and of One Mediator between God and Men, Who is only the Man Christ Jesus; and of One Holy Spirit, the Gift (and sent) of God; asserted and Defended* London: 1691.

> For tho the Expression varieth somewhat in the ordinary Greek Testaments, in that the Preposition εἰς is prefixed (altho the Complutensian Bible readeth εἰς τὸ ἕν εἰσιν in both Verses,) yet is the sense the same; this latter being spoken after the Hebrew Idiom, the former according to the ordinary Phrase. For Confirmation whereof, see *Mat.19.* comparing Ver. 5 and 6, together in the Original: Wherefore this Expression ought to be rendered alike in bother Verses, as the former Interpreters did it, thos the latter Interpreter in Verse 8, have rendred it *agree in one* putting the Gloss instead of the Translation. So that this place maketh nothing for them that hold the Holy Spirit to have one and the same Essence with the Father, unless they can prove that those who are one in Agreement must likewise necessarily be one in Essence; or that two or three cannot be one, but it must presently be in Essence. I omit for the present to speak of the Suspectedness of this place, how it is not extant in the ancient Greek Copies, and namely in that famous one of *Tecla* here in *England,* nor in the Syriack Translation, nor in most ancient Books of the Latin Edition, and rejected by sundry Interpreter both Ancient and Modern.

In John Biddle's *A Brief History of the Unitarians Called also Socinians in Four Letters written to a Friend.* Second edition, 1691, the author says on page 43:

> 1 John 5.7. *There are three that bear Record in Heaven, the Father, the Word, and the Holy Ghost, and these three are one. Answ.* 1. This Verse was not originally in the Bible, but has been added to it. 'Tis not found in the most ancient Copies of the *Greek*, nor in the *Syriac*, or *Arabick*, or *Ethiopick*, or *Armenian* Bibles. 'Tis not acknowledged by the Fathers, who treated professedly of this Question of the Trinity; 'tis wholly rejected by abundance of the most Learned Criticks and Interpreters, and by all acknowledged to be doubtful and uncertian. 2. Admitting this Verse to be genuine, yet the most Learned *Trinitarians* confess the sense is, not *these three are one God*, but these three are *one in their Testimony*, or they agree in their Testimony; for they are here considered and spoken of as Witnesses. So *Beza, Vatablus, Calvin, Erasmus,* the English *Geneva* Notes. And accordingly most of the Greek Bibles which have this Verse in them, read here as they do in the next Verse (not these three *are* one, but) these three *agree* in one; *i.e.* in on and the same testimony.

An excerpt from *Encyclopedia Britannica:*

The "sects" stimulated a "demand for popular Bible reading"

> There is evidence. . . for the existence of German Psalters from the 9th century on. By the 13th century, the different sects and movements that characterized the religious situation in Germany had stimulated a demand for popular Bible reading. Since all the early printed Bibles derived from a single family of late 14th century manuscripts, German translations must have gained a wide popularity. Another impetus towards the use of the German Scriptures in this period can be traced to mystics of the Upper Rhine. A complete New Testament, the Augsburg Bible, can be dated to 1350, and another from Bohemia, Codex Teplensis (c. 1400), has also survived. [396]

A list of quotes demonstrating, to some degree, the impact of the account of the so-called "promise" of Erasmus...

1830 Orme, W.   . . .Erasmus *promised* that if the passage...
1883 Scrivener, F.. . .a *promise* which he fulfilled in 1522.

---

396. N.M.Sa. *The New Encyclopædia Britannica*, 28 vols. Biblical Literature. Later and Modern Versions. "Gothic and pre-Reformational Bibles." (Chicago: Encyclopedia Britannica, Inc., 1988), 14:768.

1886 Miller, E.   . . .he *promised* that if any Greek manuscript. . .
1912 Kenyon, F.G. . . .Erasmus *promised* to insert it if any Greek. .
1924 Turner, C.H. . . .Erasmus kept his *promise*, and the third edition
1950 Bruce, F.F. . . .in order to redeem his *promise*.
1963 Bruce, F.F. . . .to redeem his *promise*.
1964 Metzger, B. . . .Erasmus *promised* that he would insert...
1964 Greenlee: . . .Erasmus rashly *promised* to include it
1967 Ladd, G.E.   . . .but he *promised* to include them ...
1968 Metzger, B   . . .Erasmus *promised* that he would insert...
1974 Reynolds: . . .and the *promise* had to be made good
1979 Carson: ". . .Erasmus *promised* that he would insert..."
1981 Custer: . . .make a rash *promise* that..
1983 Custer: . . .Erasmus made a rash *promise*. . .

ANTICIPATED OBJECTIONS

OBJECTION #1: de Jonge says the earliest reference to the legend of the promise is Horne in 1818. The following quote (from page 111 of his book against Travis) proves that Porson knew of the promise back in 1790:

> Erasmus said, in his answer to Lee, that if he had found a single Greek manuscript containing the three heavenly witnesses, he would have inserted them in his text.

REPLY to OBJECTION #1: Upon a first glance, this might appear as a promise, but it is essential to grasp the historical context. Let's quote from de Jonge, a major contributor on the editorial board of the recent Erasmus project, who wrote the 58 page introduction to volume IX-2 of *Erasmi Opera Omnia*. (1983)

QUOTE from main text of page 12 of de Jonge's introduction:
> ... by arguing that if ... he had found the passage in a single Greek manuscript, he would have introduced it into his edition...

QUOTE from footnote 46:

> This remark of Erasmus is sometimes misinterpreted as if he had promised to restore the so-called *Comma Iohanneum* if it could be found... It is one of the cherished legends on New Testament scholarship that Erasmus kept his promise and restored the verse when one such manuscript was produced. But this is no more than a legend. In fact, far from being a promise, Eramus' words are only a simple account of the facts owning to which he had felt obliged to exclude the *Comma Iohaneum* from his first and second edition. His words are not a promise, but a retrospective account of what he had done.

> Accordingly, the reason why Erasmus inserted the *Comma Iohanneum* in the third edition ... was not that he felt bound to keep any promise, but, as he declared himself in his annotations on *I Ioh. 5,7* and in his first apology against Stunica

(see p. 258 below), "to take away any handle for calumniating" him. It may be useful to quote here Erasmus' words in full:

"Quod si mihi contigisset vnum exemplar in quo fuisset quod nos legimus, nimirum illinc adiecissem quod in caeteris aberat. Id quia non contigit, quod solum licuit feci, indicaui quid in Graecis codicibus minus esset" (*LB* IX, 275 B-C).

OBJECTION #2 The *Comma* cannot be authentic because there is overwhelming Greek manuscript evidence against it. The Church could not be wrong for all those centuries.

REPLY to OBJECTION #2: Firstly, there is an underlying presupposition which favors one side of the debate over the universal church vs. local churchs, when the word "Church" (=the universal church) is used. The intent of the objector may be to use one word (Church) to signify "believers in all ages", which is NOT what the universal church consists of. The universal church has erred miserably in every doctrine. The question to ask is rather "Could believers be wrong about the identity of the text for all those centuries?" To such extent as the mta imagine? By no means. Hills was correct about a Maximum of Certainty, and a Minimum of Uncertainty. But the next question is "What did believers actually use?" During the Reformation, no one questions that the RT was used. So the important question is narrowed down to "What text was MOST COMMONLY USED during the Medieval and pre-Reformation ages?" To merely reply "the Vulgate" is not sufficient because it does not indicate which recension of the vulgata. However, it does point to the Latin text. The complaint of Wallace that the Latin Vulgate is often neglected, is valid. Wallace, in effect, has asked "What about the 10,000 Latin MSS?"

Secondly, the fact that certain scholars who regard the *Comma* as spurious (e.g., Porson, and Scrivener) claim that the vast majority (49 out of 50!) of these THOUSANDS of Latin Vulgate MSS contain the *Comma*, ought to be kept in mind. The claim ought to be investigated. Now if the *Comma* is spurious, then the believers in Christ were allowed to be mislead for centuries, especially when the Latin vulgate dominated. Many say it dominated for a thousand years. Suppose it dominiated from about 450 to 1450. Was the lingua franca in those years Greek or Latin?

In order to follow Burgon's methodoloy, we cannot restrict the evidence to only Greek witnesses. If non-Greek MSS abound in numbers, it becomes all the more important for a majority-text position.

The following list of Greek and Latin MSS is from Gregory's *Prolegomena* of 1894. (A Modern list would simply have a far greater quantity of listed MSS.) Although outdated, it does help one to imagine the severity of neglecting so great a mass of evidence. How can we blame the INTF in Münster, BRD, for neglecting a huge quantity of Byzantine MSS, if we neglect the mass of MSS written in the *lingua franca* of the medieval ages?

The 8th century: (SAECULUM OCTAVUM)

Codicies Graeci:

B E L O S W Y θ Ξ Ψ Ω
Evl 36.135.242.293.352.360.486b.509.525.559a.627.749

vulgata
am foss gat lux tol 3 5 20 95 (102a)115 116 131 153 154 184 228 231 234 238 493 502 510 590 610 614 669 682 698 774 850 851 934 985 1034 1237 1254 1263 1265 1267 1269 1271 1278 1444 1526 1606 1607 1608 1633 1673 1699 1843 1855 1859 1877 1880 1918 1923 1928 1937 1946 1958 1970 1973 2000 2080 2085 2105 2157 2218

The 9th century: (SAECULUM NONUM)

Codices Graeci

aleph^{evv} E^{paul} F^{ev} F^{paul} G$^{b\ act}$ G^{paul} H^{act} K^{ev} K^{epp} L^{act} M^{ev} M^{paul} N^{paul} O O^{aefg} p^{act} e^{pp} a^{poc} T^f V W^{cdefgho} X X^b Γ Δ Λ Π

Evv 33.256.461.565.566.567.892.1080.1161.
Act 112.323.374.
Evl 17.34.46.63.64.65.66.72a.127.130.152.172 (vix saec. IV).173.182.194.206a.237a.244.245b.246.247.248.249.250.286.296.312.317. 353.362.368.370.454.490.511.514.541.542.543.566.567.580.640.668.672.689.703.720.730.733.805.806.807.808.830.845.907.
Apl 13.70a.70b.73.80.84.

Vulgata: cav em iac ing mt ter vallic san^{paul} 25.63 64 109 113 159 185 186 187 206 209 235 239 240 241 242 243 254 442 611 618 654 657 671 672 791 804 812 813 814 815 817 831 846 852 893 (894?)895 (896?)897 913 914 921 924 925 926 927 994 1022 1027 1035 1045 1058 1065 1082 1095 1120 1183 1184 1185 1186 1199 1216 1222 1223 1224 1225 1226 1227 1228 1229 1230 1233 1248 1249 1264 1266 1268 1270 1272 1273 1274 1280 1281 1285 1286 1289 1317 1324 1329 1343 1363 1396 1406 1419 1429 1447 1451 1474 1478 1479 1482 1486 1489 1517 1521 1525 1611 1627 1666 1672 1683 1714 1725 1768 1777 1791 1807 1838 1874 1878 1881 1883 1893 1895 1901 1904 1907 1919 1921 1922 1924 1925 1931 1935 1939 1941 1944 1948 1953 1967 1968 1971 1974 1991 1992 2083 2084 2088 2138 2139 2140 2142 2144 2158 2161 2164 2166 2171 2219

P. 215 was absent in the original

Dan
6/5/91

Appendix Four:

A New Reformation: Is it needed today?

A variety of denominations is crying out for a new Reformation.[397] In my view, a new Great Awakening is far preferable. One of the problems of the Reformation is the inevitable consequency of conductual-averagism. Verduin defines this as the event in which "Christian behavior and ordinary behavior become indistinguishable." Verduin, who is Christian Reformed by denomination, speaks in defense of the Donatists![398] He speaks of Christendom as the "fallen" Church which was

> filling the country side with clerics who gave no evidence of being regenerate and all sorts of evidence that they were not. It was against this alarming development that the Donatists protested- saying that a cleric who lives in sin cannot convey salvation.[399]

Verduin, Th.B, A.M., who attended Calvin College, Calvin Seminary, and obtained a masters degree in history from University of Michigan in 1945, then shifts to the age of the Reformation and quotes from Luther:

> Luther himself acknowledged that his Reform had done little to correct conductual-averagism, but had left things in the main as they had been before. It is a sad fact that he sought to justify this, moreover. [400]

Verduin continues: "In an attempt to get away from the evidently indisputable fact that the Stepchildren [i.e.,the Anabaptists] were doing much better, he said"

> Doctrine and life are to be distinguished, the one form the other. With us conduct is as bad as it is with the papists. We don't oppose them on account of conduct. Hus and Wycliff, who made an issue of conduct, were not aware of this . . .but to treat of doctrine, that is really to come to grips with things.[401];lm-5

---

397. One of the most recent exhortations is from Michael Scott Horton, founder of an a orgainization whose name, CURE, Christians United for Reformation, suggests they regard the Reformation as a cure-all. The last chapter in *Agony of Deceit* (Chicago: Moody Press, 1990), is a call toward a new Reformation.
398. But this is how Baptists also view the Donatists. See, e.g., David Benedict, D.D. *History of the Donatists* (1875, Gallatin, TN: Church History Reseach and Archives, 1985)
399. *Reformers and Their Stepchildren*, 96.
400. *Reformers and Their Stepchildren*, 108.
401. *Luthers Werke*, vol. 1, p. 296, as quoted by Verduin, 108.

Verduin continues: "The Reformed preachers at Berne admitted as much in a letter which they sent to the City Council"

> The Anabaptists have the semblance of outward piety to a far greater degree than we and all the other churches which in union with us confess Christ: and they avoid the offensive sins that are very common among us.[402]

(Dr. Kenneth Good, in his excellent contribution *Are Baptists Reformed?* (Lorain, OH: Regular Baptist Heritage Fellowship, 1986) demonstrates how the Reformers departed from *sola scriptura*, in his chapter "Baptists Differ from the Reformed in Their Views of the Word of God.")

(Those who are still clamoring for a new Reformation are kindly encouraged to consider what the church historian, Philip Schaff said:

> The Reformation everywhere had its defects and sins, which it is impossible to justify. How cruel was the persecutions of the Anabaptists. . .And how sad were the moral state and the the rude theological quarrels in Germany. No wonder that Melanthon longed for deliverance from the *rabies theologorum*. I hope God has something better and greater in store than the Reformation.[403]

The situation of G. Witzel is only one example of those dissatisfied with the Reformation. "Seeing in Lutheranism, disagreement between doctrine and life, he at a later time returned to the Roman Catholic Church"[404]

Those calling for a new Reformation are also encouraged to read the accounts of the Great Awakening of 1740-1742, and to compare the visible effects on the souls of individuals.

---

402. W.J. McGlothlin, *Die Berner Täufer* (1902), as quoted by Verduin, 109.
403. *The Life of Philip Schaff*, 462, cited by J.T. Christian in *History of the Baptists*
404. "Witzel" *NSHE* 12:400.

Appendix Five:

A selection of German Bibles examined in several test-passages (distinctive Received Text non-Majority Readings)

TBS =(1976) Received Greek NT of the Trinitarian Bible Society
'p' =(xiii) Peripignan Codex of the 13th century (S. France)
AUG =(c.1350) Augsburg Codex (German) "2° Cod 3"
WYC =(c.1380) Wycliffe Bible
TEP =(c.1400) Tepl Codex (German)
G01 =(1466) pre-Lutheran German; (Strassburg; J. Mentel)
G02 =(1470) pre-Lutheran German; (Strassburg; H. Eggestein) [not av.]
G03 =(1475) pre-Lutheran German; (Strassburg;J.Pflanzmann)[Ga LIII 55a]
G04 =(1476) pre-Lutheran German; (Augsburg; G. Zainer) [Ga LIII 43.2]
G05 =(~1476) pre-Lutheran German; (Nuremberg: Sensenschmidt & Frisner) [LIII 55.2]
G06 =(1477) pre-Lutheran German; (Augsburg: G. Zainer) [Ga LIII 38.2]
G07 =(1477) pre-Lutheran German; (Augsburg: Anton Sorg) [Ga LIII 56.2]
G08 =(1480) pre-Lutheran German; (Augsburg: Anton Sorg) [Ga LIII 56a]
G09 =(1483) pre-Lutheran German; (Nurenburg: A. Koberger) [Ga LIII 39]
G10 =(1485) pre-Lutheran German; (Strassburg: J.R. de Grüningen) [Ga LIII 40.2]
G12 =(1490) pre-Lutheran German; (Augsburg: Schönsperger) [Ga LIII40.4]
G13 =(1507) pre-Lutheran German; (Augsburg: Hans Otmar)[not av.]
G14 =(1518) pre-Lutheran German; (Augsburg: Silvan Otmar)[not av.]
CPG =(1514) Complutensian Polyglott
ZÜR =(1531) *Die Zürcher Bibel von 1531* (1983 repr.:Theologische Verlag)
LTH =(1545) Luther's last edition in his lifetime
BGL =(1734) *Novum Testamentum graecum* by J.A. Bengel
H/F =(1982) *New Testament according to the Majority Text* Hodges-Farstad
UBS =(1983) United Bible Society Greek NT 3rd edition, corrected
M^{pt}, M^I =readings from a large quantity of MSS, not followed by H/F

modern German:
L1956 = "den Text Martin Luthers(in der Fassung der Revision von 1956)" [*Tetrapla 1964; Das Neue Testament in vier Übersetzungen*]
Z1964 = "den Text der Zürcher Bibel",[*Tetrapla 1964; Das Neue Testament in vier Übersetzungen*]
G1973 = German: Biblisch-pastoralen Arbeitstelle der Berliner Bischofskonferenz
L1984 = German: *Die Bibel nach der Übersetzung Martin Luthers* (in der "revidierten Fassung von 1984" (Stuttgart: Deutsche Bibelgesellschaft, 1985)
E1985 = German: Elberfelder (3rd ed. 1986) [*Das Neue Testament; Sechs Bibelübersetzungen in einer Übersicht*, 1989]
G1989 = German: Evangelische Haupt-Bibelgesellschaft zu Berlin und Altenburg
----

Matt 6:13
TBS πονηροῦ. ὅτι σοῦ ἐστιν ἡ βασιλεία καὶ ἡ δύναμις καὶ ἡ δόξα εἰς τοὺς αἰῶνας
TEP ubeln.
G03 übeln. Amen.
G04 übel amen.
G05 übel Amē .
CPG πονηροῦ.

H/F πονηροῦ. ὅτι σοῦ ἐστιν ἡ βασιλεία καὶ ἡ δύναμις καὶ ἡ δόξα εἰς τοὺς αἰῶνας
LTH   vbel. Denn dein ist das Reich, und die Krafft, vnd die Herrligkeit in Ewigkeit Amen.
ZÜR   übel. Dañ dein ists reych, macht vnd herrligkeit, Amen.
L1912 Übel. Denn dein ist das Reich und die Kraft und die Herrlichkeit in Ewigkeit. Amem.
L1956 Übel. Denn dein ist das Reich und die Kraft und die Herrlichkeit in Ewigkeit. Amen.
Z1964 Bösen.
L1984 Bösen. [Denn dein ist das Reich und die Kraft und die Herrlichkeit in Ewigkeit. Amen.]⁴⁰⁵
E1985 Bösen.

Matt 10:3
TBS καὶ ματθαῖος ὁ τελώμης
TEP und Mathes der offensnder
G01 vnd matheus der offen súnder
G03 vnd mathias der offen sűnder
G04 vnd Matheus der offen sunder
G05 und Matheus des offen sunder
G06 vñ Matheus o' offen sünd'

---

405. A note reads "Dieser Abschluß des Gebetes findet sich schon in einer Gemeindeordnung von Anfang des 2.Jahrhnderts, wird aber in den neutestamentlich Handschriften erst später bezeugt"

G07	vnd Matheus der offensünder
G08	und Matheus o offensünder
G09	und matheus ὁ offensünder
G10	vnd matheus der offensünder
G12	vnd matheus der offensünder
CPG	και ματθαίος ο Τελώμης
H/F	και ματθαιος ο Τελώμης
ZÜR	vnd Mattheus der zoller
LTH	vnd Mattheus der Zölner
BGL	καὶ ματθαῖος ο τελώμης

1. Matt 10:8

(B)	νεκροὺς ἐγείρετε λεπροὺς καθαρίζετε [Vaticanus]
TBS	λεπροὺς καθαρίζετε νεκροὺς ἐγείρετε [Aleph C D 1 vg]
TEP	derstet de toten
G01	derstet die dotten
G03	erktee die toten, gereinigt die aßsetzige
G04	Erkuckend die totten reynigent die außsetzigen
G05	erkuckend die todten reymgend die uszsetzige
G06	Erkückēr die totē
G07	erkückend die todten
G08	erkücket die todté
G09	Erkücket die tödten
G10	Erkücket die todten
G12	erkücket die todten
CPG	_____ _____ λεπρούς καθαρίζετε
ZÜR	weckēd die todten auf
LTH	Wecket die Todten auff
KJV	raise the dead
BGL	λεπροὺς καθαρίζετε °νεκροῦς ἐγείρετε
L1956	weckt Tote auf
Z1964	wecket Tote auf
G1973	weckt Tote auf
H/F	_____ _____ λεπροὺς καθαρίζετε [M]
UBS	νεκροὺς ἐγείρετε, λεπροὺς καθαρίζετε (aleph* B C*) accd to H/F
L1984	weckt Tote auf
E1985	weckt Tote auf
G1989	weckt Tote auf

Dr. Hills says that B supports the reading "raise the dead". He is correct, but my color facsimilie of B shows there is a transposition of words in B, differing from the Received Text order. However, Hills is only referring to the expression "raise the dead".

2. Matt 27:35a

TBS	ἵνα πληρωθῇ τὸ ῥηθὲν ὑπὸ τοῦ προφήτου, [Eus 1 syr^h SYR^{Tr-mg} it vg]

TEP daz da gesagt ist durch den weissagen sagent
G01 das derfullt wurde das gesait ist durch den weyssagen sagent
G03 dz erfüllt wurd dz geseyt ist durch dē weyssagen sagēt
G04 das erfullt wurd das geseit ist durch den weyssagen sagent
G05 dz erfult wurd daz geseyt ist durch den wyssage sagent
G06 dz erfült würd dz geseit ist durch den weisgen sagent
G07 das erfült würd das geseyt ist durch den weyssagen sagent
G08 das erfült würd daz geseit ist durch den weis-sagten sagēt
G09 das erfült wurd das gesagt ist durch den weyssagē, saged,
G10 das erfüllt würde das gesaget ist durch den weissagē, sagend,
G12 das erfüllt word das gesagt ist durch den weyssagen sagend
CPG ∞∞∞∞∞ ∞∞∞∞∞ ∞∞∞∞∞ ∞∞∞∞∞ ∞∞∞∞∞ ∞∞∞∞∞ ∞∞∞∞∞ ∞∞∞∞∞ ∞∞∞∞∞ ∞∞∞∞∞
ZÜR das erfullt wurde das gesagt ist durch den propheten
LTH das erfüllet würde das gesagt ist durch den Propheten
KJV that it might be fulfilled which was spoken by the prophet,
BGL ἵνα πληρωθῇ τὸ ῥηθὲν ὑπὸ τοῦ προφήτου
L1956 *damit erfüllt würde, was gesagt ist durch den Propheten
Z1964 ___ ____ ___ ___ _____.
G1973 ___ ____ ___ ___ _____.
H/F ___ ____ ___ ___ _____
UBS ___ ____ ___ ___ ___ (omitted without a footnote)
L1984 ___ ____ ___ ___ _____.
E1985 ___ ____ ___ ___ _____.
G1989 ___ ____ ___ ___ ___"In der späteren Überlieferung finden sich zusätzlich die Worte:" etc.

Matt 27:35b
TBS Διεμερίσαντο τὰ ἱμάτιά μου ἑαυτοῖς, καὶ ἐπὶ τὸν ἱματισμόν μου ἔβαλον κλῆρον. [Eus 1 syr^h SYR^Tr-mg it vg]
TEP Si teilten in mein gewant und auf mein gewantd legten si daz lozz
G01 Sy teilten in meine gewand.vnd auf meine gewand legten sy daz loß
G03 Sy teiltē im meīe gewand, vñ auff meine gewand legten sy dz loß
G04 Sy teylten in meine gewand,vnd auff meinem gewandt legten sy das loß
G05 Sie teylten yn mine gewand. und vff mimem gewandt legten sie das losz
G06 Sy teyltē im mein gewāde, vnd auf meinē gewand legtēd sy das loß
G07 Sy teylten m̄ meme gewand, vñ auff memem gewand legten sy das loþ
G08 Sÿ teilten im mein gewade/uñ auf meinem gewand legtent sÿ das loß
G09 Sy teylten me meine gewand, vñ uber meine gewand legten sy das loß
G10 Sie teylten ine meine gewannd,vnnd,über meyne gewand legten sye das loß
G12 Sy teylten im meine gewand, un über meine gewand legten sy dz loß
CPG ∞∞∞∞∞ ∞∞∞∞∞ ∞∞∞∞∞ ∞∞∞∞∞ ∞∞∞∞∞ ∞∞∞∞∞ ∞∞∞∞∞ ∞∞∞∞∞ ∞∞∞∞∞ ∞∞∞∞∞
ZÜR Sy habend meine kleyder vnder jnen geteylt, vnnd über mein gwand habend sy das looß geworffen

LTH Sie haben meine Kleider vnter sich geteilet, Vnd vber mein Gewand haben sie das Los geworffen

KJV they parted my garments among them, and upon my vesture did they cast lots.

BGL Διεμερίσαντο τὰ ἱμάτιά μου ἑαυτοῖς, καὶ ἐπι τὸν ἱματισμόν μου ἐβαλον κλῆρον.

L1956 Sie haben meine Kleider unter sich geteilt und haben über meinen Rock das Los geworfen.

Z1964 ___ ___ ___ ___ ___ ___ ___.

G1973 ___ ___ ___ ___ ___ ___ ___.

H/F _____

UBS _____ (omitted without even a footnote)

L1984 ___ ___ ___ ___ ___ ___ ___.

E1985 ___ ___ ___ ___ ___ ___ ___.

G1989 _____ (omitted with footnote) "In der späteren Überlieferung finden sich zusätzlich die Worte:" etc.

John 3:25

TBS μετὰ Ἰουδαίων {p66 aleph* 1 it} [plural]
TEP mit den Juden [plural]
G01 mit den iuden [plural]
G03 mit den iuden [plural]
G04 mit den iuden [plural]
G05 mitt den juden [plural]
G06 mit den juden [plural]
G07 mit den juden [plural]
G08 mit den juden [plural]
G09 mit den iudē [plural]
G10 mit dē iuden [plural]
G12 mit den juden [plural]
CPG μετά ιουδαίων [plural!]
ZÜR mit den Juden [plural]
LTH sampt den Jüden [plural]
KJV and the Jews [plural]
BGL μετὰ ιουδαίων [plural]
L1956 und einem Juden [singlar]
Z1964 mit einem Juden [singular]
G1973 und einem Juden [singular]
H/F μετὰ Ἰουδαίου [M p75 B A] [singular]
UBS μετὰ Ἰουδαίου [singular]
L1984 und einem Juden [singular]
E1985 mit einem Juden [singular]
G1989 und einem Juden [singular]

Acts 7:37

TBS αυτου ακουσεσθε [C]
TEP den werdet ir horn
'p' audite (*deux lettres gratées* te)
G03 den wert ir hören (p. 445a)
G04 den wert ir hören
G05 den wert ir hören (p.lxxx)
CPG _____ _____.
.Mⁱ αυτου ακουσεσθε
H/F _____ _____.
LTH: Den solt jr hören
ZÜR... den sollend ir hören
KJV him shall ye hear
L1912 denn sollt ihr hören
L1956 _____ _____ __ _____.
Z1964 _____ _____ __ _____.
L1984 _____ _____ __ _____.
E1985 _____ _____ __ _____.

Acts 8:37a

TBS εἶπε δὲ ὁ Φίλιππος, Εἰ πιστεύεις ἐξ ὅλης τῆς καρδίας, ἔξεστιν. [E it vg Cyprian Irenaeus]
'p' *Tunc dixit philippus. si credis ex toto corde tuo licet.*
AUG Do sprach philipp' Ob du gelaubst auss gantzē h'tzen,ib ist der zimlich getauft w'rten.
TEP Und philipp sprach. Ob du glaubst von allem dinem herrzan Gotz, es gezimt.
WYC Forsoth Philip seide,If thou bileuyst of al the herte,it is lawful
G01 vnd philipp sprach. Es gezimpt ob du gelaubst von gantzem hertzen
G03 vnd philip sprach Es getzimpt ob du glabst vō gantzē hertzen
G04 vñ philippus sprach.Es gezimpt.Ob du gelaubest auß gantzem hertzen
G05 vnd philippus sprach,es gezimpt ob du geloubest vsz gantzem hertzen
G06 vnnd philippus sprach. Es gezymptl Ob du geaubest auß gantzem hertzen
G07 vnd philippus sprach, Es gezimpt,Ob du gelaubest auß gantzem hertzen
G08 und philippus sprach, Es gezympt,Ob du gelaubest auß gantzem hertzen
G09 vñ philippus sprach. Es gezyint. Ob du gelaubest auß gātzē hertzē
G10 Unnd philippus sprach, Es gezympt,Ob du glauBest auß gantzem hertzen
G12 und philippus sprach, Es gezÿmpt,Ob du gelaubst auß ganczem herczē.
CPG ∞∞∞∞∞∞ ∞∞∞∞∞∞ ∞∞∞∞∞∞ ∞∞∞∞∞∞ ∞∞∞∞∞∞ ∞∞∞∞∞∞ ∞∞∞∞∞∞ ∞∞∞∞∞∞
ZÜR Philippus aber sprach: Glaubst du von ganzem herzen so mags wol sein
LTH Philippus aber sprach Gleubestu von ganzem hertzen So mags wol sein.
KJV and Philip said, if thou believest with all thine heart, thou mayest.
BGL εἶπε δὲ ὁ Φίλιππος, Εἰ πιστεύεις ἐξ ὅλης τῆς καρδίας° ἔξεστιν.
L1956 *Philippus aber sprach: Wenn d von ganzem Herzen glaubst, so mag es geschehen.
Z1964 Philippus aber sagte zu ihm: Wenn due aus ganzem Herzen glaubst, darf es geschehen

G1973 ___ __ _ [in margin:"gehört nicht zum ursprünglichen Text"]
H/F ___ __ _ _ ___ ___ __ ___ ___ ___ ___
UBS ___ __ _ _ ___ __ __ ___ ___ ___ ___
L1984 ___ __ _ ("Vers 37 findet sich erst in der späteren...")
E1985 ___ __ _ ("spHs. fügen hinzu: <Philippus aber sprach. . .")
G1989 ____(Vers 37 findet sich erst in der späteren Überlieferung:

Acts 8:37b
TBS ἀποκριθεὶς δὲ εἶπε, Πιστεύω τὸν υἱὸν τοῦ θεοῦ εἶναι τὸν Ἰησοῦν Χριστόν [E it vg Cyprian Irenaeus]
'p' et respondet spado. {et} dixit. Credo filium esse dei ihm xpm.
AUG Und er antwurtent sprch Ich gelaub den gotz sun sein ih'm xp'm
TEP Er antwurt und sprach. Ich glaub Jhesum Kristum zesein den sun Gotz.
WYC he answeringe, seith, I bileue the sone of God for to be Jhesu
G01 Er antwurt vnd sprach. Ich gelaube ihesus cristum zesein den sun gotz.
G03 Er antwurt vnd sprach Ich glaub ihesum cristum zesein den sun gottes
G04 Er anwurt. vñ sprach.Ich gelaub das ihesus cristus sey der sun gotz.
G05 er antwurt vñ sprach Ich geloub das iesuys christus sye der sun gottes
G06 Er antwurt, vñ sprach, Ich geaub das ihesus cristus sey der sun gottes
G07 Er antwurt, vñ sprach, Ich gelaub das Jhesus cristus sey der sun gots,
G08 er antwurt unnd sprach, Ich gelaub das ihesus cristus seÿ dersun gotes
G09 Er antwurt, vñ sprach, Ich gelaub das ihesus christus sey der sun gots
G10 Er anrwurt vnd sprach, Ich glaub das iesus cristus sei der sun gotts
G12 Er antwurtet, vñ sprach, Ich gelaub das ihesus cristus seÿ der sun gotes
CPG ∞∞∞∞∞∞ ∞∞∞∞∞∞ ∞∞∞∞∞∞ ∞∞∞∞∞∞ ∞∞∞∞∞∞ ∞∞∞∞∞∞ ∞∞∞∞∞∞ ∞∞∞∞∞∞
∞∞∞∞∞∞
ZÜR Er antwortet, vnd sprach: Ich glaub das Jesus Christus sey Gottes sun.
LTH Er antwortet vnd sprach, Jch gleube das Jhesus Christus Gottes Son ist
KJV And he answered and said, I believe that Jesus Christ is the son of God
BGL ἀποκριθεὶς δὲ εἶπε, Πιστεύω τὸν υἱὸν τοῦ θεοῦ εἶναι τὸν Ἰησοῦν Χριστόν
L1956 Er aber antwortete und sprach: Ich glaube, daß Jesus Christus Gottes Sohn ist.
Z1964 Er aber antwortete und sprach: Ich glaube, daß Jesus Christus der Sohn Gottes ist.
G1973 _____ __ __[in margin:"gehört nicht zum ursprünglichen Text"]
H/F _____ __ __ ___ ___ __ ___ ___ __ ___
UBS _____ __ ___ ___ __ ___ ___ ___ __ ___
L1984 _____("Vers 37 findet sich erst in der späteren Überlieferung:...")
E1985 _____("spHs. fügen hinzu: <Er aber antwortete. . .")
G1989 _____("Vers 37 findet sich erst in der späteren Überlieferung:...")

Appendix Five (con't)

---

5. Acts 9:5

TBS σκληρόν σοι πρὸς κέντρα λακτίζειν. |629 it^{gig,r} vg^{some} E 431 sy^p|
'p' Durum est tibi contra stimulum calcitrare
AUG dir ist hirt wid'r wegung zegen ißn
TEP hert ist dir zestreiten wider den gart
WYC It is hard to thee, for to kyke akens the pricke.
G01 Hert ist dir zestreyten wider den garten.
G03 Hetzt ist dir zestreiten wider den garten
G04 Hőrt ist dir zestreitē wider die anfechtung des fleysch.
G05 hert ist dir zeitriten wider die anfechtung des fleysches
G06 Hózdt ist dir zestreyttē wid' die anfechtüg des fleisch
G07 Hózt ist dir zestreitten wider die anfechtung des fleysch
G08 hózbt ist dir zestreitten wid die anfechtung des fleisch
G09 Schwer ist dir zestreytē wid' dy anfechtüg fleyschs.
G10 Schwer ist dir zestreytten wyder die anfechtung des fleischs
G12 Schwoz ich dir zůstreyten wider die anfechtung des fleyschs
CPG ∞∞∞∞∞ ∞∞∞∞∞ ∞∞∞∞∞ ∞∞∞∞∞ ∞∞∞∞∞ ∞∞∞∞∞ ∞∞∞∞∞ ∞∞∞∞∞
∞∞∞∞∞
ZÜR Es wirt dir schwår werden wider den sticher zefüssen
LTH Es wird dir schweer werden wider den Stachel lecken
KJV it is hard for thee to kick against the pricks
BGL ____ ___ ____ _____ _____.
L1912 *Es wird dir schwer werden, wider den Stachel zu lecken
L1956 __ ___ __ _____ _____ _____ _____ __ _____.
Z1964 __ ___ __ _____ _____ _____ _____ __ _____.
G1973 __ ___ __ _____ _____ _____ _____ __ _____.
H/F __ ___ __ _____ _____ _____ _____ __ _____.
UBS __ ___ __ _____ _____ _____ _____ __ _____.
L1984 __ ___ __ _____ _____ _____ _____ __ _____.
E1985 __ ___ __ _____ _____ _____ _____ __ _____.
G1989 __ ___ __ _____ _____ _____ _____ __ _____.

6. Acts 9:6

TBS τρέμων τε καὶ θαμβῶν εἶπε, Κύριε, τί με θέλεις ποιῆσαι; καὶ ὁ Κύριος πρὸς αὐτόν, [vg^{some} E 431 sy^p]
'p' quis tremens. dixit. Domine quit me uis facere
AUG schrikent sprach herr was wild du mich machen
TEP und der schrocken und pidment sprach er: O herr waz wilt du daz ich tu?
WYC And he tremblinge and wondringe, seide, Lord, what wolt thou me for to do.
G01 Vnd erschrocken vnd pidempt sprach er.O herr:waz wild das ich tůn
G03 Und erschrocken vñ bidment spprach er O herz was wilt dz ich thů
G04 Vnd erschrocken vnnd pidempt sprach er.Herr,was willt das ich thůn

G05 Und erschrocken umd bidempt sprach er, herr was wilt das ich thůn.
G06 vnd erschrocken vñ pidmempt sprach er Herr was willt daz ich thůn.
G07 vnd erschrocken vnd pidempt sprach er, Herz was wilt das ich thůn:
G08 und erschzocken uñ pedempt sprach er Herr was wilt das ich thůn
G09 Uñ erschrocke vñ bidempt sprach er. Herz was willt das ich thu.
G10 Und erschrockend vnd Bidempt sprach er. Herz wz wilt dz ich tu.
G12 Und erschocken, vnd bidment sprach er Her was wilt das ich thů.
CPG ∞∞∞∞∞ ∞∞∞∞∞ ∞∞∞∞∞ ∞∞∞∞∞ ∞∞∞∞∞ ∞∞∞∞∞ ∞∞∞∞∞ ∞∞∞∞∞ ∞∞∞∞∞ ∞∞∞∞∞
ZÜR Und er sprach mit zitteren vñ zagen: Herr, was wilt du das ich thůn sólle:
LTH Vnd er sprach mit zittern vnd zagen, Herr, was wilt du das ich thun sol
KJV and he trembling and astonished said, Lord, what wilt thou have me to do?
BGL ____ __ __ ____ ____ ____ __ __ ____ ____ __ .
L1912 Und er sprach mit Zittern und Sagen: Herr, was willst du, daß ich tun soll?
L1956 ___ __ ____ __ ____ ____ ____ ___ ___ __ ___ _.
Z1964 ___ __ ____ __ ____ ____ ____ ___ ___ __ ___ _.
G1973 ___ __ ____ __ ____ ____ ____ ___ ___ __ ___ _.
H/F ____ __ ____ __ ____ ____ ____ ____ __ __ ___ .
UBS ____ __ ____ __ ____ ____ ____ ____ ___ __ ___ .
L1984 ___ __ ____ __ ____ ____ ____ ___ ___ __ ___ _.
E1985 ___ __ ____ __ ____ ____ ____ ___ ___ __ ___ _.
G1989 ___ __ ____ __ ____ ____ ____ ___ ___ __ ___ _.

Acts 10:6
TBS οὗτος λαλήσει σοι τί σε δεῖ ποιεῖν
'p' (Hic decit tibi quid te oporteat facere, *la 2ᵉ m.ajoute*)
TEP der sagt dir waz dir gezimt zetun.
CPG ____ ____ __ __ __ ____.
G03 Der sagt dir, was dir getzimt zetůn
G04 Der sagy dir, was dir gezympt cze thůn
G05 Der sagt dir was dir gezimpt zethůn
ZÜR... der wirdt dir sagen was du thůn solt.
L1575. Der wird dir sagen, was du thun solt.
KJV he shall tell thee what thou oughtest to do
L1912 der wird dir sagen, was du tun sollst
L1956 ___ ____ ___ ____ __ __ __ ____.
Z1964 ___ ____ ___ ____ __ __ __ ____.
H/F ____ ____ __ ____ __ __ ___ .
L1984 ___ ____ ___ ____ __ __ ____.
E1985 ___ ____ ___ ____ __ __ ____.

Acts 10:21

TBS   τοὺς ἄνδρας τοὺς ἀπεσταλμένους ἀπὸ τοῦ Κορνηλίου πρὸς αὐτόν
CPG   τοὺς ἄνδρας τοὺς ἀπεσταλμένους ἀπὸ τοῦ Κορνηλίου ειπε πρὸς αὐτόν
H/F   ____ ____ ____ _____ _____ ____ ____ _____.
'p'   (qui missi erant a cornelio, *la 2ᵉ m. ajoute*)
TEP   Wan Peter staig ab zu den mannen und sprach: Secht ich binz der den ir socht wolhz ist di sacho um di ir soit kumon. Si sprachon zu im: Cornelius den centrio ain gerechter man und furchtend Got
G03   Uñ petrus steig ab zů den mannen er sprach Secht ich bī es den ir sůcht, welchs ist die sach vm̄ die ir seyt kůmen Sy sprachen zů im Cornelius ein centurio ein gerecte man vnd vŏrchtēt got
G04   Vnnd petrus gieng ab zů den mannen vñ sprach. Secht ich bins den ir sůcht. Wŏlchs ist die lache vm̄ die ir seyt kummen. Sy sprachen czů im. Cornelius ein centurio ein gerechter man vnd vŏrchtent got.
G05   Und petrus gienge ab zů den mānen vnd sprach Secht ich bins dē ir ssicht Wŏl-- (page torn from Tübingen copy)
ZÜR   die vomm Cornelio zů im gesandt
LTH   die von Cornelio zu jm gesand waren
KJV   which were sent unto him from Cornelius
L1912 die von Kornelius zu ihm gesandt waren
L1956 ____ ____ _____ ___ ___ _____ _____.
Z1964 ____ ____ _____ ___ ___ _____ _____.
L1984 ____ ____ _____ ___ ___ _____ _____.
E1985 ____ ____ _____ ___ ___ _____ _____.

Act 15:34
'p'   (defective: cannot be checked)
TBS: ἔδοξε δὲ τῷ σίλᾳ ἐπιμεῖναε αὐτοῦ.
MPᵗ: ἔδοξε δὲ τῷ σίλᾳ ἐπιμεῖναε αὐτοῦς.
CPG: ἔδοξε δὲ τῷ σίλᾳ ἐπιμεῖναε αὐτο.
TEP: Wan es wart gesehen Sile do zu bleiben
H/F: ____ __ __ ____ _____ _____.
ZÜR: Es duncket aber Silan gůt da zebleyben.
LTH: Es gefiel aber Sila, das er da bleibe.
KJV: it pleased Silas to abide there still
L1912 Es gefiel aber Silas, daß er dableibe
L1956 *Es schien aber Silas gut, dort zu bleiben
Z1964 Silas aber fand für gut, dort zu bleiben
L1984 ____ ____ ____ ___ ___, ___ __ _____.
E1985 ____ ____ ____ __ __, ____ __ _____.

Acts 20:28
TBS: ἐκκλησίαν τοῦ θεοῦ
UBS3 ἐκκλησίαν τοῦ θεοῦ
H/F: ἐκκλησίαν τοῦ κυρίου καὶ θεοῦ
CPG: εκκλησιαν του κυριου και θεού
MPᵗ: ἐκκλησίαν τοῦ κυρίου καὶ θεοῦ

MPᵗ: ἐκκλησίαν τοῦ κυρίου τοῦ θεου
TEP: kirchen Gotz
ZÜR: gemeynd Gottes
LTH: gemeine Gottes
KJV: church of God
E1985 Gemeinde Gottes

Acts 24:6
TBS: ἐκρατήσαμεν καὶ κατὰ τὸν ἡμέτερον νόμον ἠθελήσαμεν κρῖνειν.
UBS3 ἐκρατήσαμεν ___ ___ ___ _____ _____ _____ _____
H/F: ἐκρατήσαμεν ___ ___ ___ _____ _____ _____ _____.
CPG: ἐκρατήσαμεν καὶ κατά τον ημέτερον νόμον ηθελήσαμεν κρῖναι
MPᵗ: ἐκρατήσαμεν καὶ κατὰ τὸν ἡμέτερον νόμον ἠθελήσαμεν κρῖναι.
424: ἐκρατήσαμεν καὶ κατὰ τὸν ἡμέτερον νόμον, ἠβουλήθημεν κρίναι κατὰ τὸν ἡμέτερον μόμον.
TEP: wir wolten in urtailen nach unser ee.
ZÜR: vnd woltend jn gerichtet haben nach vnserem gsatz
LTH: vnd wolten jn gerichtet haben nach vnserm Gesetz.
KJV: we took, and would have judged according to our law.
L1912 und wollten ihn gerichtet haben nach unserm Gesetz
L1956 *und wir wollten ihn richten nach unserem Gesetz
Z1964 den wir ach festnahmen und nach unserem Gesetz richten wollten
L1984 ___ ___ ___ _____ "Die Verse 6b-8a finden sich erst in der späteren Überlieferung"
E1985 ___ ___ ___ _____ "einige sppHs. fügen hier ein: <und nach..."

Acts 24:7
TBS: παρελθὼν δὲ Λυσίας ὁ χιλίαρχος μετὰ πολλῆς βίας ἐκ τῶν χειρῶν ἡμῶν ἀπήγαγε,
UBS3 _____ __ __ _____ _ _____ ____ _____ ____ __ ___ _____ ____ _____.
H/F: _____ __ __ _____ _ _____ ____ _____ ____ __ ___ _____ ____ _____.
CPG: παρελθών Δὲ Λυσίας ὁ χιλίαρχος βία πολλή εκ των χειρών ημών αφείλετο και προς σε απέστειλε
MPᵗ: παρελθὼν δὲ Λυσίας ὁ χιλίαρχος μετὰ πολλῆς βίας ἐκ τῶν χειρῶν ἡμῶν ἀπήγαγε,
424: ἐλθὼν δὲ ὁ χιλίαρχος Λυσίας βία πολλῇ ἐκ τῶν χειπῶν ἡμῶν ἀφίετο καὶ πρός σε ἀπέστειλε,
TEP: Wan Lisias der tribuner der uberkam er derlost in von unsern henden mit grozzem gewalt
ZÜR: Aber Lysias der oberhauptmann fürkam das, vnnd fürt jnn mit grossem gewalt auß vnseren henden
LTH: aber Lysias der Heubtman vnterkam das, vnd füret jn mit grosser gewalt aus vnsern henden
KJV: But the chief captain Lysias came *upon us*, and with great violence

took *him* away out of our hands.
L1912 aber Lŋsias, der Hauptmann, kam dazu und führte ihn mit großer Gewalt aus unsern Händen
L1956 *aber Lysias, der Oberhauptmann, kam dazu und führte ihn mit großer Gewalt aus unseren Händen
Z1964 der Oberst Lysias aber kam dazu, ließ ihn mit großer Gewalt aus unsern Händen hinwegführen
L1984 ___ ___. ___ ___. ___ ___ ___ ___ ___ ___.
E1985 ___ ___. ___ ___. ___ ___ ___ ___ ___ ___.

Acts 24:8a
TBS: κελεύσας τοὺς κατηγόρους αὐτοῦ ἔρχεσθαι ἐπὶ σέ.
UBS3 ___ ___ ___ ___ ___ ___ ___.
H/F: ___ ___ ___ ___ ___ ___ ___.
CPG: κελεύσας και τοὺς κατηγόρους αὐτοῦ ἔρχεσθαι.
M^{pt}: κελεύσας τοὺς κατηγόρους αὐτοῦ ἔρχεσθαι ἐπὶ σέ.
424: κελεύσας τοὺς κατηγόρους αὐτοῦ ἔρχεσθαι πρὸς σέ
TEP: er hies sein befager kumen zu dir
ZÜR: vnnd hieß seine verkleger zů dir komen
LTH: vnd hies seine Verkleger zu dir komen.
KJV: commanding his accusers to come unto thee
L1912 und hieß seine Verkläger zu dir kommen.
L1956 *und hieß seine Ankläger zu dir kommen.
Z1964 und befahl seinen Anklägern, vor dich zu kommen
L1984 ___ ___ ___ ___ ___ ___.
E1985 ___ ___ ___ ___ ___ ___.

I Tim 3:16
AUG das geoffenbart ist in dem fleische
TEP di da ist der offent in dem fleisch
G01 die do ist eroffent im fleisch
G03 de do ist eroffer im fleisch
G04 die da ist eröffēt im fleysch
G05 die da ist eroffent im fleysch
G06 die do ist eroffent im fleisch
G07 die da ist eroffent im fleysch
G08 die do ist eröffēt im fleisch
G09 die da ist eroffent im fleysch
G10 die da ist eroffent im fleysch
CPG^{Gk} θεός εφανερώθη εν σαρκί
CPG^{Lt} quod manifestū est ī carne;
ZÜR welche da ist geoffenbaret im fleysch
LTH Gott ist offenbaret im Fleisch
BGL Θεὸς ἐφανερώθη ἐν σαρκὶ
L1912 Gott ist offenbart im Fleisch

L1956 ER ist offenbart im Fleisch
Z1964 Der goeffenbart worden ist im Fleisch
G1968 *Er ist offenbart im Fleisch,*
G1973 Er wurde offenbar im Fleisch,
L1984 Er ist offenbart im Fleisch,
E1985 Der geoffenbart worden ist im Fleisch
G1989 Er ist offenbart im Fleisch,

R. Porson said "If we are certain of any reading having constantly kept it place in the Latin copies, we are certain that they never read otherwise than QUOD in I Tim III. 16, instead of DEUS."[405]

1 John 2:14a
TBS: ὅτι ἐγνώκατε τὸν ἀπ' ἀρχῆς. ἔγραψα ὑμῖν, νεανίσκοι, ὅτι ἰσχυροί
UBS3 ὅτι ἐγνώκατε τὸν ἀπ' ἀρχῆς. ἔγραψα ὑμῖν, νεανίσκοι, ὅτι ἰσχυροί
H/F: ὅτι ἐγνώκατε τὸν ἀπ' ἀρχῆς. ἔγραψα ὑμῖν, νεανίσκοι, ὅτι ἰσχυροί
CPG: ___ _____ __ __ ____. _____ ___, _____, ὅτι ἰσχυροί
KJV: because ye have known him *that is* from the beginning. I have written unto you, young men, because ye are strong

7. 1 John 5:7b
TBS ἐν τὸ οὐρανῷ, ὁ πατήρ, ὁ λόγος, καὶ τὸ ἅγιον πνεῦμα·καὶ οὗτοι οἱ τρεῖς ἕν εἰσι.
'p' in celo. Pater. uerbum. sp̄s sc̄s. Et hii tres; unum sunt.
AUG ī dem hīm̄el. det vat' d'sūn ōd' daz wort. vn̄ d' hīlige geist und die drī sīnt aīnez
TEP im hīmel; der Vater, das Wort, und der heilige Geist, und dise drei sint ain
G01 im himel, der vatter, das wort, vnd der heilig geist, vnd dise drey seind ein
G03 im himel, der vater, das wort; vnd dez heilig gaist, vn̄ dise drey seind ein
G04 im himel Der vatter,das wort,vnd der heylig geist, vnd dise drey seind eyns
G05 im himel Der vatter, das wort, vn̄ der heylig geyst, vnnd dise dry sind eins
G06 ī himel. Der vater dz wort vn̄ d' heylig geyst, vnd dise drei seind eins
G07 im hymel, Der vater,das wort vnd der heylig geyst, vnd dise drey semd eins.
G08 im himel. Der vater dz wort uñ d heilig geist, un dise drei seind eins
G09 im̄ hymel. Der vater, das wort, vn̄ der heylig geyst, vn̄ dise drey sind eins.
G10 imm hymel. Der vatter das wort,vnd der heilig geist, vnd dyse drey seind eins,

---

405. *Letters to Travis,* 143.

G12 im hymmel,Der vater,das wortt,vmd der heylige geyst, vñ dise drey sind eins
CPG εν τω ουρανω, ο πατήρ και ο λόγος καὶ το ἅγιον πνεῦμα,καὶ οἱ τρεῖς εις το εν εἰσί.
H/F ___ ___ _____ . _ _____ _ _ _____ ___ ___ _ _____ _____ .
ZÜR im himel: Des vatter, das wort, vnnd der heylig geyst, und die drey dienend in eines.
LTH ___ _____ ___ _____ ___ _____ _____ _____ ___ ___ _____ .
KJV in heaven, the Father, the Word, and the Holy Ghost; and these three are one.
BGL °ἐν τὸ οὐρανῷ, ὁ πατήρ, ὁ λόγος, καὶ τὸ ἅγιον πνεῦμα·καὶ οὗτοι οἱ τρεῖς ἕν εἰσι.
G1963 ___ _____ _____ ___ _____ _____ ___ _____ _____ .
G1968 ___ _____ _____ ___ _____ _____ ___ _____ _____ .
G1973 ___ _____ "Dieser Einschub gehört nicht zum ursprünlichen Text".
H/F ___ _____ _____ ___ _____ _____ ___ _____ _____ .
UBS ___ _____ _____ ___ _____ _____ ___ _____ _____ .
E1985 ___ _____ _____ ___ _____ _____ ___ _____ _____ .
G1989 ___ _____ _____ ___ _____ _____ ___ _____ _____ .

1 John 5:8
TBS καὶ τρεῖς εἰσιν οἱ μαρτυποῦντες ἐν τῇ γῇ
'p' Quit tres sunt; qui testimonium dant in terra.
AUG und drie sint di da gezuuchnisse gebent (i dem himel...)
TEP und drei sint, de gebent gezeuig uss der erden
G01 Vnd drey seind die gebent gezeúg (im himel...)
G03 Und drey seind die gebēt gezeúg (im himel...)
G04 Vnd drey seind die da gebent gezeugknuß (im himel...)
G05 und dry sind die da gebent gezugknusz (im himel...)
G06 Vñ drei seind die do gebent zeúgknuß (ĩ himel...)
G07 Un drey seind die da gebent gezeűgknuß (im hymel...)
G08 uñ drey seind die do gebēt zeűgknűß (im himel...)
G09 Und drey sind die da geben gezewgknuß (im̃ hymel...)
G10 Unnd drey sind dye da geBen gezewgknuß (imm hymel...)
G12 umd drey sind die da geben gezeugknuß (im himmel...)
CPG καὶ τρείς εισιν οι μαρτυποúντες επι της γης
ZÜR Unnd drey sind die da zeűgend auff erden
LTH ___ _____ ___ _____ _____ ___ _____ _____ .
KJV and there are three that bear witness in earth
BGL καὶ τρεῖς εἰσιν οἱ μαρτυποῦντες ἐν τῇ γῇ,
G1968 ___ _____ ___ _____ _____ ___ _____ _____ .
G1973 ___ ___ "Dieser Einschub gehört nicht zum ursprünglichen Text".
H/F ___ _____ ___ __ _____ ___ _____ _____ .
UBS ___ _____ _____ __ _____ ___ __ __ .
E1985 ___ _____ _____ __ _____ ___ _____ _____ .

Appendix Six:

The Tübingen collection of Lutheran Bibles:

1591 =Biblia, das ist Die gantze Heilige Schrifft/Teutsch D.Martinus Luther.
1594 =Biblia, Das ist Die gantze Heilige Schrifft/veteutscht durch Doct. Mart. Luther
1596 =Biblia, das ist...Ga LIII.3
1603 =Biblia, das ist die gantze Heilige Schrift, deutsch durch Martin Luther
1634 =Biblia...Deutsch, D. Mart. Luth. mit ausgehenden Versiculn...
1649 =Biblia, Das ist Die gantze Heilige Schrifft Deutsch, D. Mart. Luth.
1659 =Biblia, Das ist:Die gantze H.Schrift Altes und Neues Testaments Teutsch, D. Martin Luthers
1670 =Biblia, Das ist die gantze Heilige Schrift, Deutsch, D. Mart. Luth

Acts 8:37a
1591   Philippus aber sprach: Glaubest du von gantzem hertzen,so mags wol sein.
1594   Philippus aber sprach: Glaubest du von gantzem Hertzen,so mags wol seyn.
1596   Philippus aber sprach: Glaubest du von gantzem herzen, so mags wol seyn
1603   Philippus aber sprach, Gleubestu von gantzem Hertzen, so mags wol sein.
1634   Philippus aber sprach: Glaubest tu von gantzem Hertzen, so mags wol seyn.
1649
1659   Philippus aber sprach: Glaubest tu von gantzem hertzē, so mags wol seyn.
1670   Philippus aber sprach, Glaubest du von gantzem Hertzen, so mags wol seyn.

Acts 8:37b
1591   Er antwortet vnnd sprach: Ich glaube, Daß Jesus Christus Gottes Sohn ist.
1594   Er antwortet vnd sprach: Ich glaube, daß Jesus Christus Gottes Sohn ist.
1596   Er antwortet vñ sprach: Ich glaube daß Jesus Christus Gottes sohn ist
1603   Er antwortet und sprach,Ich glaube das Jhesus Christus Gottes Sohn ist
1634   Er antwortet und sprach: Ich glaube Daß Jesus Christus Gottes Sohn ist.
1659   Er antwortet und sprach: Ich glaube daß Jesus Christus Gottes sohn ist.
1670   Er antwortet und sprach, Ich glaube das Jesus Christus Gottes Sohn ist

1 John 5:7b

1591 .. ..: ... .,... ...., ..., ...
1594 im Himmel: Der Vatter, das Wort, vnd der heilige Geist, vnd die drey sind eins.
1596 im himmel: Der vater, daß wort, und der heilige Geist, und die drey sind eins.
1603 .. ..: ... .,... ...., ..., ...
1634 im Him̃el, der Vater, das Wort, vnd der heilige Geist, vnd die drey sind eines.
1659 im himmel, der vater, das wort, und der heilige geist, und die drey sind eins.
1670 im Himmel, der Vatter, das Wort, und der heilige Geist, Und diese drey sind eins.

1 John 5:8a
1591 Denn drey sind, die da zeugen auff Erden,
1594 Denn drey sind, die da zeugen auff Erden
1596 Und drey sind, die da zeugen auff erden,
1603 Denn drey sind, die da zeugen auff Erden,
1634 Und drey sind, die da zeugen auff Erden,
1659 Und drey sind, die da zeugen auff erden,
1670 Und drey sind, die da zeugen auff Erden,

Appendix 7: Reply to Evangelist Gary Hudson's attack

Reply to an alleged refutation of the grammatical argument
First, a display of reading is presented.

m:pl= masculine plural
n = neuter
f = feminine
\> = implies

MS 629
(7) ὅτι τρεῖς εἰσιν οἱ μαρτυροῦντες ἀπο τοῦ οὐρανου πατήρ λόβος καὶ __ μνεῦμα ἅγιον καὶ οἱ τρεῖς εἰς το ἐν εἰσι. (8) καὶ τρεῖς εἰσιν οἱ μαριθυροῦντες ἐπι της γης, τὸ πνεῦμα τὸ ὕδωρ, καὶ τὸ αἶμα

TBS (1976)
(7) ὅτι τρεῖς εἰσιν οἱ μαρτυροῦντες ἐν τῷ οὐρανῷ, ὁ πατήρ, ὁ λόβος, καὶ τὸ ἅγιον μνεῦμα καὶ οὗτοι οἱ τρεῖς ἐν εἰσι.(8) καὶ τρεῖς εἰσιν οἱ μαριθυροῦντες ἐν τῇ γῇ, τὸ πνεῦμα, καὶ τὸ ὕδωρ, καὶ τὸ αἶμα, καὶ οἱ τρεῖς εἰς τὸ ἕν εἰσιν.

Mr. Hudson argues that the *Comma* is spurious because of what Scrivener said about the missing article. But Scrivener was speaking about 629. Actually, one missing article, while others were present doesn't prove interpolation or anything. But an entire verse (vss. 7-8) missing, leaving a grammaticaly difficulty does prove something.

(6) οὗτός ἐστιν ὁ ἐλθὼν δι'ὕδατος[n] καὶ αἵματος[n], Ἰησοῦς Ξριστός οὐκ ἐν τῷ ὕδατι[n] μόνον ἀλλ' ἐν τῷ ὕδατι[n] καὶ ἐν τῷ αἵματι[n], καὶ τὸ <u>πνεῦμά[n]</u> ἐστιν τὸ <u>μαρτυροῦν[n]</u>, ὅτι τὸ πνεῦμά[n] ἐστιν ἡ ἀλήθεια[f].

Why are the 3 witnesses treated as masculine in v. 8? Some objecting to the *Comma* have replied that they are treated as maculine in v. 8 to "personalize" them. But that doesn't explain v. 6. Note that the Spirit, πνεῦμα, as the third *person* of the Trinity, was not provided as a masculine, to "personalize" the Spirit. It remained neuter.

(6) This is he that came by water and blood, *even* Jesus Christ; not by water only, but by water and blood. And it is the Spirit that beareth witness, because the Spirit is truth.

(7) ὅτι τρεῖς[m:pl] εἰσιν οἱ[m:pl] μαρτυροῦντες[m:pl] <u>ἐν τῷ οὐρανῷ, ὁ πατήρ[m], ὁ λόβος[m], καὶ τὸ ἅγιον μνεῦμα[n] καὶ οὗτοι οἱ τρεῖς ἐν εἰσι.</u>

(8) <u>καὶ τρεῖς[m] εἰσιν οἱ μαριθυροῦντες[m:pl] ἐν τῇ γῇ,</u> τὸ πνεῦμα[n], καὶ τὸ ὕδωρ[n], καὶ τὸ αἶμα[n], καὶ οἱ[m:pl] τρεῖς[m:pl] εἰς τὸ ἕν εἰσιν.

Comma omitted > 7.m:pl= 8.n+n+n; *Comma* not omitted > 7.m:pl =7. m+m+n, and 8.m:pl= ń+n+n (where ń =m, from m+m+n in v. 7). In other words, m:pl= n+n+n is hard to see alone, unless it is preceed immediately by the explanatory pattern m:pl= m+m+n, with the masculine nouns πατήρ and λόγος.

In this display of verses 7-8, the *Comma* is underlined. The collective term "that bear witness" in v. 7 is masculine, and if the *Comma* is removed, it refers to three neuter nouns (Spirit, water, and blood). The result is n+n+n= m:pl, without masculinity superinduced upon the leading noun, which is a grammatical difficulty. In the *Comma* in included, the result is m+m+n= m:pl (v. 7) and m:pl= n+n+n (v. 8), with masculinity superinduced upon the leading noun "by its previous position in the masculine group."[406]
The argument by Evangelist Gary Hudson is that, in v. 8, "the Spirit was used collectively"! But if it is collective, why is it singular? Why doesn't it say "the Spirits"? He implies that if f+f+f= n:pl occurs in 1 Cor 13:13, then n+n+n= m:pl is possible in 1 John. But how does n+n+n= m:pl follow from f+f+f= n:pl ? He doesn't explain. The final clause in verse 8 is decisive. καὶ οἱ[m:pl] τρεῖς[m:pl] εἰς τὸ ἕν εἰσιν. "These three" imply masculine nouns. But without the *Comma*, where are the masculine nouns?

Cor 13:13

νυνὶ δὲ μένει πίστις[f], ἐλπίς[f], ἀγάπη[f], τὰ τρία[n] ταῦτα· μείζων δὲ τούτων ἡ ἀγάπη.

The three abstract nouns (faith, hope, love) are feminine. The collective term (these three) is neuter. f+f+f= n:pl.

---

406. R.L. Dabney "The Doctrinal Various Readings of the New Testament Greek" *The Works of Robert L. Dabney* 3:377-82.

Appendix 8: Reply to Dr. Stewart Custer

1983   WAITE, D.A./QUOROLLO vs. S.CUSTER/PRICE. *Debate on W/H Text vs. Textus Receptus.* (October 11) Marquette Manor Baptist Church, Shumborg, IL. Cassette #1175. Collingswood, NJ: Bible For Today.

A quote from Dr. Custer's 10 minute segment:
> Now Erasmus made a rash promise. He said "If you can show me a Greek manuscript that has that text in it, I will print it in there." Of course that was a minor detail. They went back and summoned their scribes and got them to translate the Latin Vulgate into Greek and put that verse in. [It] came right back to him. The ink was hardly dry on the manuscript. Presented it to him. Those two manuscripts are 61 --One of them is in Dublin, today. The date is the 16th century, the time of Erasmus. The other one is 629. It's in the Vatican right now. Those are the only two manuscripts out of those 5000 that have verse 7 in it. There are two other manuscripts that have it written- in the margin, centuries after this fact, that are utterly worthless for evidence. Those two manuscripts, they held Erasmus to. Told him frankly that if he didn't put that verse in, they'd excommunicate him. He, being a good Roman Catholic, put it in. He did it over protest, knowing that there was no Greek manuscripts that had that, except ones that they had just produced.

A review of Dr. Custer's claims on the *Comma*:

claim: Erasmus made a rash promise.
Fact: De Jonge demonstrated in 1980 that no evidence exists for such a promise.

claim: "It [MS 61] came right back to him"
reply: The reading in MS. 61 was pointed out to Erasmus "between May 1520 and June 1521."[407]

claim: "The ink was hardly dry"
reply: C.R. Gregory speculates the MS was produced in Oxford in 1520. If Erasmus didn't see it until June 1521, how could the ink be wet? Without any proof, this is deliberate exaggeration.

claim: "Presented it to him. Those two manuscripts are 61. . ."
reply: This is not a coherent thought. He may have spoke ahead of himself.

---

407. Raymond Brown, "Appendix IV: Johannine Comma", *The Anchor Bible*, vol.30: *The Epistles of John*, (NY:Doubleday, 1982), 779.

Perhaps, he intended to say that both 61 and 629 were presented to Erasmus. Later, he provides another clue, that in fact this may have been what he intended to say.

claim: "the only two MSS out of those 5000 that have verse 7 in it.[408]
note: The given ratio, 2/5000, has a wrong numerator and denominator.
fact: The year prior to this debate, 1982, R.E. Brown listed 8 Greek MSS. How was it reduced to 2 MS ?
note: The ratio 2/5000 also has a wrong denominator.
fact: As of 1987, only 498 Greek MSS contain the section where this verse can be checked. See *ANTF 9* (1987), p. 163-66

fact: The numerator must reflect the quantity of MSS which contain 1 John 5. Custer said 5000, but it cannot be greater than ~500!
fact: 2/5000 is a exaggeration of the 8/498.

claim: It is in the margin of 2 MSS "centuries after the fact"
fact: All 5 MSS with the *Comma* in the margin, are dated BEFORE "the fact" of the 16th century. [409]

claim: "if he didn't put the verse in, they'd excommunicate him."
fact: This is a fabricated claim. There was no threat of excommunication based on the omission of the *Comma*. [410]

claim: "Erasmus, being a good Catholic . . ."[411]

But why then did the stanch Catholics refer to him as a "Lutheran at heart" prior to 1524, (when he had completed his first 3 Greek editions)?

"Hochstraten of Colegne, Egmond, Aleander, and other stanch romanists constantly taunted Erasmus with the accusation that were he not a Lutheran

---

408. Custer is now "counting noses", but his count is wrong.
409. Metzger does says the marginal reading of 635^{mg} has a 17th century hand. But other opinions must be heard.
410. Modern accounts imply that Stunica and Lee had one objection with Erasmus, the omitted *comma*. A reading of *Erasmi Opera Omnia* IX-1, IX-2 shows they were outspoken with hundreds of objections. The claim that excommunication was contingent on this one omitted verse, further promotes the "one-objection against Erasmus" myth.
411. D. Kutilek in his article "Erasmus and his theology" *Biblical Evangelist*, Oct 16, 1985 said "He was a lifelong devoted Catholic."

at heart he would publicly rebuke the heretic [Luther]."[412]

Roland Bainton, throughout his book *Erasmus of Christendom* (1969), portrays Erasmus as "rejected by the Catholics as subversive and by the Protestants as evasive" (p. vii). He was "rancorous toward Pope Julius but chary of alienating him, because only popes can grant dispensations from certain canonical regulations and Erasmus stood in need of dispensations." (p. 103). Privately he wrote "a scathing epigram" (p. 104) against Pope Julius.

Why would Luther, who despised Catholocism, select a Greek translation made by a lifelong devoted Catholic, and call it his "wife"? E. Emerton said "There can be no doubt that Erasmus was in sympathy with the main points in the Lutheran criticim of the Church."[413] Of Erasmus, "his name has generally had an evil sound in Roman Catholic ears."[414]

No one doubts that Erasmus was a Catholic. The mta, and now even some of the MTA, delight to remind the RTa of this. But the real question is asked and answered by C.H. Turner;

> Was Erasmus an adherent of the Pope or of Luther? His friends and his enemies alike answered the question according to their prepossessions. Bombasius begged him to enter the arena as a Papal champion: Melanthon was assured that 'Erasmus nobiscum est'.[415]

Melanthon's quote means "Erasmus is with us."

> But Erasmus refused to be drawn. He temporized, and published in March 1524 *Apologia contra conclusiones Stunicae*. He would not break with either side.

What was the attitude of Erasmus towards the Bohemian Brethren, who regard the Pope as Antichrist? The following excerpts is taken from P.S. Allen's account[416] of the correspondence between Erasmus and Jan Schlecta, who was describing the Bohemian Brethren (the reply of Erasmus is dated Nov 1, 1519):

---

412. E.G. Schwiebert, in *Luther and His Times* (St. Louis, Concordia Publ.,1950) p.686.
413. *NSHE* 4:165.
414. *NSHE* 4:166.
415. *Early Printed Editions of the Greek Testment*, 24.
416. "The Bohemian Brethen" *The Age of Erasmus* (Oxford: Clarondon Press, 1914) 285-87.

Sch: They choose their own bishops, rude unlettered laymen. . .
Era: Their practice of electing their own priests and bishops has authority in antiquity;
Sch: They salute one another as Brother and Sister;
Era: With the titles of Brother and Sister I see no fault to find: it is a pity they are not more widely used among Christians.
Sch: and [they] recognize no authority but the Bible.
Era: To prefer God's word in the Bible to the judgements of Doctors is sound. . .
Sch: Their priests celebrate mass without vestments,
Era: To celebrate mass in everyday dress is not contrary to the truth. . .
Sch: and they keep no holy days but Sundays, Christmas, Easter, and Whitsun.
Era: About festivals they seem to follow the usage current in the days of Jerome.

In 1505, the Dominican Jacobus Lilienstayn wrote *A Treatise against the erroneos Waldensian Brethren, commonly known as the Pickards, without rule, without law, and without obedience, of whom there are many in Moravia, more than in Bohemia*. The Bohemian Brethren replied in 1507, with their *Apologia*. They "presented it to Erasmus at Antwerp with the request that he would read it through. . ."[417] and give his comments. Erasmus said as far has he had gone, he found no error. "He declined, however to bear testimony about it, as this would bring them no help, and only danger to himself."[418] P.S. Allen translates a few lines of Erasmus here, in which he refrained from publicly announcing his agreements with the Bohemian Brethren:

> "You must not think that any words of mine will bring you support; indeed, my own influence, such as it is, requires the backing of others. If it is true that my writings are of any value to divine and useful learning, it seems to me unwise to jeopardize their influence by proclaiming publicly the argeement between us: such actions might lead to their being condemned and torn from the hands of the public. Forgive me for this caution, you will perhaps call if fear: and be assured that I wish you well and will most gladly help you in other matters."

The attitute of Rev. Hugh Pope, O.P.(professor of N.T. exegesis in Collegio

---

417. Ibid. p.295-96.
418. Ibid.

Angelico at Rome), towards Erasmus is noteworthy:

> But the real trouble was Erasmus' lack of theology. . .He seemed to take pleasure in suggesting doubts about almost every article of Catholic teaching; the Mass, confession, the primancy of the Apostolic See, clerical celibacy, fasting and abstinence, and so forth. Small wonder, then, that he came to be regarded as the man who paved the way for the Reformation. . .[419]

A devoted Catholic, in that day, would respect the "Latin Vulgate" and the 365 Vaticanus readings collected by J.G.Sepulveda, which agreed with it. But Erasmus rejected these. Summarizing an aspect of E. Bulkeley's debate (1588) with the Rhemists, Rev. Pope says "When the Rhemists acclaim the Vulgate as the best of versions, Bulkeley pronounces those by Erasmus[52] and Beza to be Better."[420]

Now let us return to Martini, an issue raised by Dr. Qurollo in the debate, but which Dr. Custer dodged. From the *UBS World Report*, March 1980, we read the announcement "Professor Carlo Martini. . .has been appointed Archbishop of Milan." The article continues that "Professor Martini, 53, is a Jesuit. He was formerly rector of the Gregorian University, the most renowned Roman Catholic institution for theological studies. The archdiocese of Milan is considered one of the most important dioceses in Italy. In this century two Archbishops of Milan have been elected Pope- Pius XI and Paul VI." The RTa are still waiting for the fundamentalists mta, to explain why they trust four liberals and a Jesuit in line to become the next pope, with the identity of the New Testament!

claim: "except ones that they had just produced"
note: This provides a second clue that Custer was claiming the Catholics produced two Greek MSS.
reply: Metzger says of MS. 61 "It was on the basis of this *single*, late witness that Erasmus was compelled to insert[421] " the *Comma*.

Conclusion of evaluation: The bloated ratio implying 5000 MSS contain the 5th chapter of 1 John 5, the fabrications about "the ink was hardly dry" the threat of "excommunication" over refusing to put in a verse, form a very

---

419. H. Pope *English Versions of the Bible*, revised by Rev. S. Bullough, O.P.(St.Louis & London: Herder, 1952) 105.
420. Ibid. p.290. In footnote 52, Rev. Pope say "Erasmus was Bulkeley's 'god', and Bulkeley constituted himself Erasmus' 'prophet'". But note that Bulkeley was a Protestant.
421. Metzger, *Text of the New Testament*, 2nd ed. 62.

amusing fairy tale.

Appendix 9:

Is the Received Text part of our Baptist Heritage?

A.T. Robertson, the world famous Greek scholar, regarded the *Johannine Comma* as spurious. Thus, some have suggested that Baptists ought to follow the example of noted 19th century Southern Baptists such as J.A.Broadus and J.P. Boyce, who (with A.T.Robertson) rejected the RT. This ought to be addressed. Two aspects should be considered: 1)the Baptist perspective of the doctrine of the perpetuity of the local churches, and 2) the antiquity of the Greek Received Text. Concerning the first point, which states (as a German Reformed scholar and former director of the Münster and Berlin Archives, Ludwig Keller, said) that "Baptist churches existed for many decades and even centuries before the Reformation"[422] though they did not call themselves "Baptists". Secondly, if we consider that Burgon admitted that "the Received Text is full 1500 years old-(yes, and a vast deal older)"[423] it ought not to surprise any Baptists, that the Received Text is not only part of the Reformed, and Lutheran heritage, but even for centuries before theirs, it has been part of the Baptist heritage. It will not suffice to say that the Particular Baptist, D.A. Carson, betrayed his Baptist heritage,[424] when he attacked the Received Text in his *King James Version Debate*, unless Baptists also admit that not only W.H. Whitsitt,[425] but also J.A. Broadus, and his student, A.T. Robertson, have betrayed their Baptist heritage when they adopted the textual methods of the Anglican scholar Hort, the Presbyterian Warfield, and the Lutheran, Tischendorf. The signatories of the 1st and 2nd London Baptist Confessions of Faith of the 17th century did not depend on Hort, Tischendorf, or Warfield. However, Broadus, Robertson, and J.P. Boyce did. Baptists must admit, that despite their reputation, learning, and various contributions, they went astray in New Testament textual criticism. For example, A.T. Robertson, praises the work of the Anglican, Hort, in this manner on p.viii:

> No one outside Hort, in his famous *Introduction* and Appendix (vol. II, *The New Testament in the Original Greek* by Westcott and Hort in 1882) had so clearly set forth the principles of textual criticism

---

422. *Baptist Quarterly Review*, VII, 28-31, cited by J.T. Christian, *History of the Baptists*, 1:88
423. *Revision Revised*, 392
424. D.A. Carson was a speaker at the 1982 Councils on Baptist Theology
425. Whitsitt "went to Europe and studied. . .under such outstanding scholars as Constantine von Tischendorf. . ." W.H. Brackney, *The Baptists*, (NY,CN, London: Greenwood Press, 1988), 281. A.T.

that the student could readily grasp the science and apply it.

When Warfield's book on textual criticism went out of print, Robertson urged him to revise it. But Warfield declined and even asked Robertson many times to revised it. Not even W.H. Davis, was able to revise it. Robertson continues on p. viii:

> In shear desparation I have come back to it [the project to revise Warfield's handbook] that my own students and others may have the method of Hort with sufficient fulness for the student.[426]

Theodore Letis, an RTa, has demonstrated the defects of Warfield's "common sense approach" to textal criticism, in *The Contribution of Edward Freer Hills to the Revival of the Ecclesiastical Text*. Warfield mainly followed the method of Hort. The Baptist scholar merely patterned his thinking from the Presbyterian,[427] Warfield. In modern days, this is repeated with the Baptist, D.A. Carson,[428] who largely followed the liberal Presbyterian, Bruce M. Metzger.)

Robertson was under the tutelage of Whitsitt, among others (p. 252).

426. For anyone who is familiar to Burgon's thorough refutation of the "method of Hort" in *Revision Revised*, they will find this comment of Robertson's to be a grievous statement. It ought to be a warning to any young Baptists aspiring to become proficient in Greek studies.

427. A.T. Robertson was also greatly influenced by Tischendorf. Though Tischendorf's edition VIII of the Greek NT differed from his seventh in 3572 places, Robertson used it anyway! On p. vii, Robertson says without any shame "Until it passed out of print I used Warfield's *Introduction to the Textual Criticism of the New Testament* and Tischendorf's *Novum Testamentusm Greace*, ed. VIII.

428. It was astonishing how dependent Carson was upon Metzger in *The King James Version Debete*. It causes one to wonder if his confidence in Metzger abided, after the appearance of the *Reader's Digest Bible* (1982), and the *New Revised Standard Version* (1990).

Appendix 10:

***

Mansucript evidence for and against the *Johannine Comma*.

***

The sources for this digest:

C.R. Gregory *Textkritik des Neuen Testamentes* vol 2. (1902)

Kurt Aland *Text und Textwert der Griechischen Handschriften des Neuen Testaments* (1987)

J.R. Clemons *An Index of Syriac MSS Containing the Epistles and the Apocalypse* (1968)

Philip Schaff, referring to 1 John 5:7,8 commented

> It is a wonder that Dean Burgon has not come up to the defense of this forlorn post. He might summon any number of *Latin* witnesses.[429]

Actually, had Burgon had done that very deed, it would have been profitable, since a century has passed and the question of the complete Latin evidence for the *Comma* remains neglected. Porson's estimate (which Scrivener agreed with) that perhaps 49 of every 50 Latin Vulgate MSS contain the verse remains unverified. We do not know if some are actually Old Latin. We do not even have an estimate of how many contain the fifth chapter of 1 John. Additionally, the Syriac MSS continue to be neglected. Armenian MSS have also been neglected. In 1958, A.W. Adams still gave a false impression of their scarcity. In 1959, E.F. Rhodes listed 267 Armenian MSS in the Erevan repository. But as of 1977, at Erevan, there are "more than 1,500 Gospel manuscripts and 100 complete Bible manuscripts, not to mention incomplete and fragmentary manuscripts." Metzger says "more manuscripts of this version are extant than of any other ancient version, with the exception of the Latin Vulgate" *Early Versions of the N.T.* p.157.

In 1953 G. Zuntz said "The agreement between our modern editions does not mean that we have recovered the original text." (This restlessness of Zuntz is fascinating!) He continued "It is due to the simple fact that their editors, whatever theories, they may hold or reject, *follow one narrow section of the evidence*, namely, the non-Western Old Uncials."[430] [emphasis mine]

Even today, the mta, and MTA each follow *one narrow section of the*

---

429. *Companion to the Greek Testament and the English Version* (London: MacMillan, 1883) 193.

430. Zuntz. *The Text of the Epistles; A Disquisition upon the Corpus Paulinum.* 8.

evidence. The mta depend largely upon early Greek uncials, though, they do seem to consider Old Latin MSS, and editions of early versions. The MTA (of the 1990's) are worse in that they depend only on the narrow section of evidence consisting of late Greek cursives, plus a narrow section of the Greek papyri.

What was Dean Burgon's view concerning this mass of documents?
> So far from regarding the whole body of ancient authorities as untrustworthy, it is precisely "the whole body of ancient authorities" to which I insist that we make our appeal, and to which we must eventually defer. I regard them therefore with more than reverence.[431]

abbreviations:
[f =fragmentary, p =part is included, i =incomplete]
"hostile"= MSS which omits the *Comma* in 1 John 5
"silent" = MSS with mysterious *Lücke* (gaps) in 1 John 5:7-8
h = number of hostile witnesses
H = number of hostile witnesses including variants

---------------------------------3rd century----------------------
GREEK MSS (silent:)
(5 MSS) p9 p20 p23 p72+ p78   See footnote.[432]

---------------------------------4th century----------------------
GREEK MSS without the *Comma*:
[h =2] Aleph B   silent: p81

---------------------------------5th century----------------------
GREEK MSS without the *Comma*:
[h =3] A 048; 1757   silent: p54+
LATIN MSS extant:
a^2 *b e h i k n s, m* 694

---------------------------------6th century----------------------

---

431. *Traditional Text of the Holy Gospels Vindicated and Established.* p.10
432. Upon my request for a copy of the page from these 5 papyri with the position of 1 John 5:7, the INTF refused my request and returned my check. Michael Welt of the INTF replied on Feb 21, 1991: "There are no papyri which come into consideration, which cover the area around 1 John 5 that allow you to recognize the interesting lacuna. So I'm sending back to you the check for DM 7,50." Now I'm even more curious.

GREEK MSS without the *Comma*:
[h =1] 0296

LATIN MSS extant
d f q r s t e gue ; *for fuld gue*^lect *harl per san* 19 246 615 1610 1612 1947 1949 2082 2225
SYRIAC MSS: Do scholars say they contain the 5th chap of 1 John?
--An index says these do:(4 MSS) LONw63; LONw125; LONw126; LONw127;

---------------------------------7th century----------------------
GREEK MSS with the 5th chap of 1 John:
none;   silent: p74

LATIN MSS containing the *Comma*:
(? MSS) perhaps "some" from: *bold reg taur* 137 253 707 1221 1284 1457 1609 1972 1986

SYRIAC MSS: Do scholars say they contain the 5th chap of 1 John?
--An index says these do:(4 MSS) LONw64; LONw128; ROM266; SIN5;
--An index says 'partly':(01 MS) LONw129-7i;

---------------------------------8th century--------------------
GREEK MSS without the *Comma*:
(1 MS) ψ+
LATIN MSS containing the *Comma*:
(? MSS) perhaps "most" from: *am foss gat lux tol* 3 5 20 95 96 (102a) 115 116 131 153 154 184 228 231 234 238 493 502 510 590 610 614 669 682 698 774 850 851 934 985 1034 1237 1254 1263 1265 1267 1269 1271 1278 1444 1526 1606 1607 1608 1633 1673 1699 1843 1855 1859 1877 1888 1918 1923 1928 1937 1946 1958 1970 1973 2000 2080 2085 2105 2157 2218.
SYRIAC MSS: Do scholars say they contain the 5th chap of 1 John?
--An index says these do:(5 MSS)BIR103; LON13; NYK286; SIN15L; SIN54;
--An index says 'partly':(01 MS) CHG199f;
--They haven't checked!!:(01 MS) UNL)G1b?;

---------------------------------9th century------------------------
GREEK MSS without the *Comma*:
[h= 8] K L P 049; 1424+ 1841+ 1862 1895
[note: 1424 also omits the *pericope* (John 7:53-8:11); and L also omits the *angel at the pool* (John 5:3b-4)]

LATIN MSS which contain the *Comma*:
...ix) perhaps "most" from: Δ^M Θ^H Θ^A Θ^M Σ^{C+} Σ^A ϕ^T ϕ^B ϕ^G ϕ^V τ^{68} cav em iac ing mt ter vallic san^{paul} 25 63 64 109 113 159 185 186 187 206 209 235 239 240 241 242 243 254 442 611 618 654 657 671 672 791 804 812 813 814 815 817 831 846 852 893 (894?) 895 (896?) 897 913 914 921 924

925 926 927 1022 1027 1035

1045 1065 1082 1095 1120 1183 1184 1185 1186 1199 1216 1222 1223 1224 1226 1227 1228 1229 1230 1223 1248 1249 1264 1266 1268 1270 1272 1273 1274 1280 1281 1285 1286 1289 1317 1324 1329 1343 1363 1396 1406 1419 1429 1447 1451 1474 1478 1479 1482 1486 1489 1517 1521 1525 1611 1627 1666 1672 1683 1714 1725 1768 1777 1791 1807 1838 1875 1878 1881 1883 1893 1895 1901 1904 1907 1919 1921 1922 1924 1925 1931 1935 1939 1941 1944 1948 1953 1967 1968 1971 1974 1991 1992 2083 2084 2088 2138 2139 2140 2142 2144 2158 2161 2164 2166 2171 2219 2247 2249 2312

SYRIAC MSS: Do scholars say they contain the 5th chap of 1 John?
--An index says these do:(5 MSS) BEI)Hall; LONw121; PAR85; SIN17; UNL3;
--An index says 'partly':(3 MSS)LONw161p; LONw781.7p; LONw793.13p;
--They haven't checked!!!:(01 MS)CHG198?

---------------------------------10th century-------------------
GREEK MSS without the *Comma*:
[H=30] 056 0142; 82 175 221 307 314 450 454 457 602 605 619 627 832 920 1066 1611 1720 1739 1829 1836 1845 1851 1874 1880 1891 2125 [h= 28] 456 2464

LATIN MSS with the *Comma*:
(? MSS) perhaps "most" of: $\Delta^L \Delta^B \Lambda^L \Sigma^T$ mm *136 156 158 170 203 204 213 230 232 449 604 613 616 617 769 802 803 827 930 935 953 958 1031 1036 1105 1187 1188 1203 1231 1244 1353 1364 1386 1408 1409 1413 1418 (1419a) 1427 1440 1441 1442 1443 1452 1469 1483 1487 1572 1574 1575 1612a 1625 1632 1693 1696 1697 1700 1701 1755 1756 1769 1771 1821 1851 1882 1888 1897 1902 1903 1908 1909 1910 1915 1916 1917 1926 1943 1950 1951 1985 1987 1993 2053 2055 2120 2125 2137 2167 2168 2169 2172 2185 2288 2289*

SYRIAC MSS: Do scholars say they contain the 5th chap of 1 John?
--An index says these do:(9 MSS) NHM249; LEN8; LON1; LON72; PAR89; PARsyr335; PARsyr360; PARsyr361; PARsyr363;
--An index says 'partly':(3 MSS) BIR635f; LONw1622p; SIN6Tp;
--They haven't checked!!!:(2 MSS) LONw223L?; L)OR2288?;

---------------------------------11th century-------------------
GREEK MSS without the *Comma*:
[H=80] 35 42 81 93 103 104 133 142 177 181, 250 256+ 302 312 323 398 424 431 451 458, 459 464 465 466 491 506 517+ 547 606 607, 617 623 624 625 635 638 639 641 699 796, 901 910 919 945 1162 1175 1243 1244 1270 1311, 1384 1521+ 1668 1724+ 1730 (1734) 1735+ 1738 1828 1835, 1837 1838 1846 1847 1849 1854 1870 1871 1888 2138 2147 2298 2344 2587 2723 [h=75] +variants 436 1448 1875 2475 2746

SYRIAC MSS: Do scholars say they contain the 5th chap of 1 John?
--An index says these do:(9 MSS) CMB)Add.1968; MRD4; MRD5; LON14; OXF333; PAR28; PRI)Gar1; UNL5; ROM510;
--An index says 'partly':(2 MSS) LONw820p; PRI)Gar2;
--They haven't checked!!:(01 MS) LONw245L?;

---------------------------------12th century-------------------
GREEK MSS without the *Comma*:
[H=79] 1 2 3 36 43 57 88T 94 97 105 110, 189 203 226 319 321 326 330 337 378 440 452 618 620 622 632+ 637 656 808 876 917, 922 927 1058 1115 1127 1241 1245 1315 1319 1360, 1390 1505 1573+ 1673 1737 1752 1754 1843 1853 1863, 1864 1867 1868 1872 1885 1893 1894 1897+ 2127 2143, 2186 2191 2194 2242 2243 2289 2412 2625 2805+ [h= 70] +variants 76 1359 1490 1646 1718 1743 1889 2401 2541

[note: 1241 also omits the *pericope*]

SYRIAC MSS: Do scholars say they contain the 5th chap of 1 John?
--An index says these do:(18 MSS) ALQ15; CMBool.2; CMB)Add.2810; CMB)Add.1700; CAM175; MAN2; MOS7; MOS8; LEY2344; LON15; NYK293; OXF)syr.d7; PAR29; PAR30; PAR50; PARsyr364; ROM275; ROM470;
--An index says 'partly':(none)
--They haven't checked!!:(3 MSS) CAM10?; MLN25L?; ROM211?;

---------------------------------13th century-------------------
GREEK MSS without the *Comma*:
[H= 98] 6 38 141 172+ 180 204 234 263 309 325, 327 328 365 383 384 390 421 442 460 462, 468 469 479 483 592 601 614 665 676 720, 757 912 914 915 941 1069 1070 1072 1094 1103, 1107 1149 1161 1242 1251 1292 1297 1398 1400 1404, 1501 1509 1594 1595 1597 1642 1717 1719 1722 1728, 1731 1736 1740 1742 1758 1780 1827 1839 1852 1855, 1857 1858 1860 1865 1873 2261 2374 2400 2404 2423, 2483 2492 2502 2516 2558 2627 2696 2712 2718(-s) [h= 89] +variants 51 206 218 999 1456 1352a 1563 1727 1850

SYRIAC MSS: Do scholars say they contain the 5th chap of 1 John?
--An index says these do:(32 MSS) BIR368; CMB)Add.1967; CMB)Add.1969; L)OR.2695; L)OR.4051; L)OR.5265; DIY10; DIY11; HAV)RoH28; JER9; LON2; LON16; LONw65; LONw122; LONw123; NYK260; NYK295; PAR31; PAR32; PAR48; PAR297; PARsyr365; PRI379; PRI317; PRI)Gar3; PRI)McC1; WSH405; UNL6; UNL138; UNL)D; ROM16; ROM471;
--An index says 'partly':(6 MSS) LONw131i; LONw167p; LONw229p; NYK257f; PAR46i; UNL1Lp;
--They haven't checked!!:(6 MSS) CAM19?; CAM52?; CAM53?; LONw229?; MLN329?; MOS9?;

------------------------------14th century------------------
GREEK MSS without the *Comma*:
..xiv) 5 18 131 201 209 216 254-c 308 363 367, 386 393 394 404 425 453 489 498 582 603, 604 608 621 630 633 634 643 680 743 794, 824 913 921 928 935 959 986 996 1022 1040 1075, 1099 1100 1102 1106 1248 1249 1354 1482 1495 1503, 1523 1524 1548 1598 1599 1609 1610 1619 1622 1637, 1643 1678 1721 1723 1725 1726 (1732) 1733 1744 1746, 1747 1761 1762 1765 1769 1842 1856 1877 1890 1892, 1899 1902 2080 2085 2086 2197 2200 2356 2431 2466, 2484 2494 2495+ 2527 2626 2653 2716 2774 2777 [h= 100] + variants 62 223 254 429 628 1732 1741 1753 1831 1832 1881 1896+ 2180 2279 2508 2511 2705 1067 1409 [H= 119]

SYRIAC MSS: Do scholars say they contain the 5th chap of 1 John?
--An index says these do.(4 MSS) BIR334; MLN)B.20; LONw124; PAR474;
--An index says 'partly':(01 MSS) OXF34;
--They haven't checked!!:(3 MSS) IST59L?; MLN33L?; ROM22L?;

------------------------------15th century------------------
GREEK MSS without the *Comma*:
[H= 55] 69 102 149 205 322 368 385 400 432 467, 616 636* 642 664 801 1003 1105 1247 1250 1367+, 1508 1617 1626 1628 1636 1649 1656 1661 1729 1745, 1750 1751 1763 1767 1830 1840 1844 1876 1882 2221, 2288 2352 2523 2544 2554 2652 2691 2704 2736 [h= 49] +variants 4 1405 2131 2675-c 444 615

SYRIAC MSS: Do scholars say they contain the 5th chap of 1 John?
--An index says these do:(7 MSS) BIR551; BIR41; AMScod13; LON18; UTI)Wm; UNL140; UNL)Peck;
--An index says 'partly':(01 MSS) ROM277p;
--They haven't checked!!:(4 MSS) AMS158?; LONw235?; L)OR.229?; PMP77L?;

------------------------------16th century------------------
GREEK MSS without the *Comma*:
..xvi) 90 296 631 1618 1704 1749 1768 1861 2130 2218 2255 2378 2501 [h= 13] +variants 522 1702 [H= 15]

SYRIAC MSS: Do scholars say they contain the 5th chap of 1 John?
--An index says these do:(7 MSS) CMB)Ff2.15; MLN70; PAR49; ROM276; UNL31; ROM17; ROM486;
--An index says 'partly':(01 MS) ROM118p;
--They haven't checked!!:(01 MS) ROM25?;

------------------------------17th century------------------
GREEK MSS without the *Comma*:
[h= 6] 1101 1748 1869 1903 2674 2776

SYRIAC MSS: Do scholars say they contain the 5th chap of 1 John?
--An index says these do.(9 MSS) BIR148; ALQ17; BEI)1; FLO2; JER33; PAR1p5; PRI)Cab.C37; STR4117; ROM461;
--An index says 'partly'.(none)
--They haven't checked!!:(01 MS) MOS11?;

---------------------------------18th century--------------------
GREEK MSS without the *Comma*:
{h= 1} 1104

SYRIAC MSS: Do scholars say they contain the 5th chap of 1 John?
--An index says these do.(14 MSS) ALQ18-18; ALQ19-18; AQR3-18; BIR480-18; BIR540-18; CAM176-18; MAN12-18; MRB7-18; MRD7-18; MOS10-18; LEY2350-18; OXF36-18; OXF)syr.e6-18; PMP104-18;
--An index says 'partly'.(01 MS) CMBool.31-18i;
--They haven't checked!!:(3 MSS) CAM33-18?; NYK308L-18?; NYKunnmb-18?;

---------------------------------19th century--------------------
SYRIAC MSS: Do scholars say they contain the 5th chap of 1 John?
--An index says these do:(2 MSS) BIR356-19; PMP237-19;
--An index says 'partly':(01 MSS) BIR331a-19p
--They haven't checked!!:(01 MS) AQR4-19?;

---------------------------------20th century--------------------
SYRIAC MSS: Do scholars say they contain the 5th chap of 1 John?
--An index says this does:(01 MS) MAN11-20;

---------------------------------undated------------------------
SYRIAC MSS: Do scholars say they contain the 5th chap of 1 John?
--An index says these do:(14 MSS) CHA560-?; CHA561-?; CHA562-?; LUN)N.1212-?; SMR382-?; TUR11-?; UNL)Harr-?; OXF35-?; PRI345-?; MAN15-?; GEN13-?; MRD6-?; ECH)Ter-min-?; LEY2791-?; ATL)Yonan-(5-11);
--An index says 'partly':(3 MSS) LONw78325-?p; PAR61-?p; ROM475M-?p
--They haven't checked!!:(8 MSS) NYK251-??; NYK252-??; ROM352L-??; SMR381-??; SIN20a-??; UNL)A-13? UNL)H-??; CHA)I327-??;

Total Greek MSS without the *Comma*: 445 +53 variants = 498

Summary of 498 Greek MSS containing 1 John 5,
in which the *Comma* is omitted:

GREEK papyri: hostile witnesses
0 MSS -----none from the 2nd century
0 MSS -----none from the 3rd century
0 MSS -----none from the 4th century
0 MSS -----none from the 5th century

0 MSS -----none from the 6th century
[total GREEK papyri with testify against the *Comma* = 0]

papyri: silent witnesses
5 MSS from the 3rd century
1 MS from the 4th century
1 MS from the 5th century
1 MS from the 7th century
[total papyri with curious gaps in 1 John 5:7-8 = 8 MSS]

GREEK uncials and miniscules :
2 MSS/498= 0.40% from the 4th century
3 MSS/498= 0.60% from the 5th century
1 MS/498= 0.20% from the 6th century
0 MSS------none from the 7th century
1 MS-------0.20% from the 8th century
8 MSS/498= 1.60% from the 9th century

[6 MSS/498= 1.20% are 6th century or earlier]
[15 MSS/498= 3.01% are 9th century or earlier]

[483/498 =96.98% are 10th century or later]
30 MSS/498= 6.02% from the 10th century
80 MSS/498= 16.06% from the 11th century
79 MSS/498= 15.86% from the 12th century
98 MSS/498= 19.67% from the 13th century
119 MSS/498= 23.89% from the 14th century
55 MSS/498= 11.04% from the 15th century
15 MSS/498= 3.01% from the 16th century
06 MSS/498= 1.20% from the 17th century
01 MS/498=   0.20% from the 18th century

Greek MSS which
alter Mt 19:16-17: Al B ..D (et al.
.omit ..Jh 5:3b-4: Al B C ..(et al.
.omit ...Mt 6:13b: Al B ..D ...S vg (et al.
omit Jh 7:53-8:11: Al B ....L W p66 p75
omit ..Mr 16:9-20: Al B ....sy^s
omit 1 John 5:7-8: Al B ....(et al.

****

145 Syriac MSS include the 5th chapter of 1 John
----

24 Syriac MSS include a portion of 1 John 5:

35 Syriac MSS are yet unexamined as to whether they include 1 John 5!
--Dated: 27 MSS
--Undated: 8 MSS

---

65 Syriac MSS which seem to indicate the canon excluded 1 John 5

ALQ27π-19m ALQ28L-19m ALQ29π-19m ALQ30π-19m ALQ31π-19m AQR3π-17m
AQR10π-19m AQR11L-19m BEI)11L-15m BEI)12L-16m BEI)13L-16m BEI)14L-?m
BIR485-19m BIR227π-18m CMB)Add.2035π-19m CMBool.17π-17m CAM9π-13m
CHA)II4L-18m CHA)II7L-18m CHA)II11π-?m CHA65L-?m CHA102L-?m
CHA120L-?m KIR1-13m KIR7-m LEN15-6m LEN21L-8m LEN22L-13m
LONw118-12m LONw133-6m LONw134-6m LONw135-6m LONw136-6m
LONw137-6m LONw138-7m LONw139-7m LONw141-7m LONw145-10m
LONw147-13m LONw153-13m LONw162.3.3-10m LONw224π-10m LONw234π-14m
LONw244π-10m LONw247π-13m LONw335π-13m LONw427.3-7m LONw752.1-9m
LONw780-9m L)OR.2287-9m MRB9-?m MRD17π-16m PRI)Cab.C50-17m ROM23π-?m
SIN3-7m SIN13π-11m SIN214π-13m SIN215π-13m SIN216π-13m SIN218π-13m
SIN228π-?m SIN229π-13m SIN235π-13m UNL4-9m UNL8-6m

Syriac MSS which are defective at 1 John 5:

CMB)Add.2810x-12n/a
BIR42-9; BIR634-9; BOS7-7; CMBool.11-18; CMBool.21-18; CMB)Add.1970-18;
CMB)Add.1974-17; CMB)Add.1985-18; CMB)Add.1986-18; CMB)Add.2023-13;
CMB)Add.2053-13; CMB)Add.2917-16; CHA69-?; CHA79-?; CHA157-?; DAM2-18;
DUB1509-15; ESC1528-?; LEN7-?; LEN23π-?; LEY2345-18; LON66-10; LONw80-7;
LONw96-10; LONw117-13; LONw132-11; LONw140-7; LONw142-7; LONw143-7;
LONw144-8; LONw146-11; LONw148-13; LONw149-13; LONw150-13; LONw151-14;
LONw152-14; LONw220π-9; LONw221π-9; LONw222π-9; LONw745-7; LONw787-?;
LONw854-7; L)OR.8607-12; MRB7.1-?; MLN30-5; MLN31-6; NYK294-12; OXF19-17;
OXF97.1-? OXF)syr.02-18; PAR60-16; PAR72L-15; PAR74L-16; PAR75L-16;
PAR76L-16; PAR82L-16; PAR83L-16; PAR84-9; ROMk7uol6.8-19; UNL11-8.

Appendix 10: Latin MSS:

Earlier in this work, a suggestion was made concerning a comment Dr. E.F. Hills had made. The proposed improvement was to say that God *chose* to preserve his text in a public way "that all the world may know where it is and what it is." It was not a necessity upon God. He chose not to leave his elect people wandering in darkness. Thus the questions that concerns us is: What text was used prior to Jerome? and What text what used during the middle ages? Also: In which major language were these texts written? Generally speaking, Latin was the major language. Sturz has objected that for about 1000 years

> "the Western part of the church was largely ignorant of the Byzantine text, being shut up, for the most part, to the Latin Vulgate which differs in many respects from the Byzantine text."

But it is wrong to presuppose, for "about one thousand years" that *only* the Latin Vulgate text was the dominant text used, for even Kenyon and Metzger speak of Old Latin exemplars which are "remarkable" for their longevity into the Middle Ages". Those who argue likewise with Sturz, overlook not only these remnant pre-Jerome exemplars of the Middle Ages, but also overlook the persecutions of the Middle Ages and the widespread destruction of Latin MSS.

Pertaining to the use of the texts in the Middle Ages, and on the importance of the Latin language, some useful essays/books are Adolf Harnack's "Über den Privaten Gebrauch der Heiligen Schriften in der Alten Kirche" in *Beiträge zur Einleitung in das Neue Testament* (Leipzig: J.C. Hinrich, 1912); Bonifatius Fischer's "Zur Überleiferung altlateinischer Bibeltexte im Mittelalter" in *Lateinische Bibelhandschriften im Frühen Mittelalter* (Freiburg: Verlag Herder, 1985), and Carl Vossen's *Latein; Muttersprache Europas* (Düsseldorf: Verlag Hub. Hoch., 1978). Vossen's subheadings for chapter two include "Die Übergangszeit", "Die karolingische Renaissance", "Das scholastische Latein", "Latein als geistiges Band des Mittelalters", "Das Humanistenlatein der Renaissance", and "Die neulateinische Epoche."

F.H.A. Scrivener said the passage 1 John 5:7-8 "is found in the printed Latin

Vulgate, and in perhaps 49 out of every 50 of its manuscripts," [433] Many have said it occurs only in the late Vulgate MSS, but according to Horne, Richard Porson said "it is actually found in twenty-nine Latin MSS, the fairest, the oldest, and the most correct in general."[434]

J.H. Ropes of Harvard said that Caspar René Gregory "probably examined more mansucripts of the New Testament than any other man that ever lived,"[435] His symbols for Greek MSS was adopted. Hence, the Gregorian notation. Strangely, his symbols for Latin MSS has been neglected. Dr. Walter Thiele, who today is perhaps the world's leading expert on Latin MSS, in the 1950's assigned his own symbols to the selection of Latin MSS he works with. In his works "c" is Ω^C, "dem" is Ω^D, etc.

In the edition of the *Vetus Latina* by the VLI, Thiele's worked on the Johannine epistles. From the church fathers and from his large selection of Latin MSS he worked with, he cited the evidence (in 1966) for the *Comma* as follows:

> KCT V(Var) (Comma Iohanneum) 67 64 LRYSUCΣX 91 94 95 54* $\Delta\,\Theta M\,\Phi\,V\,2\Omega DC$ 59, Paris lat.315, lat.11533, Vat. lat.10511*, Vat.lat.12958, Leningrad Q.v.I, 16^2, Wien 1190^2, CY;PS-CY cent; POT?;PRIS;PS-ATH sy; PS-HI ep?; FID Am >Constitutum Constatini?; FID Aldama?; AN Casp; PS-VIG tri; Var > PS-HYG, PS-JO II.; PS-AU spe, sol; EUGE-C; FU; FEnd; PS-FU Pin; PROL; CAr cpl; KA C?, Sp; PS-AM tern?; BEA; Wilhelm v. St. Thierry; *et* ~ $\Omega^{OW}\Lambda H2O2M2$ 54^2, Paris lat.4^2, Vat. lat.10511^2, Vat.Pal.lat.93; EUCH int (Var); BED cath (Var); PS-EUS-P (Var): > 61 629 88^2[436]

Among these unexamined Latin MSS, we cannot yet even declare whether any are actually Old Latin MSS. The following array of 6000 question marks is displayed to provide some idea of the quantity of MSS which are being neglected. (Let us assume 2000 Latin MSS are already displayed by a symbol in appendix 10.)

? ?
? ?
? ?

---

433. *A Plain Introduction* 3rd ed. p. 650.
434. Porson *Letters* p. 152. As provided by T.H. Horne (1922) 505 n3.
435. *Dict. of Amer. Biogr.* 7:601.
436. W. Theile "Epistulae Catholicae" *Vetus Latina; Die Reste der altlateinischen Bibel* vol 24/2 (Freiburg: Verlag Herder, 1966)

? ?
? ?
? ?
? ?
? ?
? ?
? ?
? ?
? ?
? ?
? ?
? ?

? ?
? ?
? ?
? ?
? ?
? ?
? ?
? ?
? ?
? ?
? ?
? ?
? ?
--1000
? ?
? ?
? ?
? ?
? ?
? ?
? ?
? ?
? ?
? ?
? ?
? ?
? ?
? ?
? ?

? ?

? ?
? ?
? ?
? ?
? ?
? ?
? ?
? ?
? ?
? ?
? ?
? ?
? ?
? ?
? ?
--2000
? ?
? ?
? ?
? ?
? ?
? ?
? ?
? ?
? ?
? ?
? ?
? ?
? ?
? ?

? ?
? ?
? ?
? ?
? ?
? ?
? ?
? ?
? ?
? ?
? ?
? ?
? ?

--3000

? ?
? ?
? ?
? ?
? ?
? ?
? ?
? ?
? ?
? ?
? ?
? ?
? ?
? ?
? ?

? ?
? ?
? ?
? ?
? ?
? ?
? ?
? ?
? ?
? ?
? ?
? ?
? ?
? ?
? ?

--4000

? ?
? ?
? ?
? ?
? ?
? ?
? ?
? ?
? ?
? ?
? ?
? ?
? ?
? ?

? ?
? ?

? ?
? ?
? ?
? ?
? ?
? ?
? ?
? ?
? ?
? ?
? ?
? ?
? ?
? ?
? ?

--5000
? ?
? ?
? ?
? ?
? ?
? ?
? ?
? ?
? ?
? ?
? ?
? ?
? ?
? ?

? ?
? ?
? ?
? ?
? ?
? ?
? ?
? ?
? ?
? ?

????????????????????????page 258????????????????
??
??
??
--6000

Appendix #11: Theology/character of the opposers:

(d. 1662) J. Biddle "unitarian"[437] (d. 1680) C. Sandius "the Arian"[438]

(d. 1712) R. Simon "Roman Catholic", "quarrelsome in disposition"[439]

(d. 1727) I. Newton "His leanings to Arianism"[440]

(d. 1729) S. Clarke "was accused of Arianism"[441]

(d. 1741) T. Emlyn "first unitarian minister in England"[442]

(d. 1742) R. Bentley: it was his "arrogance which...provoked the feud"

(d. 1752) W. Whiston "Arian theologian"[443]

(d. 1754) J.J. Wettstein "became suspected of Socianian tendencies"[444]

(d. 1762) G. Benson "He was undoubtedly a Socinian"[445]

(d. 1777) W. Bowyer "depended upon the judgement of J.J.Wettstein"[446]

(d. 1791) J.D. Michaelis "secretly he had tried to renounce"[447] orthodoxy

(d. 1791) J.S. Semler "alchemy, mystical theosophy, and freemasonry"[448]

(d. 1794) E. Gibbon "had so little sympathy for the aims of the Church"[449]

(d. 1804) J. Priestly "embraced Arianism"[450]

(d. 1808) R. Porson had "doubts...especially about...the trinity"[451]

(d. 1812) J.J. Griesbach "with...Semler, with whom he lived as a student"[452]

(d. 1812) J.S. Buckminster "was liberal, a forerunner of the Unitarian movement"[453]

(d. 1821) J. Barrett "indulged in cursing and swearing."[454] (d. 1832) A. Clarke "he denied his eternal sonship"[455]

(d. 1853) A. Norton "the position of conservative Unitarianism."[456] (d. 1880)

---

437. *DNB* 5:13.
438. Porson, *Letters to Travis*, ii.
439. *NSHE* 10:422.
440. W. Orme, *Memoirs of the Controversy*, 43.
441. *DNB* 10:444.
442. *DNB* 17:356.
443. *NSHE* 12:338.
444. F.H.A. Scrivener, *A Plain Introduction* 3rd ed.,460.
445. *DNB* 4:256.
446. B.Metzger *Text of the New Testament*.
447. *NSHE* 7:364.
448. *NSHE* 10:355.
449. *NSHE* 4:483.
450. *NSHE* 9:254.
451. *Secrets of Mount Sinai*
452. Orchard & Longstaff, *J.J. Griesbach; Synoptic and text-critical studies 1776-1976*
453. *NSHE* 2:290.
454. *DNB*
455. *DNB* 10:414.

J.S. Porter "unitarian divine"[457]
(d. 1881) S. Sharpe "a Unitarian scholar"[458]
(d. 1884) E. Abbot "Unitarian layman" [459]
(d. 1901) J. Thayer "was a Unitarian"[460]
(d. 1930) A. von Harnack held "liberal theological views"[461]

(1615-1662) John Biddle's comments against 1 John 5:7,8 are found in his *A Brief History of the Unitarians called Also Socinians in Four Letter written to a Friend.* 2nd ed. (1691). See letter #4. On 1 Tim 3:16 he says (p. 40) "It appears by the Syriac, Latin, Ethiopick, Armenian, Arabick, and most ancient *Greek* Bibles. . .that the Word *God* was not origially in this Text, but added to it:"

(1644-1680) Christopher Sandius: "In the year 1670, the Arian Sandius made a formidable attack upon this verse. . ."[462]

(1638-1712) Richard Simon: "French Roman Catholic", who "on May 21, 1678, was expelled from the Oratorians because of the publication of his *Histoire critiqe du Vieux Testament*" *NSHE* 10:422.

(1638-1725) Daniel Whitby: wrote on the Trinity, in which "he began with the orthodox doctrine. . .[Oxford,1691], but his views changed, and his *Last Thoughts*. . .reveals him as a convinced Unitarian." *DNB* 12:339.

(1642-1727) Isaac Newton "His leanings to Arianism, which were no doubt promoted by his acquaintace with Clarke, Whiston, and other eminent persons of that school, are to be deplored."[463]

(1675-1729) Samuel Clarke "was accused of Arianism, the general tendency of the book [*Scripture Doctrine of the Trinity*] being clearly in that direction" *DNB* 10:444

(1663-1741) Thomas Emlyn: "Emlyn was the first preacher who described himself as a unitarian, a term introduced by Thomas Firmin. . .He maintains, however, that he 'never once' preached unitarianism, advocating his theology

---

456. *Dict of Amer Biog* 13:568.
457. *DNB* 46:185.
458. F.F. Bruce, *English Bible; History of Translations* (1961) 130.
459. *NSHE* 1:4.
460. *The Kingdom of the Cults* (rev. ed.) 59.
461. *EBrit* 5:712.
462. Porson, *Letters to Travis*, ii.
463. W. Orme, *Memoirs of the Controversy*, 43.

only through the press." *DNB* 17:358.

(1662-1742) Richard Bentley was a Trinitarian. He even lived with Stillingfleet for six years 1683-89. In 1720 he published his proposals to reconstruct Jerome's Vulgate. He then intended to compare this with the oldest Greek manuscripts. By this means he "believed that he could restore the Greek test as generally received by the church at the time of the Council of Nice (325 A.D.)" *DNB* 4:314.

(1667-1752) W. Whiston: His new inquiries led him to the view that "the accepted doctrine of the Trinity was erroneous", he was "banished from the university" *DNB* 51:11 "-and in Oct., 1710, he was deprived of his professorship." *NSHE* 12:338. In 1988, Harold P. Scanlin misleadingly portrayed Whiston as a "controversial Baptist"[464] But Scalin failed to provide the rest of the account. Hugh Pope says "Only in 1747, after the publication of his *Primitive New Testament*, did Whiston, then eighty years old, abandon communion with the Church of England and join the Baptists."[465]

(1693-1754) J. J. Wettstein "became suspected of Socinian tendencies, . . .so that in the end he was deposed from the pastorate (1730), driven into exile" F.H.A. Scrivener, *A Plain Introduction* 3rd ed.,460.

(1699-1762) George Benson: "one of the professors 'spoke of him with abhorrence as an avowed Socinian' (*Biog. Britannica*)" *DNB* 4:256.

(1684-1768) Nathaniel Lardner: "he 'was much inclined' to the Arianism adopted by Samuel Clarke" *DNB* 32:149.

(1725-1791) J.S. Semler "felt a profound disinclination toward all manner of Pietism" [see also H. Hoffman's *Die Theologie Semlers* (Leipzig: 1905)]

(1733-1804) Joseph Priestly: "By reading with care, 'Dr. Lardner's Letter on the Logos', I became what is called a Socianian soon after my settlement at Leeds [Sept. 1767];" *Autobiography of Joseph Priestely*, (reprint of *Memoirs*, 1806, Somerset: Adams & Dart, 1970) 93.

(1759-1808) Richard Porson: "Byron described him as the most bestial of all the disgusting brutes that he knew. Porson, he wrote, was sulky, abusive, and intolerable, adding, 'In private parties he was always drunk or brutal,

---

464. "Bible Translation as a Means of Communication New Testament Criticism to the Public" *Technical Papers for the Bible Translator* 39 (Jan 1988) 103.
465. *English Versions of the Bible* (1952) 526.

and generally both'. He became librarian to the London institution, but scarcely attended to any of his duties, frequently coming home dead-drunk long after midnight." (p.30) R.C. Jebb says Byron's account refers "to the years 1805-8" *DNB* 46:159. "In any case, his doubts about orthodoxy-and especially about the doctrine of the Trinity-were all too obvious." (p. 31) James Benltly, *Secrets of Mount Sinai*

(1745-1812) J.J. Griesbach: "Here [at Halle] he soon came in contact with Johann Salomo Semler, with whom he lived as a student, and also after his great tour abroad (40:18)"[466] Also: ". . .-even in the eyes of the Weimar government -Griesbach was regarded as a representative of a more liberal theology. . ." Gerhard Delling,"Johann Jakob Griesbach: his life, work and times" *J.J. Griesbach; Synoptic and Text-Critical Studies 1776-1976* (Cambridge: Cambridge Univ. Press, 1978) 15.

(1784-1812) Joseph Stevens Buckminster: "In theology he was liberal, a forerunner of the Unitarian movement;. . .He superintended the publication of the American edition of Griesbach's Greek Testament (1808);" *NSHE* 2:290.

(1753-1821) John Barrett: "He was very attentive to his religious duties, but freely indulged in cursing and swearing." He was vice-provost and professor of oriental languages of Trinity College, Dublin.

(1762-1832) Adam Clarke "on the person of Jesus Christ, while maintaining his divinity, he denied his eternal sonship"[467]

(1786-1853) Andrews Norton "occupied the position of conservative Unitarianism." In 1833, he wrote *A Statement of Reasons for Not Believing the Doctrines of Trinitarians*.

(1801-1880) John Scott Porter: "His views were Arian, and he became the editor (1826-8) of an Arian monthly, the 'Christian Moderator'" *DNB* 46:185 "and followed Priestely in maintaining the presence of an unhistorical element in the initial element in the initial chapters of St. Matthew and St. Luke" (p. 186)

(1799-1884) Samuel Sharp: was "president of the British and Foreign Unitarian Association in 1869-70" *DNB* 51:426.

(1828-1901) Joseph Henry Thayer "was a Unitarian who denied Christ's

---

466. Note 40 is B.R. Abeken: J.J. Griesbach, in F.C.A.Hasse (ed.), *Zeitgenossen*, 3rd series, vol.1 part 8, Leipzig, 1829.
467. *DNB* 10:414.

deity" and "and denied the visible second coming of Christ"[468]

(1851-1930) Adolf von Harnack: "because of his liberal theological views, especially with resect to the historical Christian creeds, his appointment to the post at Berlin was opposed by the supreme council of the Evangelical Church of Prussia". . .Throughout his life, . . .he was denied ecclesiastical posts." *EBrit* 5:712.

---

468. Walter R. Martin. *The Kingdom of the Cults* rev. ed. (Mineapolis: Bethany, 1977) 59, 71.

the
BIBLE
FOR
TODAY

900 Park Avenue
Collingswood, NJ 08108
Phone: 856-854-4452
www.BibleForToday.org

B.F.T. #2008

www.ingramcontent.com/pod-product-compliance
Lightning Source LLC
Chambersburg PA
CBHW082036230426

43670CB00016B/2679